MANCHESTER

THE PHOTOGRAPHIC COLLECTION

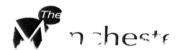

MANCHESTER

THE PHOTOGRAPHIC COLLECTION

CHRIS MAKEPEACE

SUTTON PUBLISHING

This edition first published in 2003 by
Sutton Publishing Limited • Phoenix Mill
Thrupp • Stroud • Gloucestershire • GL5 2BU

Manchester in Old Photographs was first published in 1996 by Sutton Publishing Limited
Manchester in Old Photographs: A Second Selection was first published in 1998 by Sutton
Publishing Limited
Manchester in Old Photographs: A Third Selection was first published in 2000 by Sutton
Publishing Limited

British Library Cataloguing in Publication Data
A catalogue record for this book is available from the British Library.

ISBN 0 7509 3349 6

Typeset in 9/11pt Photina.
Typesetting and origination by
Sutton Publishing Limited.
Printed and bound in Great Britain by
J.H. Haynes & Co. Ltd, Sparkford.

CONTENTS

Part One – Manchester in Old Photographs

Part Two – Manchester: A Second Selection

Part Three – Manchester: A Third Selection

PART ONE

MANCHESTER
IN OLD PHOTOGRAPHS

*This incident, photographed in the 1890s, appears to have taken place
at the junction of St Mary's Gate and Deansgate when tram H33,
based at one of the depots in the Harpurhey area, was operating the
service between central Manchester and Alexandra Park. The incident
also appears to have attracted a large crowd of bystanders, while some
of the passengers on the upper deck look down on what has happened
with interest as the tram wheels are re-railed.*

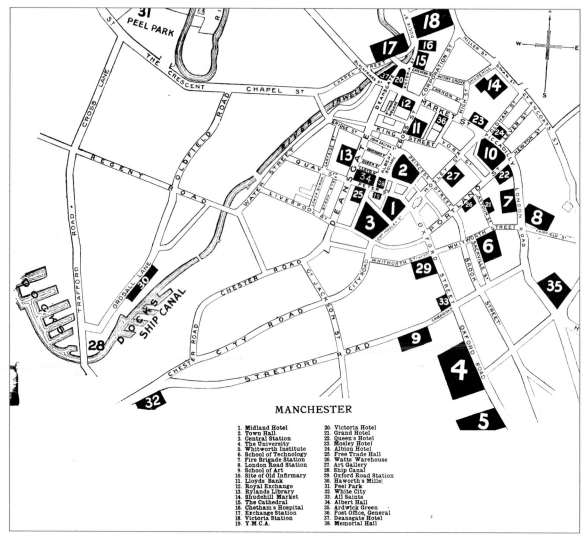

MANCHESTER

1. Midland Hotel
2. Town Hall
3. Central Station
4. The University
5. Whitworth Institute
6. School of Technology
7. Fire Brigade Station
8. London Road Station
9. School of Art
10. Site of Old Infirmary
11. Lloyds Bank
12. Royal Exchange
13. Rylands Library
14. Shudehill Market
15. The Cathedral
16. Chetham's Hospital
17. Exchange Station
18. Victoria Station
19. Y.M.C.A.
20. Victoria Hotel
21. Grand Hotel
22. Queen's Hotel
23. Mosley Hotel
24. Albion Hotel
25. Free Trade Hall
26. Watts Warehouse
27. Art Gallery
28. Ship Canal
29. Oxford Road Station
30. Haworth's Mills
31. Peel Park
32. White City
33. All Saints
34. Albert Hall
35. Ardwick Green
36. Post Office, General
37. Deansgate Hotel
38. Memorial Hall

This map of Manchester was published in about 1905 and shows the main roads and public buildings in the centre of the city. The main street pattern shown here has changed little over the past ninety years, although some of the roads have now been pedestrianized and many of the small courts and streets, which lay between Market Street and Shudehill, have disappeared either as a result of the blitz or post-war redevelopment. Many of the buildings shown on this map are still standing today although in some cases they have been found new uses or have been refurbished.

INTRODUCTION

When Angus Bethune Reach visited Manchester in 1849, he described the town as 'Queen of the Cotton cities . . . this great capital of the weavers and spinners of the earth, the Manchester of the power-loom, the Manchester of the League, our Manchester – is but a thing of yesterday . . . considerably within two-thirds of a century the scattered villages of Manchester, Salford, Hulme, Pendleton, Chorlton and two or three others, became the vast cotton metropolis which has lately succeeded in swaying the industrial and commercial policy of England.' Twelve months earlier the editor of the *Builder* had commented that 'Manchester has been pointed to as the type of one grand idea – Machinery – an idea which belongs to our own age exclusively, and is full of great results hardly yet foreshadowed.' These two comments sum up Manchester's growth to the mid-nineteenth century, namely that it was a product of recent developments. Between 1751 and 1851 the population of central Manchester had risen from around 17,000 to over 186,000, after which it started to decline although, as a result of absorbing the surrounding districts, the total population of the city continued to rise until the 1930s, peaking at around 737,000 just before the Second World War.

Although Manchester developed rapidly between 1750 and 1850, the period often described as that of the Industrial Revolution, the origins of Manchester can be traced back to the Roman occupation of Britain in the first century AD. Around AD 79 the Romans established a small fort on a sandstone buff, overlooking the confluence of the rivers Irwell and Medlock. In the beginning the fort consisted of an earthen rampart with a wooden stockade at the top and protected by a double line of ditches. The fort was rebuilt on several occasions, the last time being about AD 200 when stone replaced the wood. Outside the walls a small civilian settlement developed which included metal working facilities as well as the usual type of buildings one associates with a garrison – inns, shops, temples and a bath-house. Radiating from the fort were a number of roads, the most important of which was that from Chester to York. Other roads led to places like Melandra (near Glossop), Ribchester, Castleshaw (above Oldham) and Coccium (believed to be Wigan).

After the Romans left in about AD 410 little is known about what happened in Manchester. Place name evidence suggests that there was both Saxon and Danish influence, but archaeological evidence is non-existent. There is a brief reference to Manchester in the Anglo-Saxon Chronicle for 919, but its full meaning and what King Edward did in Manchester is not clear. The only certainty during this period is that the settlement migrated from around the fort to another defendable site overlooking the confluence of the rivers Irwell and Irk. Even in the Domesday Book there is only the briefest of references to Manchester. It indicates that Manchester was within the Hundred of Salford, that King Edward was Lord of the Manor of Salford (implying that the manor of Manchester was subordinate to the manor of Salford), that there was a parish church in Manchester dedicated to St Mary, and that the church held certain lands free from all taxes except the geld.

Medieval Manchester was not a large settlement. It was centred around the residence of the lords of the manor, now Chetham's School, the parish church, now the cathedral, and the market-place, with the main roads being Deansgate, Old Millgate, Long Millgate, Withy Grove and a small section of Market Street. The importance of the town as a centre is illustrated by the grant of an annual fair in 1222 and the attempt in 1301 to grant it a charter. Although the charter was rescinded in 1359 it established a pattern of local government for Manchester which continued to operate until 1792, when the first police commissioners were appointed. After this the Court Leet continued to operate in tandem with them until the borough council was elected in 1838. The Court Leet was finally abolished in 1845 after the council had paid the Mosley family £250,000 for the manorial rights. There is also evidence that from the late thirteenth century there were people in Manchester who earned their living not from farming but by trading, and had shops in the town.

Although Manchester was not a borough it was a market town and the centre of an extensive medieval parish, which covered most of modern Manchester as well as part of Salford and several surrounding areas. In 1421 Thomas de la Warre, who was not only the lord of the manor but also a priest, secured for the church a charter which established a college of clergy to provide for the spiritual needs of the people of the parish. In addition he gave the church his manor house as a home for the clergy, buildings which are now part of Chetham's School. The charter, although suspended from time to time, remained in operation until 1847 when the Diocese of Manchester was created and the collegiate church became Manchester Cathedral.

By the sixteenth century Manchester was also becoming the leading town in south-east Lancashire. Much of its wealth was generated from the woollen trade, there being a number of wealthy woollen merchants in Manchester at that time. The wool appears to have been imported from Ireland and distributed to local people to turn into cloth, who then returned it to the merchants who took it to London to sell. One of the wealthiest of these clothiers, or cloth merchants, was Humphrey Chetham, whose funeral when he died in 1653 cost over £1,200, while another merchant family, the Mosleys, purchased the Manor of Manchester in 1596.

During the Civil War Manchester supported the Parliamentary forces and was even besieged for a short while in 1642. However, like other areas, it welcomed the restoration of Charles II, the conduit in the market-place flowing with claret on the day of his coronation. The accession of William and Mary in 1689 resulted in the establishment of the first Nonconformist chapel in the town and the erection of St Ann's Church to cater for those who did not agree with the High Church, pro-Jacobite views expressed at the collegiate church. The division of Manchester into two factions became apparent in 1715 when a mob supporting the Old Pretender attacked and seriously damaged Cross Street Chapel, and again in 1745 when many of the supporters of the Hanoverians left the town before Bonnie Prince Charlie arrived. The High Church faction tended to see the Low Church faction and Nonconformists as allies, so when proposals were made in the early eighteenth century for a workhouse to be governed by a body drawn equally from the three groups they opposed it, presumably because they thought they would be in a permanent minority. The same applied when proposals were made for a borough charter shortly afterwards.

In many respects 1745 marks the end of a period in Manchester's history. Up to then Manchester was a market town and a regional centre, but as the eighteenth century progressed Manchester's importance began to increase dramatically helped by developments affecting the textile industry. During the eighteenth century cotton began to replace wool as the main component of cloth which was manufactured in the area. At the same time developments took place which resulted in the weaving of broad cloth, using the flying shuttle, which upset the balance between spinning and weaving. The flying shuttle was still capable of being used domestically, but the machines required to speed up yarn production required water power. Both Arkwright's water-frame and Crompton's mule operated more efficiently with a mechanical means of power, and in the case of the mule far more efficiently with steam power as its size could be increased to over 1,000 spindles. Initially water was used, but from the 1790s steam power came to be used to drive machines. It was with the development of a rotative motion enabling steam engines to drive machines that Manchester began to expand very rapidly. Manchester was ideally situated to take advantage of the new form of power. Land on the edge of the town was relatively cheap, it was flat and there was cheap bulk transportation available not only to bring the raw cotton from Liverpool and take the finished products away, but also to bring coal in to produce the steam. A further factor was the presence of a large labour force which was growing at an amazing rate in the 1790s and early 1800s. People were coming into Manchester seeking work. New housing was required, which in itself created employment as well as the very poor housing conditions made famous by people like J.P. Kay and Frederick Engels.

The first cotton mills were built in Chorton-on-Medlock and Ancoats in the 1790s, their six to seven storeys overshadowing the houses. For the first time, people began to be ruled not by hours of daylight and their own free will but by the factory hooter or bell. When these early mills opened they relied on natural light, but after 1805 gas lighting was gradually introduced which allowed employees to work longer and longer hours. For the first time it was possible to see the conditions under which people lived and worked and the consequences of poor housing and long hours for men, women and children. This may have encouraged observers to begin to collect statistical information not only on working conditions but also on disease and living conditions, and to publish the results of their findings. Two of Manchester's leading societies in this field were the Manchester Statistical Society, founded in 1833 and the Manchester and Salford Sanitary Association, formed in 1851.

As well as manufacturing cotton Manchester was also the centre of the cotton trade. The Royal Exchange was where manufacturers and others met to exchange commercial information and strike deals. At the same time firms with mills outside Manchester established warehouses where customers could see the company's products, one of the best known of which was that of the Rylands company. Other warehouses were developed by wholesalers who sold not only the cloth, but also the goods made from the cloth, firms like J. & N. Philips and J. & S. Watts. All these firms were connected in some way with the cotton industry, which it was said made for the home market before breakfast and for export for the rest of the day'. At the same time as Manchester developed as the centre of the cotton industry there began to develop various financial facilities such as banking and insurance. These were essential for the smooth running of an increasingly complex business life in the city.

The demands of the cotton industry had an effect on the industrial base of Manchester and surrounding districts. Gradually the demand for a wider range of colours that did not wash out led to developments in the bleaching and dyeing industries, which in turn put pressure on the chemists to develop synthetic colours. To produce these the chemical industry began to develop using, at first, the by-products of the gas industry. The knock-on effect of the demands of the cotton industry were enormous.

The use of steam to drive machines also affected industry in the area. As machines went faster so wood was replaced by metal. No longer was it possible to adapt a part if it did not fit; parts had to be accurately made. This gave rise to new machines that reproduced the same part accurately many times over, and later machines developed to make these machines. Gradually the skilled workman was able to be replaced by a semi-skilled man and ultimately by a man whose job it was merely to operate the machine. Manchester developed an engineering industry of its own. Developing from the manufacture of textile machines, engineers began to make machine tools which encouraged others to produce large products such as bridges, railway engines and, in this century, motor cars and aircraft.

In order for the technological developments to have their full effect other developments in transportation were essential. The opening of the Bridgewater Canal in 1764 provided Manchester with a means of bulk transport which was relatively cheap and efficient. When the canal was extended to Liverpool in 1777 raw cotton and finished products could be imported and exported easily. The canal network could also be used to carry coal to the mills as well as building materials and, very importantly, food. Until a cheap means of bulk transport had been developed the size of towns had been limited by the amount of food that could be grown and transported into the town. With canals there came the opportunity to draw on the rich agricultural areas of north Cheshire and south Lancashire. Thus it was possible to feed 70,000 people without the risk of riots.

The nineteenth century saw further changes in transport with the development of railways. Manchester became the centre of a railway network stretching throughout the country. Not only were people carried, but increasingly freight became the largest revenue earner. However, as the railways took over the canals there were complaints about the rising cost of transport to and from Liverpool. This ultimately led to the movement which resulted in the building of the Manchester Ship Canal between 1887 and 1893. It was Mancunians who lead the movement and who played a leading role in the battle to secure Parliamentary approval between 1882 and 1885, and it was Manchester City Council that came to the company's rescue in the early 1890s when funding became difficult. When the Manchester ship canal was opened the dream of linking Manchester directly to the sea came true. More recently international travel has been fostered by the development of Manchester International Airport for both freight and passenger services. In many respects, this is a continuation of the transport changes started back in the eighteenth century which helped Manchester become a major city.

When Manchester became a borough in 1838 it was not without its opponents, who felt that the existing system of local government was adequate. The new borough council inherited a town with few regulations and many problems. The council, however, was prepared to tackle some of these, but it was a slow process. The passing of the 1844 Police Act was the first of many attempts to try to improve conditions in the town. Likewise the decision to obtain water from outside the town's boundaries was revolutionary, but essential if conditions were to improve. It should be noted that the police commissioners were not slow at seizing a chance if one arose, as is well illustrated by the decision in 1817 to sell gas to the public, although they did not have permission or the authority to do so. The borough council took the opportunity to supply the surrounding areas with gas, water and electricity. This provision of an infrastructure for the surrounding districts gradually bound them to the city and made their take-over a lot easier at the end of the nineteenth and in the early years of the twentieth century.

Over the last two centuries there have been many developments in which Manchester has played a leading part. Technological developments have helped industry develop, but also there is the important field of 'ideas'. The Manchester Literary and Philosophical Society provided a forum which brought together scientists, technologists and engineers while the trading connection encouraged the growth of the free trade movement in the mid-nineteenth century.

It is said that from 'little acorns big oaks grow'; in the case of Manchester, from the small Roman fort of AD 79 and the associated civilian settlement so the great city of Manchester developed, although it was over 1,700 years before the town became one of the country's leading settlements with a commercial and economic influence which was enormous. It has been said that Manchester liked to call itself 'the second city of the Empire'. Manchester was, and still is, justly proud of its achievements especially over the last 250 years. Reach was right when he described the town as 'Queen of the Cotton cities' while the editors of the volume published for the visit of the British Association in 1962 called Manchester 'The centre of a region'. Manchester may not be large in terms of population, but its conurbation and its influence covers very large area indeed. It may still be true that 'What Manchester thinks today, the rest of the country thinks tomorrow.'

CHAPTER ONE

STREET SCENES

The main streets of any thriving town are bustling and full of life. Manchester in the late nineteenth and early twentieth century was no exception to this with people hurrying about their daily business. De Tocqueville commented in 1835 that 'crowds are ever in a hurry . . . their footsteps are brisk, their looks preoccupied . . .'. Fourteen years later, A.B. Reach, writing for the *Morning Chronicle*, described the main streets as 'busy and swarming . . . crowded at once with the evidences of wealth and commerce . . . crowds of busy pedestrians of every class . . . bustling from counting-house to counting-house, and bank to bank . . .'. These descriptions of Manchester's streets would have been applicable in the twentieth century as much as in the nineteenth century.

The photographs in this section take the reader on a tour of central Manchester from Piccadilly along Portland Street, Oxford Street, St Peter's Square, Mosley Street, Albert Square, Peter Street, Deansgate, the Market Place and Market Street back to Piccadilly. Many changes have taken place in the buildings which line these street, changes brought about by the blitz and redevelopment with further changes being made as a result of the 1996 IRA terrorist bomb. For a city to be alive changes have to take place. Old buildings will have to be replaced, although the extent of the changes will depend on the type of buildings involved and the potential for finding suitable new uses for them when their original use has become obsolete.

One important change that has occurred since many of these photographs were taken is the change from horse-drawn vehicles to vehicles powered by the internal combustion engine. Congestion existed in the nineteenth century just as it does today and complaints were made about the danger of crossing roads. Attempts are being made to remove traffic from the centre of Manchester with pedestrianization schemes like those for King Street, St Ann's Square and Market Street. One result of pedestrianization is that it is now possible to stand back and look at the upper floors of buildings without the fear of stepping backwards into a moving vehicle. Often it is the upper floors of buildings which reveal interesting details, such as dates of construction, the name of the building and even initials of the owner or builder.

Photographs of street scenes paint a far more vivid picture of the town than a large number of words. From a photograph it is possible to gain an impression of the buildings, which building stood next to which and even who occupied various shops. As well as what the buildings looked like, photographs can also be used to show the type of vehicles which used the street, the posters which appeared on walls, the dress of the people and even the street furniture. The more street scenes are examined, the more detail can be discovered, especially if the illustrations are used in conjunction with other sources such as directories and newspapers.

Photographs of street scenes come from many sources – some have been taken by individuals, others by official bodies and yet others have been transformed into postcards. Fortunately, many of the postcards of central Manchester show busy streets rather than just buildings and so they are more lively than they might otherwise be.

It is to be hoped that this section on the streets of central Manchester will enable the reader to build up a picture of the town before the blitz and post-war reconstruction and redevelopment.

Until the late eighteenth century Piccadilly, or Lever's Row as it was then known, marked the southern extent of Manchester. In 1812 Lever's Row was renamed Piccadilly, a name which was already in use for the section between Newton Street and what is now the approach to Piccadilly station. Originally Piccadilly was lined with private houses, some of whose occupants were associated with the Infirmary, which dominated the area and stood where Piccadilly Gardens are now sited. During the nineteenth century the houses were replaced by hotels, shops and offices, although one still survives between Lever Street and Newton Street to show what the original buildings must have looked like. This particular illustration was taken towards the end of the nineteenth century, looking south from where Royal Buildings are now situated. On the extreme left is the Albion Hotel, which, according to a French visitor, had one of the best cuisines in Europe in the mid-nineteenth century. The Albion Hotel closed in 1926 and was replaced by Woolworth's store. On the extreme right is the Queen's Hotel, which was originally a series of town houses. The Queen's Hotel was well known in the late nineteenth century for its turtle soup, which was sold in a condensed form to other hotels and for important occasions. The hotels which were found in and around Piccadilly had a large number of guests from various parts of the United Kingdom as well as from abroad. Many were businessmen who had come to do business with Manchester's firms, but also a number of people who could be described as tourists stayed in them as well.

For over 150 years Piccadilly was dominated by the Manchester Royal Infirmary, on the left of the picture. The original Infirmary building was little more than a very large Georgian house with a wing fronting on to Portland Street. Shortly after it was completed, another wing was added facing Mosley Street. Gradually other alterations were made which resulted in the masking of the original Georgian building. By the third quarter of the nineteenth century discussions were being held about the possibility of the Infirmary moving to a new site where it would be able to expand. At the same time, concern was beginning to be expressed about the sanitary state of the building and the cost of putting things right. In 1902 the decision was taken to move the hospital to a 'green-field' site in Chorlton-on-Medlock, close to the eye hospital. The decision was made in the light of new developments in the field of medicine, such as the arrival of the X-ray and the fact that bed occupancy rates showed that almost every day of the year there were only a few empty beds. The new hospital was completed in 1908 and the patients were moved in December that year. This photograph was taken in 1908 just before the Infirmary closed. In front of the Infirmary is the Esplanade, which was created in 1853 when the ponds and fountains were filled in and the area paved over and statues added.

Even before the Infirmary had moved to its new premises the debate about what the site in Piccadilly should be used for was opened. Various suggestions were made including a new Royal Exchange and a new art galley. The issue was debated at council meetings and in the columns of the local papers, but there was general agreement that the old buildings should be demolished. Work started early in 1910 and by April only the front portico remained. This spectacular photograph was taken in April 1910 when the columns which graced the front façade of the building were demolished.

Opposite: To many people Piccadilly is regarded as the centre of Manchester. This photograph shows one of the hotels which was to be found in the area, the White Bear. This building had originally been the town house of the Lever family of Alkrington, but had been sold in about 1772 and converted into a coaching inn. Although the front was altered on several occasions, when the building was demolished in about 1906 some of the original structure of the building was discovered at the rear. To the right of the White Bear is the Mosley Hotel, which had moved from Market Street to Piccadilly in 1828, when its original location was required for road improvements. In the 1890s the hotel was rebuilt with many improved facilities. The Mosley Hotel closed after the First World War and the building was replaced by the Piccadilly Cinema.

With the demolition of the old Infirmary an open space was created in the centre of one of the busiest parts of Manchester. Before any use could be agreed, the city council was faced with the problem of finding a new home for the Free Reference Library as their existing premises had been declared unsafe. As a temporary measure huts were erected to house the library, but the final decision on where it should go and what should happen to the old Infirmary site was delayed by the outbreak of war in August 1914. The site had already been landscaped as a temporary measure and this was retained after the war, providing an important open space in this part of Manchester. This picture, taken in about 1927, shows Piccadilly Gardens, while in the background is Browns warehouse, designed by Edward Walters, the façade of which is now the Portland Hotel. The warehouse on the extreme right was demolished in the early 1970s, its replacement office block becoming the offices of the now abolished Greater Manchester County Council in 1975.

As pedestrians walk along the Esplanade at Piccadilly, they pass several statues erected in the nineteenth century. The one shown in this photograph is of the Duke of Wellington, which was unveiled in 1856. The statue, sculpted by Matthew Noble and unveiled before a crowd of 100,000, represented Wellington not as a military leader but as a parliamentary statesman, a decision which did not meet with universal approval. However, a concession was made to Wellington's military career by including a pile of dispatches at his feet and two panels depicting the Battle of Waterloo and the Battle of Assaye in India.

Opposite: Until the late nineteenth century Portland Street ended where it met David Street (later Princess Street). Beyond the junction there were canal wharves from the Rochdale Canal, including a site occupied by Pickfords. The buildings closest to the junction of Portland Street and Princess Street were erected in the early nineteenth century although several were modernized in the late nineteenth century. For instance, the building with a gable was re-fronted in about 1883 for Armstrong's, who were stationers. It is interesting to note the advertisements on the gable wall, which indicate the kind of things the public were being encouraged to buy in the early years of the twentieth century. The junction here was always very busy, hence the policeman in the centre of the road directing traffic.

The first modern warehouse was erected by Richard
Cobden, to the designs of Edward Walters, on Mosley Street
in about 1838. Twenty years later what has been described
as the most magnificent of Manchester's cotton warehouses
was completed for the firm of S. & J. Watts on Portland
Street. The building was designed by Travis and Magnall
and cost almost £100,000. The design was said to have
included four different styles of Renaissance architecture.
At the end of the nineteenth century S. & J. Watts employed
over 1,000 people, and claimed that all orders received in
the morning post were dispatched that same day. In the
1970s the building closed as a warehouse, and after several
scares about its future was converted into a hotel.

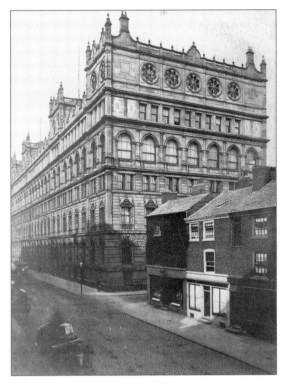

In 1890 the Refuge Assurance Company decided to build its own offices on a site which had recently become available at the junction of Whitworth Street and Oxford Street, as the rented premises they occupied had become overcrowded. Alfred Waterhouse was chosen to design the new offices. He presented his plans for a six-storey building in January 1891, and the work was completed and the offices ready for occupation by mid-summer 1895. Within a decade these new offices had also been filled and so Paul Waterhouse, the son of Alfred, was commissioned to design an extension, which was completed in 1912. To link the two blocks the clock tower was constructed; it became a landmark in this part of Manchester. A further extension was added in the 1930s. When the Refuge Assurance Co. moved to Wilmslow at the end of the 1980s their former offices were converted into a hotel, now called the Palace, which has retained the late Victorian and Edwardian splendour of large open plan offices. This view, taken just before the First World War, shows the clock tower from the entrance to Oxford Road station.

This view is of the corner of Whitworth Street West and Oxford Street and was taken from the approach to Oxford Road station. On the left is St Mary's Hospital, which was opened in 1892 as a replacement for an overcrowded building on Quay Street. Shortly after the hospital was opened St Mary's merged with the Southern Hospital for Women and Children, and a new building was erected on High Street in Chorlton-on-Medlock. The central Manchester building continued to be used until the 1960s, when it was closed and eventually demolished. On the extreme right is the Palace Theatre, opened in 1891 and refurbished in about 1912. The white building in the centre is the St James building, which was completed in about 1912 by the Calico Printers Association. It was named after the St James Theatre and Hall which stood on the site from about 1880 until 1909. The St James Theatre was said to the home of 'heavy drama' while it was at the St James Hall that the Tiller girls first went through the routines that were to make them so famous in the twentieth century.

The construction of Oxford Street started in 1790 with the intention of linking central Manchester with the Manchester to Wilmslow Turnpike Road, which passed through villages like Withington and Didsbury. When the new road was constructed the River Tib, which flowed around the southern side of St Peter's Square, had to be culverted. Gradually Oxford Road became lined with buildings, but it was not until the late nineteenth century that the part nearest the River Medlock and the southern boundary of the Manchester township was developed, as the eastern side of the road consisted mainly of canal wharves associated with the Rochdale Canal. There were, however, a few factories and mills close to the canal at this point. On the opposite side of Oxford Street were the works of Sharp Stewart and Co., who made textile machinery as well as railway locomotives. This view shows the junction of St Peter's Square and Oxford Street, probably in about 1910. The buildings on the right, which included the Princes Theatre, were demolished after the Second World War and were replaced by Peter House. In 1905 the buildings on the right hand side were occupied by a cocoa merchant, a cricketers' outfitters and a boot maker, while the offices included several merchants and a maker-up of cotton goods. On the opposite side of the road at the same time was a branch of Boots, a portmanteau manufacturer, a fruiterer and the well-known Princes' Café, founded by a Mr Tamvaca in 1870.

If you follow the buildings on the left of the previous photograph into St Peter's Square, the buildings shown in this particular illustration would have been seen. This photograph was taken in about 1929. The buildings on the corner, of which only part can be seen, were known as St Peter's Chambers and were occupied mainly by surgeons, while next door was Duncan & Foster Ltd, caterers. The tall building was a mixture of shops at street level and offices on the upper floors. In 1931 the shops included a tailor, a hairdresser, a wallpaper dealer and a gramophone dealer and musical instrument seller. The upper floors were mainly occupied by firms associated with the textile industry. All the buildings were demolished in the early 1970s and replaced by Elisabeth House.

On the corner of St Peter's Square and Peter Street stood an impressive block of buildings which were erected in the 1860s and 1870s to replace what was described as 'a motley collection of buildings'. Although they have the appearance of town houses, they were in fact designed to be offices. When this photograph was taken at the beginning of the twentieth century, these buildings included a café, a tailor, professional offices and one property, No. 3, which provided offices for doctors. These buildings were demolished in 1928 when work started on the construction of the new central library.

When the Manchester Reference Library was forced to move from its premises in the former Town Hall at the corner of Cross Street and King Street in 1912, it had to move into temporary accommodation in Piccadilly. Plans to erect a new central library were delayed by the First World War so it was not until the early 1920s that the city council could once more start to plan for a new library. A site was chosen at the corner of St Peter's Square and Peter Street, and Vincent Harris was selected to design the new building. Work started in 1929 with the foundation stone being laid in 1930 by Ramsay MacDonald, the prime minister. Gradually the steel frame of the library rose above the surrounding area as this photograph shows. The structure of the dome and the central circular reading room can also been seen. The library was completed in 1934 at a cost of £413,000, and was officially opened by George V, who also laid the foundation of the Town Hall Extension, also designed by Vincent Harris, on a site between the library and the existing Town Hall.

St Peter's Square was linked to Piccadilly by Mosley Street, named after the Mosley family who were lords of the manor of Manchester from 1596 to 1845. Originally many of the buildings which were erected on Mosley Street were private houses although many had warehouses and workshops at the rear. There were a few public buildings to be seen, such as the Portico Library, the Manchester Assembly Rooms and Mosley Street Independent Chapel. In 1823 the Royal Manchester Institution was formed with the aim of trying to encourage Mancunians to appreciate the fine arts such as painting and sculpture. Charles Barry was commissioned to design a suitable building for the collection of paintings and sculptures which it was hoped would be collected. Work on the new art gallery started in 1825 and was completed by 1834. In 1882 the Art Gallery, together with its collections, was passed to Manchester City Council, who still own the building and the collections. This view shows the Art Gallery with the Union Club, established in 1825, in the background. The building housing the Union Club was designed by Richard Lane and completed in 1835.

This photograph of the junction of Mosley Street and York Street in about 1910 clearly illustrates the problems Manchester had with traffic congestion in the early twentieth century, with lorries carrying goods to and from warehouses mingling with trams and a large number of pedestrians trying to cross the road. In the background is Colwyn Chambers, completed in about 1892.

In the late eighteenth century a number of societies were formed in different parts of the country to bring together men who had a common interest in science and technology. In 1781 the Manchester Literary and Philosophical Society was founded by twenty-four men, many of whom were medical men at the infirmary. Initially the Society met at Cross Street Chapel, but in 1799 it moved to its own building on George Street. The membership included many of the leading scientists of the period. Among the earliest members were the Henrys and John Dalton, whose work on colour blindness and whose atomic theory were revolutionary. Other important scientists who were members included J.P. Joule, Edward Frankland, Henry Roscoe and Carl Schorlemmer. Other members included William Fairbairn, an engineer, J.B. Dancer, manufacturer of scientific instruments and James Mudd, photographer. The Society provided a meeting place for scientists and engineers to exchange ideas on the latest developments. Their building was damaged in the Christmas blitz of 1940, which resulted in the loss of important historic scientific papers. This photograph shows the Society's house in the early twentieth century.

The Literary and Philosophical Society not only had an ordinary membership, but also a number of honorary members, who were usually prominent scientists of the day. Among those who were given this honour were Bunsen, developer of the Bunsen burner, Neils Bohr, J. J. Berzelius, who put Dalton's atomic theory on a firm experimental basis, and D. I. Mendeleev, pictured here in the centre of the front row. Mendeleev was responsible for the discovery of the periodic table, which advanced the atomic theory announced by Dalton in 1812 at a meeting of the Society.

One of the least photographed streets in Manchester is Princess Street, formerly David Street, which links Cross Street with Mosley Street, Portland Street and Whitworth Street. The street originally came into existence in about 1792 when the first houses were erected close to the River Tib, overlooking the site of St Peter's Church. This photograph shows the part of Princess Street opposite the town hall where most of the original properties were domestic in scale, but were eventually replaced by larger, more imposing buildings. Further along, beyond the junction with Portland Street, Princess Street becomes a street of warehouses, many of which were erected in the 1860s and 1870s.

The building at the corner of Cross Street and John Dalton Street was originally a private house, but it was converted into a public house known as the Princes Tavern in about 1828. The importance of this building is not in its architecture, nor events which went on when it was a public house, but in the fact that Thomas de Quincey, author of *Confessions of an English Opium-eater*, was born in the building in 1785. The building was sold at auction for £14,300 in 1885 and demolished in 1889. It was replaced by a red sandstone building which until recently was used by a building society. When the new building was erected a cartouche was included on the Cross Street façade giving details about the birth of de Quincey.

Manchester's Town Hall is often regarded as one of the finest Victorian buildings in the country. It was designed by Alfred Waterhouse and completed in 1877. Although the city council wanted Queen Victoria to officially open the building she declined the invitation and so the honour fell to Alderman Abel Heywood, Mayor of Manchester. The new Town Hall was built fronting on to the newly created Albert Square, the centre-piece of which was the Albert Memorial. When the Town Hall was opened there were three days of celebrations including a grand procession where representatives of the various trades in the city marched in front of the mayor carrying symbols of their trade. If the illustration is examined carefully, it will be seen that the Albert Memorial appears to be partly surrounded by scaffolding and that there are barriers in front of the Town Hall. The photograph was probably taken early in 1894, when the Albert Memorial was restored in readiness for Queen Victoria's visit in May of that year to open the Manchester Ship Canal.

Albert Square was created in the mid-1860s when a number of small workshops and back-to-back houses were demolished to create a square in which Manchester's tribute to Prince Albert could be located. The Albert Memorial, handed over to the city in 1867, was designed by Thomas Worthington to house a statue of the Prince that had been given to Manchester by Alderman Goadsby. Within a short space of time several other statues were added. The first was of James Fraser, Bishop of Manchester, which was unveiled in 1888. The next one, unveiled in 1891, was of John Bright, who was one of the leaders of the Anti-Corn Law League and Free Trade in Manchester. Bright's statue can be seen in this photograph of Albert Square between the wars, just to the left of the Albert Memorial. The final statue to be added was of William Gladstone, unveiled in 1901, and on the left of the picture. The original paved area in Albert Square was very much smaller than it is today, as this photograph shows. Since 1945 the roadway has been reduced so that by the time of writing Albert Square has been almost completely pedestrianized.

Peter Street was created in 1793 to link Oxford Street, which was then under construction, with Deansgate and Quay Street. As a result vehicles wanting to get to the Castlefield and the Bridgewater Canal or Mersey Irwell Navigation did not have to work their way down Market Street, but could take the new road. This saved time and reduced congestion in central Manchester – the aim of building the road was to try to reduce congestion on Market Street. To many people Peter Street is associated with Peterloo, the Free Trade Hall, Theatre Royal, the Midland Hotel and the Gaiety Theatre. This view shows the side of Peter Street facing the Free Trade Hall and Theatre Royal. The building on the right is the Comedy Theatre, later renamed the Gaiety Theatre. The Comedy Theatre was built in 1884 as a replacement for the Gaiety Theatre of Varieties which was destroyed by fire in the previous year. As a theatre it had a reputation for having poor sight lines for the audience in certain parts of the building, a problem which was never properly resolved. In 1903, after a change of ownership, it was renamed the Gaiety Theatre, although it did not result in a change of the type of play put on. In 1908 Annie Horniman began the first permanent repertory theatre in the country. Horniman put on plays that were chosen for their quality. Likewise, the actors and actresses were engaged because of the quality of their performance. Among the plays that were first performed at the Gaiety under Horniman were *Hindle Wakes* and *The Whispering Well*. The Gaiety Theatre closed as a theatre in 1921 and was converted into a cinema, which was demolished in 1959.

One of Manchester's best known and probably best loved buildings is the Free Trade Hall on Peter Street. This building, designed by Edward Walters, was completed and opened in 1856, replacing two earlier temporary buildings which had been erected on the site by the Anti-Corn Law League to hold fund raising events in the 1840s. The building shown in this illustration was used not only for public meetings, but also for exhibitions, political meetings and concerts. It was the first public hall in Manchester which could be used for events irrespective of political and religious persuasions. It was also the only public building in the country which was named not after a local person or a saint, but after an economic idea, free trade. The Free Trade Hall became the home for the most famous series of concerts held in Manchester by the Hallé Orchestra. These were started in 1858 and ran continuously since then, with the exception of the Second World War, until 1996, when the orchestra moved to its new home, the Bridgewater Hall on Lower Mosley Street. Among the meetings which have taken place in the building have been suffragette meetings, meetings in support of the Manchester Ship Canal and meetings addressed by political leaders such as Churchill in January 1940. As well as events of public interest, the Free Trade Hall was also a popular venue for school speech days and on occasions celebratory dinners. It is interesting to note the canopy over the pavement which allowed those attending events to descend from their carriages or cabs and enter the building without getting wet.

As Manchester expanded outwards at the end of the eighteenth century, new roads came into existence while existing roads changed from country lanes to busy streets. An example of the latter was Liverpool Road, which until 1806 was known as Priestnor Street. One reason given for the change of name was that now Eccles New Road was open, the road between Manchester and Liverpool had been improved and this was the quickest way to reach the new turnpike road. The earliest houses on Liverpool Road were constructed in the 1790s and are shown in this photograph. In the mid-nineteenth century these houses were in multi-occupation with families living in the cellars. At street level shops predominated, selling a wide range of goods. In 1891, about five years before this photograph was taken, the shops included a clothier, ladder maker, several furniture brokers, a butcher, several beer retailers, a boot maker and a tobacconist. Although the photograph does not identify where on Liverpool Road the photograph was taken, it is possible to make an assumption that it shows the part of Liverpool Road between Southern Street and Barton Street, where in 1891 the shops were occupied by a furniture broker, a fent dealer, a ladder maker, a butcher and a hairdresser. Ten years later the fent dealer and the furniture broker had moved on, replaced by a fishmonger and a tripe dealer.

The Three Sugar Loaves public house stood at the corner of Water Street and Back Quay, across the road from the River Irwell. It is not certain when it opened, but it was certainly in existence in 1772 when the first Manchester directory was published. It is possible that it was built in the 1750s or 1760s to provide for the men who were working at the various wharves which had been established on the banks of the River Irwell by the Mersey Irwell Navigation. For a time in the 1820s it was known as the Navigation, but reverted to its original name before 1845. The building shown here must have been a rebuild of the earlier one, but it is not recorded when this took place; neither is it known when it closed and was demolished. This might have been during the Second World War or when Manchester redeveloped the area, erecting the College of Building.

The main east-west route through Manchester is along Deansgate, which until the 1870s was a narrow road causing much congestion. The council tried to secure its widening on several occasions, but all attempts failed until they agreed that property owners would be allowed to erect new premises with the same amount of floor space as in their existing buildings. This photograph of Deansgate was taken looking across the road at Barton buildings, whose relatively plain exterior hides one of Manchester's architectural gems, Barton Arcade, designed by Corbett, Raby and Sawyer and completed in 1871. Barton Arcade was one of several shopping arcades which were built in Manchester in the latter half of the nineteenth century, but the blitz and post-war redevelopment has resulted in the loss of all the others. Although the building is much admired today, when it opened some commentators were critical of the height of the shop windows, which, they said, made dressing them effectively very difficult.

When Bury New Road was constructed in the 1820s it ended in a series of narrow streets, which made access to central Manchester very difficult. In order to improve access to and from Bury New Road it was decided to construct a new road from Hunts Bank to Deansgate and St Mary's Gate. This road was known as Victoria Street and its construction divided the Market Place from Smithy Door, which stood adjacent to it and which had been used as an overflow market area in the eighteenth century. In 1876 the area bounded by Victoria Street, St Mary's Gate and Deansgate was cleared, including the remnants of Smithy Door, to enable a new building to be erected, Victoria Buildings, which was destroyed in the blitz. This photograph shows the part of Victoria Street between Victoria Buildings and the Market Place. The building with the gable in the centre is the Coal Exchange while to its right is Sinclair's Oyster Bar, which partially occupies the site of John Shaw's public house of the late eighteenth century. The tower in the background is the ventilation tower of Strangeways Prison, opened in 1868 as a replacement for the New Bailey Prison in Salford.

There has been a church on the site of Manchester Cathedral since before the Norman Conquest. In the middle ages Manchester was the centre of an extensive parish covering 60 square miles of south-east Lancashire, and like many other parishes experienced absentee clergy. In 1422 the Lord of the Manor, Thomas de la Warre, who was also a priest, secured a charter for the church which changed its status from that of a simple parish church to a collegiate church. This allowed for a number of clergy to be appointed with specific instructions to visit the outlying townships as well as conduct services in the parish church. When the church became a college its dedication was also changed to St Mary, St Denys and St George. From 1422, when the charter was granted, until 1847, when the Diocese of Manchester was created, the charter was suspended on several occasions, but the basic principle of several clergymen serving the area was maintained. One result of the collegiation of the parish church was that an extensive programme of rebuilding was undertaken in the fifteenth and early sixteenth centuries which transformed the building. Further work was undertaken in the early nineteenth century and extensive rebuilding had to be carried out in the 1870s to overcome the problems of damage to the stone work caused by pollution. After the rebuilding work of the middle ages only one major addition to the structure of the church was undertaken before the repair of damage caused by the blitz. This was the construction of a porch at the west end to commemorate Queen Victoria's diamond jubilee in 1897. This view of the Cathedral from the early twentieth century shows not only the church but also the site where Hanging Bridge is now displayed and the domes of the Corn Exchange, built between 1892 and 1903.

Linking Victoria Bridge with Corporation Street and Cannon Street is Cateaton Street, which comes from the Anglo-Saxon meaning 'hollow way', behind which runs Hanging Ditch. This view of Cateaton Street shows its junction with Victoria Street in about 1900. The small ornate building in the centre of the illustration is Minshull House, built on land given to Manchester by Thomas Minshull, an apothecary in the seventeenth century, to provide help for the poor and train them in useful occupations. The building shown here was erected in 1889 to the designs of Ball and Elce and is in the Queen Anne style. In the sub-basement of the building are one and a half arches of the medieval Hanging Bridge, which provided access to the churchyard. The building on the left was rebuilt in 1906, about the same time as the remaining arch of Hanging Bridge was exposed as a feature for visitors and Mancunians to see.

Compared with some towns, Manchester's Market Place is relatively small and by the eighteenth century was inadequate for the size of the town and its population. In addition, it attracted people into Manchester from the surrounding area. As well as market stalls, the Market Place also had the town's stocks and pillory as well as a market cross. In 1729 the space was further restricted by the construction of a building called the Exchange, which was intended to encourage merchants to meet together in one place rather than in different parts of the town. It was not a success and eventually, in 1792, the building was demolished. By the nineteenth century most of the buildings in and around the Market Place dated from the eighteenth centuries although one building, the Wellington Inn, was probably built in the sixteenth century. On this photograph, looking towards the Royal Exchange, the Wellington Inn can be identified by the name Will Chambers seen between the first and second floors of the timber-framed building in the centre of the photograph. The building on the right is the Coal Exchange, which was built in the 1860s on the site of the former Victoria Fish and Game Market, demolished in 1865. When most of the market stalls were moved to Smithfield Market in the 1820s a few were allowed to remain, but in 1891 these too were cleared away, as the presence of stalls and people combined with traffic created a dangerous situation on market days. Some stalls, however, were allowed to remain in the area between the Wellington Inn and the Coal Exchange.

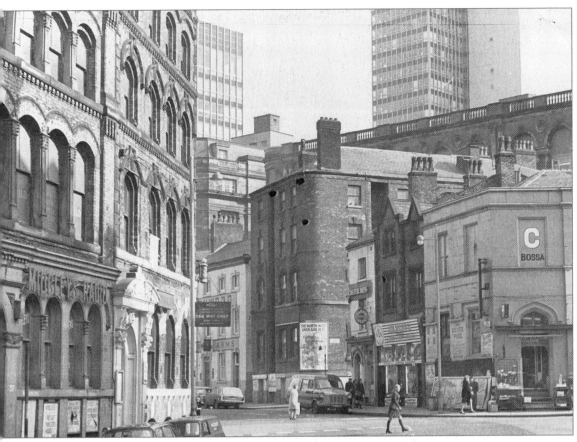

One of Manchester's oldest streets is Long Millgate, which is said to be so named because it led to one of the mills on the River Irk, owned by the Lord of the Manor, where townsmen were meant to have their grain ground. Long Millgate ran at the side of Manchester's manor house, which in 1422 was given to the collegiate church to be a home for the clergy. In 1650, the building was acquired by the executors of Humphrey Chetham, who established a school for forty buys of 'poor, painful parents that neither rogues or vagabonds be'. Backing on to Chetham's was Manchester Grammar School, founded in 1515 by Hugh Oldham, Bishop of Exeter. Long Millgate was not a straight road, there being several rather narrow sections and sharp bends. This photograph shows the junction of Long Millgate and Todd Street, close to a spot which was known as Dangerous Corner until 1829 when the road was widened. The building on the right, designed by Richard Lane and opened about 1837, was originally used for the collegiate church's Sunday school. In the background can also be seen the Manchester Arms public house, which was formerly the town house of the Howarth family. It was from the garden of this house that James Saddler undertook the first balloon ascent in Manchester in 1785. The building was demolished in the 1970s as it was in the way of the proposed underground planned for Manchester. The buildings on the left were warehouses and the Old Swan Hotel, both erected in the mid-nineteenth century when Victoria station was expanding.

The construction of Corporation Street was started in the 1840s to improve the route between central Manchester and Cheetham Hill Road and reduce the amount of traffic having to pass through the Market Place, along Old Millgate and Long Millgate to reach York Street (now Cheetham Hill Road). The work was done in two phases, Market Street to Withy Grove and the Withy Grove to Ducie Bridge in the 1850s. One result of the construction of this new road was that an alternative access to Victoria station could be constructed, although it was not until the 1870s that the present roadway in front of the station was completed. The new road enabled buildings to be erected to take advantage of their proximity to the station, although the buildings that originally faced on to Long Millgate were not turned round but continued to face Long Millgate. This illustration shows Corporation Street from near its junction with Miller Street, looking towards central Manchester. On the right can be seen the canopy over the fish dock at Victoria station, which was added in the early twentieth century to handle fish trains from the coast. In the centre of the block of buildings in the middle of the picture is the Manchester Arms public house, which was one of those that continued to have its main entrance on Long Millgate. Today all these buildings have disappeared and the site is a car park.

Opposite: Until the mid-nineteenth century the Market Place was surrounded by many small courts and passages. The construction of the first part of Corporation Street in 1846 resulted in the clearance of some of these, but many still remained. One such passage was known as Bull's Head Court, which is shown here in the 1930s. The court was originally the entrance to the stable yard of the Bull's Head Hotel which fronted on to the market-place. In the mid-nineteenth century it sold its frontage and turned a side entrance into its main entrance. The large bull's head which was over the original main entrance was moved to a new location over the new main entrance, and a sign was erected across the passage to make sure everyone knew where the hotel was. The bull's head was said to have been part of the crest of the Derby family of Knowsley Hall. Also visible in the background is a large pair of spectacles, often used to advertise opticians.

This photograph of about 1902 shows the junction of Corporation Street and Market Street. At this time the corner building was occupied by Westmacotts, one of Manchester's leading chemists. Next door was a fried fish dealer while Major Drapkin occupied No. 3 Corporation Street. The upper floors of these buildings were offices for a large number of firms. For instance, the firms above No. 9, Victoria Chambers, included a solicitor, heraldic engraver, a disinfectant manufacturer, a watch-maker and a working jeweller. The buildings on the left occupy the site where Marks and Spencers Manchester store was until June 1996.

Until 1829 access to Cross Street from Market Street was through a narrow alley at the side of a public house. With the opening of the town hall on the corner of Cross Street and King Street in 1825 the police commissioners, who formed part of the local government of the town (*see* p. 44), decided that it would enhance the town if the entrance to Cross Street were improved. The result was that the improvements were made at the same time as the alterations to Market Street were being undertaken. Another change which took place at the same time was that the whole length of Cross Street was given a single name, whereas previously there had been three or four different names to the road. Further changes took place in 1866 when the Royal Exchange was rebuilt with a façade on Cross Street, while in 1868 the *Manchester Guardian* established its offices on Cross Street, opposite the Royal Exchange.

CROSS STREET, MANCHESTER.

During the nineteenth and early twentieth century many of the original buildings which lined Cross Street were replaced by stone faced buildings which had shops at street level and offices on the upper floors. This view was taken looking along Cross Street towards the Royal Exchange. Among the buildings it shows is Lloyds Bank (centre), which was erected on the site of the former Manchester Town Hall. One important nineteenth-century resident on Cross Street was J.B. Dancer, who was a scientific instrument maker, undertaking work for scientists like Dalton and Joule. Another well-known resident was Ernest Jones, the Chartist leader, who was a barrister: he had an office in a building that once stood on the site of the building seen here advertising a summer sale.

After the cathedral the oldest church in central Manchester is Cross Street Chapel. This chapel was established in 1694 by the followers of the Revd Henry Newcombe, who had been expelled from the Collegiate Church in 1662 for refusing to accept the Restoration religious settlement. When Cross Street Chapel was established it followed the tenets of Presbyterianism, but during the eighteenth century it gradually moved away Trinitarianism to Unitarianism. The building shown here had been rebuilt in 1715 after it had been severely damaged by rioters supporting the old Pretender. The cost of repairing building was £1,500, which was met by Parliament. In 1929 Cross Street Chapel was described as the 'best brick built building in Manchester', but unfortunately it was destroyed in the Christmas blitz of 1940. A new chapel was erected on the site after the war, but now this has been demolished and a new development occupies the site.

King Street came into existence in about 1735 and was for many years a residential street. It is said that the name was given to it by supporters of the exiled Stuarts who also named a nearby square as St James's Square. For almost a century the only access to King Street was from Cross Street, but in 1829 the King's Arms Coaching House on Deansgate was demolished and an alternative entrance to the street was created. Cross Street divides King Street into two sections, each with a different character. This photograph shows the upper part of King Street looking down from Spring Gardens to Cross Street in the 1860s or '70s. This part of King Street became associated with banking and insurance in the nineteenth century and the presence of such offices was encouraged by the Bank of England, which opened in Manchester in 1825. In the photograph the classical-style building is Cockerell's Bank of England completed in 1845. Beyond the bank can be seen Town Hall Chambers which was later to be replaced by Alfred Waterhouse's offices for the Prudential Insurance Company. In the background are the buildings which were demolished when the Eagle Insurance Company built its offices on Cross Street in 1911. On the right can be seen the edge of the buildings which were also designed by Alfred Waterhouse in 1862 for the Royal Insurance Company, but which were later to be owned by the Vulcan Insurance Company.

The lower part of King Street, between Cross Street and Deansgate, developed in the nineteenth century as a shopping street with many of the houses which had been erected in the eighteenth century being replaced by shops. These new shops tended to cover the whole of the plot of land so that many are long and narrow. The street itself was much narrower than the upper part of King Street and so traffic congestion was always a problem. When this photograph was taken in 1931 parking restrictions had been introduced with the notice informing motorists which side they could park on, the date being the determining factor. Architecturally this part of King Street presents a variety of styles from the mock half-timbering of Nos 15–17 and Old Exchange Passage to the Georgian style of No. 35, the Victorian form of No. 62 and the terracotta character of Liberty's shop, dated 1906. The answer to parking and traffic congestion on this narrow street was adopted in the 1970s – cars were banned and the area pedestrianized.

In 1822 the Police Commissioners, who governed Manchester in conjunction with the manorial Court Leet, decided to replace their offices on Police Street with a purpose-built town hall. Francis Goodwin was commissioned to design the building, which was erected at the corner of Cross Street and King Street on the site of Dr Charles White's house. The new building not only included offices for the Commissioners and their officials, but also for the watch. In 1840, after two years of wrangling, the Police Commissioners handed the building over to the new borough council, who continued to use it until 1877 when the Town Hall in Albert Square was opened. The old Town Hall was then converted into Manchester's Free Reference Library, as the former library building in Castlefield had been declared structurally dangerous and condemned. The library remained in the former Town Hall until 1912 when this building was declared unsafe and the library was forced to move to temporary premises. The old Town Hall was demolished with the columns from the front being re-erected in Heaton Park. This photograph shows the former Town Hall when it was the library. The tower on the right is part of the York Hotel, which was built on the site of the house where the author Harrison Ainsworth was born.

Although many of the buildings on King Street were rebuilt in the nineteenth century, one of the original gentleman's residences has remained, No. 35. This house, which was built in about 1735 by Dr Peter Waring who was an ardent supporter of the Jacobite cause, would have had views across open countryside when completed. In about 1788 the property passed into the hands of the Jones family. When John Jones died, his sons abandoned the tea dealing and concentrated on banking. When Lewis Lloyd married into the family, the bank changed its name to Jones, Lloyd & Co. In 1863 the bank was taken over by the Manchester and District Banking Co., which is now part of the National Westminster Group who continued to use the building as a bank until the 1990s. The railings in front of the property were there to prevent people falling down and injuring themselves as street lighting was non-existent until the nineteenth century. Those who did not rail their cellars were liable to a fine imposed by the authorities.

St Ann's Square, originally known as Acres Fields, was the site of the annual fair held in Manchester from 1222 to 1820, until it was moved first to Smithfield and then to Liverpool Road. In 1708 the size of Acres Field was reduced by the Act of Parliament authorizing the construction of St Ann's Church and a surrounding churchyard 'three score yards in length and forty yards in breadth'. At the same time the right to continue to hold a fair in the area was guaranteed. Originally St Ann's Square was a tree-lined residential area, but towards the end of the eighteenth century the first shops appeared and gradually the domestic dwellings were replaced by shops and offices. This particular view shows St Ann's Square in about 1910 at its junction with Exchange Street. At that time the shops which were on the side shown in this photograph included a silk mercer, a tea dealer, chemist, boot maker, goldsmith and hairdresser while on the opposite side there was a tailor, a cook and confectioner's shop, bookseller, ladies outfitter and a photographer. In the offices above the shops there were a wide range of small businesses, most of a professional or consultancy nature. Today many of the buildings on this side of the square retain the same character and appearance as they did over a century ago. The photograph also shows the buildings on the Deansgate side of Exchange Street, facing the Royal Exchange, which have all been replaced by modern buildings.

In 1775 an Act of Parliament was promoted which allowed certain improvements to be made to Manchester, including the opening up of a road from St Mary's Gate into St Ann's Square. This road became known as Exchange Street and provided an improved access to the square as well as opening up a view of St Ann's Church. To create Exchange Street it was necessary to demolish a number of buildings both on St Mary's Gate and in the square itself. This pre-First World War view shows the ground floor level of the Royal Exchange before it was extended in 1919. The statue in the centre of the picture is dedicated to those who fought in the Boer War and was unveiled in 1908. The number of hackney carriages in the photograph are a reminder that it was from St Ann's Square that distances to and from Manchester were measured and that the square was also an official hackney carriage stand.

Market Street, originally known as Market Stede Lane, developed in a piecemeal manner as the town extended outwards over the centuries. By the eighteenth century it linked the Market Place with Levers Row and the Daub Holes (Piccadilly), but its width was irregular and it was a fairly steep road. Although improvements were made to some streets in the late eighteenth century, Manchester Street was not regarded as a priority case. It was not until 1821 that permission was obtained to undertake a major widening of the road, a project which cost over £250,000 and took well over a decade to almost complete, the final section not being undertaken until the 1870s. This photograph was taken in about 1910 and shows the corner of Corporation Street and Market Street, looking towards Piccadilly, with buildings which were demolished when the Arndale Centre was built. The shop on the corner was that of the firm of J.S. Moss, gentlemen's outfitters and tailors founded in about 1792 and described as a cash rather than credit tailor with a high class clientele. The S stands for Slazenger. It was the son of the founder who went to London and founded the well-known sports wear firm in the nineteenth century.

The final stage of the improvement of Market Street took place when Palace House was demolished in about 1870. This building got its name in 1745 as it was the home of Mr Dickenson who accommodated Bonnie Prince Charlie when he passed through the town in December 1745. This view of Market Street, looking towards Piccadilly, was taken in 1937 when the street was decorated for George VI's coronation. The lack of traffic is unusual as normally Market Street was one of the most congested streets in central Manchester which, even before the arrival of the internal combustion engine, some commentators regarded as dangerous to cross. Although it was pedestrianized in the 1980s, the original idea to remove traffic from this important road was first made by the city engineer in 1906.

Market Street in the 1960s, showing some of the buildings on the left hand side (looking towards the Royal Exchange) which were demolished to make way for the Arndale Centre. Although part of this side of Market Street around the junction with Cross Street has been demolished, there are still a number of buildings on this side which date back to the nineteenth century and show the style of building which graced both sides of Market Street until relatively recently.

Another view of Market Street in the 1960s, but this time the opposite side of the road. All these buildings were demolished to make way for the Arndale Centre. The area behind these buildings consisted of warehouses and small dark courts, many of which bore the names of those who had either owned property there or lived there. To go behind the shops on Market Street even in the 1950s and 1960s was to enter another world.

One corner that has changed dramatically in the last ninety years is that where Market Street and Mosley Street meet Piccadilly. This picture shows the corner in about 1905 when the site was occupied by the Royal Hotel. This hotel had moved here in 1827 when its original site on High Street was required for a warehouse. The building itself had been erected in about 1772 for the Potter family, who sold it in 1814 although continuing to live there until it was purchased by Henry Lacy. When the Royal Hotel opened it leased some of the property at the rear to David Bannerman for use as a warehouse, which gave rise to the comment that within twenty years Moseley Street would cease to be a residential street and become one of shops, offices and warehouses. The Royal Hotel was demolished in 1908 and replaced by Royal Buildings. In the background is the tower which was a feature of Lewis's store in the early twentieth century. It was the arrival of Lewis's which revolutionized shopping in Manchester by opening on Saturdays and catering for the rising middle and lower middle classes. Their bold approach caused friction with the more traditional shops like Finnigans and Kendals, who sought to offer a personalized service and were fearful of their new competitor.

There are a number of springs under central Manchester. Several of these were used in the sixteenth century to supply water for the conduit in the Market Place. Their existence is probably the reason for the name of Fountain Street, which runs from Market Street towards Cooper Street and Princess Street. Among the buildings on Fountain Street is the former Board of Guardians Office of the Manchester Poor Law Union and the Shakespeare Inn. This inn has a black and white half-timbered appearance, but it is not a creation of the sixteenth century, but the late nineteenth century, when there was a revolt against Gothic architecture. Further along, on the corner of Market Street and Fountain Street, can be seen the buildings which were erected when Market Street was improved.

Oldham Street takes its name not from the fact that it leads to Oldham Road and the town of Oldham, but from Adam Oldham who owned land at the corner of Piccadilly and a lane leading off the square in the late eighteenth century. By the end of the nineteenth century Oldham Street was a favourite shopping street with the ladies of Manchester. It was said that it was possible to buy everything from the cradle to the grave from the shops on Oldham Street. This photograph was taken in the 1890s.

The shops which lined Oldham Street in the nineteenth and early twentieth century became less impressive and important the further away from Piccadilly they were. This photograph shows the corner of Piccadilly and Oldham Street. On the left is Saqui and Lawrence, jewellers who occupied a building erected in about 1881, while on the opposite corner is the Albion Hotel. Other important buildings on Oldham Street in the nineteenth century included Affleck and Brown's store, which was established in 1860 and merged with Pauldens in 1930, and the Oldham Street Methodist Chapel, which was also the headquarters of the Manchester and Salford Methodist Mission.

This interesting view of Manchester was taken between the wars and shows central Manchester from the west, looking eastwards towards Piccadilly. At the bottom there is Oxford Road station with its terminal platforms for the electric trains to Altrincham. Also visible is the Refuge Assurance Offices with its distinctive tower, the Palace Theatre and St James Buildings all on Oxford Street. Behind the buildings on Oxford Street there is the Rochdale canal and the Dickenson Street power station, whose chimney is in the centre of the picture. At the top left hand corner of the view is Piccadilly Gardens. Between Piccadilly and Oxford Street are many of the textile warehouses which were important elements in the chain of producing and selling cotton and cotton goods. This view provides a unique opportunity to see this part of central Manchester from an unusual angle.

CHAPTER TWO

MARKETS & SHOPS

S urviving medieval documents relating to the manor of Manchester indicate that in the thirteenth century there were those in Manchester who earned their living by buying and selling goods. By 1552 there was a well-established market in Manchester which was subject to certain rules and regulations imposed by the Court Leet, although they might have been suggested by the lord of the manor's steward in order to ensure that trading was carried out in an organized manner. Certain trades, such as the butchers and fishmongers, were allocated specific places within the market-place and when they moved attempts were made to ensure they returned their designated locations. Officials were reported to ensure that trading took place in an open manner, and that certain standards were kept.

As Manchester became more urbanized so the demand for food from the surrounding area increased. Regulations were introduced which were intended to ensure that all those who lived in the township of Manchester were able to purchase sufficient food for their requirements before 'strangers', that is those from the surrounding area. The whole operation of buying and selling was carefully controlled by the lord of the manor as he had a financial interest in all purchases by charging a toll on goods and on shopkeepers.

During the eighteenth century the Market Place became overcrowded and spread into surrounding areas, like Smithy Door. There were also attempts in the 1780s to establish rival markets, such as the one at Newmarket off Cross Street, but these failed as the lord of the manor was prepared to take legal action to protect his interests. However, he did acknowledge that the original market-place was overcrowded and allowed some specialist markets to move into other parts of the town, such as the Apple Market to Fennel Street. Eventually, in the 1820s, it was decided that all the markets should be concentrated at Shudehill.

As Manchester was the centre of the area not only did retail markets develop, but also wholesale markets in foodstuffs as well as in other goods, such as cotton. It is the food markets that attract the most attention as it made the Shudehill area busy throughout the day, and especially in the early hours of the morning.

As well as the markets, shops also developed, many of which specialized in particular types of goods. During the nineteenth century the streets of central Manchester gradually lost their residential character and became streets of shops and warehouses. The first shop, for instance, appeared in St Ann's Square in the 1790s and gradually shops came to predominate in the area. Likewise when Market Street was widened in the 1820s, it was the shopkeepers who were most affected. The retail trade was regarded as very important in Manchester and was able to get its way in certain circumstances. For example, when Deansgate was widened in the 1870s the shops which were affected were able to make a very good deal with the council in return for giving up their existing premises.

Although many of the shops were originally owner-run businesses, gradually some started to establish branches in different parts of central Manchester while others began to develop into what might be called department stores. One of the earliest of these was Kendalls on Deangate, but after 1877 they had a rival in Lewis's on Market Street who appealed to the rising middle class white-collar workers, encouraging them to enter the shop without obligation to purchase anything.

As well as the shops central Manchester has always had a large number of street traders and barrow boys selling a wide range of goods from newspapers to flowers and fruit and vegetables. Although they tend to be spread throughout the city centre, there were certain areas where particular types of street trader could be found, such as those selling second hand books on Shudehill Hill, or the ice-cream sellers around Smithfield market and in Piccadilly.

When the lord of the manor decided to concentrate all the markets on the site at Shudehill, known as Smithfield, it was an open area with little cover except market stalls which the traders erected. The first traders were transferred to Smithfield in 1822, but a small residual market was left in the market-place. In 1845 the borough of Manchester purchased the manorial rights, including those of controlling the markets, from the Mosley family. Gradually the open market was covered over with a cast-iron and glass structure to provide better conditions for the traders. Although there were retail markets at Smithfield, they were better known for their wholesale markets, for fruit, vegetables and fish. This scene was photographed at the end of the nineteenth century, and shows the market hall erected by the council and the large number of people who were to be found in the area when the market was trading.

This scene was photographed in 1896 inside the fruit and vegetable market. Stall holders either await customers or carry on trading as if the photographer were not present, while porters wait for their next job of taking goods which had been brought by greengrocers to the carts to transport back to their shops in central Manchester and the suburbs. At the end of each day's trading goods which were perishable or which were damaged and could not be sold were often passed on to members of the public at very low prices, or just thrown away, to be scavenged by those living in areas like Ancoats or Angel Meadow.

Manchester has always had a number of street traders or barrow boys selling fruit and vegetables. This man selling Kent cherries at *2d* a pound in about 1933 was trading in front of a firm called Burma Gems. The cherries look far larger than those which can be purchased today.

These two flower sellers are trading in front of Woolworth's store in Piccadilly.

One of the best known street markets in Manchester was where second hand book sellers concentrated on Shudehill. Book bargains appear to be the object of these browsers and it certainly was a place where bargains could be found. With the development of the Arndale Centre the location for the bookstalls had to be moved. Today only one remains on a pitch at the corner of High Street and Church Street, a pale shadow of the former bustling book stalls of the inter-war years and the 1950s and 1960s.

This street trader is said to be selling 'lucky white heather'. He appears to be on Market Street in front of the Rylands building, across the road from Lewis's store.

A newspaper was published in Manchester in the 1720s, but since 1752, when the *Manchester Mercury* was first published, newspaper publishing has been unbroken in the city for almost 250 years. Some papers only lasted a few years, but others survived for several decades. Many of the newspapers which were published had specific political allegiances such as the *Manchester Guardian* for the Liberals and the *Manchester Courier* for the Tories. Although there were newspaper sellers who worked in the morning, it was often the evening papers which brought them most of their business as people purchased them on the way home to read on the train, tram or bus. This particular newspaper seller appears to have posed for the photographer possibly in Stephenson Square sometime in the 1930s.

This newspaper seller is standing in the Shambles in 1937 with copies of the *Manchester Evening Chronicle*. Th
Chronicle was one of two evening papers that were on sale in Manchester for over sixty years. It was first publishe
on 10 May 1897 when 169,000 copies were sold, mostly by boys on street corners. The first issue was six page
long, but later issues were of eight pages, and even more in the twentieth century. The paper was founded b
Edward Hulton, who also established the *Sporting Chronicle* and the *Athletic News* as well as the *Sunday Chronicle*
whose political views were inclined towards the Toryism and Tory democracy as expressed by Disraeli and whic
appealed to Lancashire working men who supported the Conservative party at the end of the nineteenth centur
Hulton sold his papers in 1924 to Allied Newspapers, later Kemsley Newspapers. About the same time the pape
moved from the premises on Withy Grove, which it had occupied for almost the whole of its life, to a new buildin
on the corner of Corporation Street and Withy Grove, which has been known variously as Kempsley House
Thompson House and Maxwell House. Hulton's papers had a strong interest in sport, which may account for th
newspaper poster the seller is holding.

n the late nineteenth century there were a number of ice-cream makers and sellers in Manchester, many of whom
ame from Italy. They tended to live close together in the Ancoats area. They made their ice-cream in their own
omes, often in the cellars, and from there set out to sell their product to the general public around the streets of
Ianchester. One of the favourite areas for these Italian ice-cream salesmen was around Smithfield Market, which
as always very busy. It is possible that this ice-cream salesman, photographed by Samuel Coulthurst in about
890, had set up his pitch in the Smithfield Market area.

Another well-known site in Manchester in the late nineteenth century was the hen market on Shudehill. In 1869 was described as 'a heterogeneous mass of hampers, hen coops and hutches containing poultry, pigeons and rabbit Most breeds of fowl are represented here . . . '. The commentator went on to report that it was also possible t purchase geese and 'occasionally peacocks, ducks, ferrets and white mice.' The dress of the tradesmen was describe as being 'dingy'. This photograph was taken some twenty years later, in about 1890, and shows a boy sellin pineapple juice in ½d and 1d glasses.

The Italian ice-cream manufacturers and salesmen gradually improved not only their products but also their stalls. This particular salesman was photographed in the 1930s at the hen market on Shudehill. According to Anthony Rea's book on the Italian community in Manchester, Luigi Rocca, who might be related to the person selling the ice in the picture, was one of the first ice-cream makers in Manchester in about 1881. The Roccas were also involved with Louis Colaluca in manufacturing ice-cream wafers in a factory on Mill Street in Ancoats, this factory being one of the three in the Manchester area between the wars manufacturing ice-cream wafers and cones.

Mrs Spring's shop in Hulme was a general grocery store. It is a reminder of the days when the corner shop sold everything from food to polishes. Clearly visible is the bacon slicer which would have been used to slice bacon to the thickness individual customers required. The left hand advertisement is for a well-known brand of tea, Hornimans, while other products include polish, yeast and something with the name 'laxpur.' Also there are jars and tins on the shelves, but their labels are not clear enough to read.

In the days before photocopying and easy reproduction methods if a business wanted labels or leaflets they would probably have gone to a firm which specialized in ticket writing. These were often small businesses located in small workshops throughout the city. One such firm was that of Frederick Tapp, whose premises were at 56 Thomas Street. Tapp established his business in about 1861 and presumably prospered as this postcard, which may have been used for advertising purposes, was produced in about 1900. The building is still there today, occupied by a firm which is still producing and selling posters for sales, special offers an so on.

There were many small specialist shops in Manchester up to 1939. Although many were located in the suburbs there were still a large number in central Manchester like this pet shop, Princess Aviaries, which described itself as a 'livestock emporium.' The owner certainly sold more than birds because the chalk notices at the side of the door refer to tortoises from 1s each, puppies, monkeys, dogs and young rabbits, while in the cage on the floor are chickens. Some of the cages higher up also appear to have birds in them while in the window an animal appears to be sleeping. The business must have been reasonably profitable as he is on the telephone at a time when such things were far from usual.

Seymour Mead was a well-known and respected grocery chain that was founded in Manchester in about 1865. The company soon acquired a reputation for selling unadulterated tea, coffee and general groceries. Seymour Mead blended their own tea for all their forty branches, a process which took two days. Once all the supplies for their own shops had been completed, Seymour Mead went on to blend tea for other grocers. This window display, photographed in 1908, was prepared for the seventh Grocers' Exhibition held at the St James Hall on Oxford Street, an event which was described as the 'shop window of the grocery trade.' As well as displaying the latest products, shops were encouraged to enter their staff in competitions such as tea matching, window-dressing, bacon slicing and butter and margarine tasting. The photograph also provides a good indication of the packaging in use at the time and prices which were paid for goods.

One of Manchester's best known shops is Kendals on Deansgate. The shop owes its origins to James Watts senior who opened a shop on the corner of Deansgate and Parsonage in 1796. Later he moved to 99 Deansgate on the opposite side of the road. In 1836 the Watts family decided to concentrate on the wholesale side of their business and sold the retail side to three employees, Messrs Kendal, Milne and Faulkner. The shop prospered throughout the nineteenth century and grew in reputation. In 1872 the old building was demolished when Deansgate was widened and a new building erected. Gradually the company extended its premises on both sides of Deansgate. On the north side of Deansgate, the old buildings were demolished and a new one constructed, so that by 1920 permission was given which allowed the two shops on opposite sides of Deansgate to be linked by an underground passage, enabling customers to pass between the two shops without going outside and having to cross the busy Deansgate. This view of part of Kendals is undated, but was probably taken in the 1930s. It shows one of the floors ready to receive its customers at the start of the day.

During the 1890s the buildings between St Mary's Street and Blackfriars Street were cleared to make way for further improvements to Deansgate. When the work took place, evidence was found of medieval buildings dating back to the fifteenth century. Among the businesses which were affected by this redevelopment was that of John A. Phillips, picture dealer, whose shop at No. 84 appears to be attracting a good deal of attention from potential customers. Next door at No. 82 was Worrals, a firm of confectioners who were there from about 1883 until 1897. This shop had been a confectioner for a number of years before Worrals had taken it over. The third shop that can be seen is that of John Owen, toy dealer, who occupied the premises from about 1858 until 1893, when it was acquired by a gentleman by the name of Barr.

Saturday afternoon was always an important shopping time for Mancunians. This photograph taken in the 1950s shows the corner of Piccadilly and Oldham Street as shoppers cross Piccadilly towards the Esplanade. In the background is Saqui and Lawrence, the jewellers, and Woolworth's store, opened in 1926.

CHAPTER THREE

ALL IN A DAY'S WORK

Manchester as a large town is a product of the industrial revolution when steam power was adapted to drive machinery and when transport improved to enable raw materials and finished products to be carried in bulk to and from the manufactories. Prior to the eighteenth century Manchester did have industry, although it was small scale and based in the home. Much of it was associated with the woollen industry, but it was the arrival of cotton and the developments in textile machinery which benefited Manchester.

Arkwright's water-frame and Hargreave's spinning-jenny were two of several machines which helped to improve production in the textile industry, but it was Crompton's mule, which to be fully effective required something more than human or water power, that brought about the biggest changes. Crompton's mule and the adoption of steam to drive machines were developed roughly at the same time with the result that one benefited from the other. A number of mule-makers who might be said to have been the origins of the engineering industry in the area established themselves in Manchester. Some of these mule-makers, when they found that some of their orders were left on their hands, began to use them to spin cotton. This is how McConnell and Kennedy started in the cotton spinning industry.

Manchester was never a very large producer of cotton, but it was the centre of the industry with the Exchange and warehouses. It was the place which brought together all those involved in the industry whether as manufacturers of yarn, makers of cotton goods or the manufacturers of machinery, bleaches and dyes. Manchester was the centre of the cotton industry, 'Queen of the cotton cities' as A.B. Reach described the town in 1849.

The emphasis on Manchester being the centre of the textile industry has tended to overshadow the fact that the town and its environs was also an important engineering centre. The products made by engineering firms in Manchester ranged from small parts for machines to railway engines. It was the increasing use of steam power and the faster running of machines that led to the development of machines made of metal where all the parts had to fit accurately. It was not possible, as it had been with wooden machines, to shave little bits off. With metal machines everything had to be made accurately. Gradually the machine tool trade developed with people like Joseph Whitworth taking a leading role. Some of the larger engineering works, such as Beyer Peacock's, were to be found just outside the Manchester boundaries in places like Gorton, where land and rates were cheaper, but which were close enough to Manchester to attract both the skilled and unskilled workers they required. Even in the twentieth century engineering in Manchester has kept pace with the changes that were going on: for instance, the establishment of Avro as aircraft manufacturers, the Belsize car factory and Ferranti (electrical engineering).

As well as engineering, Manchester and the surrounding area has developed a chemical industry, often as a result of demands from the textile industry for colours that would not wash out in water or which were different from those already in use. In many respects the demands of the textile industry encouraged the growth of the chemical industry, with firms such as ICI and Clayton Aniline being established.

Manchester had many small firms making a tremendous range of goods in the nineteenth and twentieth centuries. Only a few are recorded in this section; many more were never fully recorded or, if they were, more by chance than a deliberate policy, such as Plant's hat block manufactury in Ancoats above a stable. Although Reach said that Manchester was the capital of the weavers and spinners it was equally the capital of the engineer, the turner and the lathe operator. All were dependent on each other for their success.

This aerial photograph of Ancoats was taken in the mid-1960s and shows the earliest industrial suburb in Manchester. Running left to right across the photograph is Great Ancoats Street while the linear feature running north to south on the right hand side is the Rochdale Canal. Alongside the road at the side of the Rochdale Canal are the former Sedgewick Mill and McConnell and Kennedy Mill; both were originally engaged in the manufacture of cotton yarn. The earliest of these mills dates from the 1790s, when multi-storeyed buildings were unusual and towered over the surrounding domestic properties. To the south of Great Ancoats Street, also close to the Rochdale Canal, is Brunswick Mill, built in the 1820s, but whose fame rests on the fact that A.V. Roe made some of his earliest aircraft in the basement in about 1910. Other features which can be clearly identified are the tower of St Peter's, Blossom Street, which was consecrated in 1862 and although still standing is in a ruinous condition. In the top left hand corner is Victoria Square, built in about 1892 as a tenement block to replace some of the back-to-back houses and cellar dwellings formerly found in the area. The other obvious building which Mancunians will recognize is the *Daily Express* building on Great Ancoats Street. Today much of the area to the right of the Rochdale Canal has been cleared away, but there are large areas of the remaining part of Ancoats shown on this illustration still extant. Many of the former cotton mills are listed and part of a conservation area, but it is essential to find new uses for the mills before they deteriorate as a result of neglect.

The title of this float is 'Cotton'. What the event is and when it took place is not recorded on the photograph, but the presence of a lifeboat in the background suggests that it may have been part of the annual 'Lifeboat Saturday' held in Manchester from the 1890s onwards. The aim was to raise funds for the Royal National Lifeboat Institution, and involved not only representatives from the RNLI but also other organizations in the city. The parade was held on a Saturday afternoon so that those who had been working in the shops and warehouses in the morning could watch the parade before returning home. This photograph must have been taken after 1903 as the Midland Hotel is in the background.

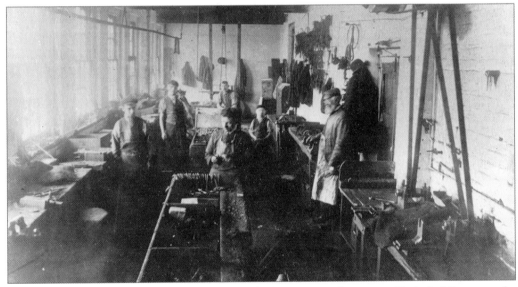

There were many small firms in Manchester in the late nineteenth century. Typical of these was the firm of Pass and Sparey, which was established in about 1880. The firm developed a high reputation for the quality of its spindles which it supplied to the textile trade in Lancashire. The firm was located on Vesta Street, close to the Ashton Canal and a few minutes walk from London Road station so they had two possible ways to send their products to clients. This photograph was taken in about 1900 with William Pass, one of the owners of the firm, keeping a careful eye on his employees and ensuring that as little production time as possible was lost as a result of having a photographer on the premises. Pass and Sparey eventually closed in about 1916 as a result of the First World War.

Although Manchester was an important manufacturing and trading centre in the nineteenth century it was also an important centre for economic ideas, especially that of free trade. In 1837 the Anti-Corn Law League was founded with the aim of securing the repeal of laws which prohibited the import of grain until the price had reached 80s a quarter. Those supporting the movement argued that it kept the price of food artificially high, while those in favour of retaining the corn laws claimed that the reason why the opponents of the corn laws wanted their abolition was so that they could pay lower wages. The organization which developed to run the campaign to secure the repeal of the corn laws was based in Newall's buildings on Market Street, shown in this illustration of 1866 shortly before its demolition to make way for an enlarged Royal Exchange. The Anti-Corn Law League was also responsible for the construction of the early Free Trade Halls in the 1840s, and when they achieved their aim in 1846 they formed a company to build the Free Trade Hall to mark their success and named it after their main economic idea – free trade.

This view shows the Royal Exchange at the corner of Market Street and Cross Street in the early twentieth century. The first Exchange on this site had been opened in 1809, providing a meeting place for businessmen to exchange commercial information and strike deals. In 1851, after Queen Victoria's visit to Manchester and her reception at the Exchange, she granted the title of 'Royal' to the organization. In 1866 it was decided to rebuild the Royal Exchange as it was too small for the growing membership. The new building, designed by Mills and Murgatroyd, was opened in two stages, in 1871 and 1874. By the beginning of the twentieth century its membership had exceeded 10,000 with days of 'High Change' being Tuesdays and Thursdays. The massive portico on the Cross Street façade was demolished in about 1912 to enable Cross Street to be widened.

This is the scene outside the Royal Exchange on Cross Street in about 1910 as businessmen hurry about their business or exchange information and news. It was said that as much business was transacted outside the Exchange as on the floor of the building itself. Across the road from the Royal Exchange can be seen the offices of the *Manchester Guardian*, founded in 1821 as a supporter of the moderate radical movement in Manchester. Later it became associated with liberalism in British politics. The *Manchester Guardian* moved to these offices in about 1868 after it had taken over the *Manchester Evening News*. The *Manchester Guardian* was regarded as the voice of Manchester's free trade movement.

Opposite: It is difficult to associate the chemical industry with the textile industry, but the demands of bleachers and dyers for a wide range of colours, and colours which would not wash out in water, encouraged the development of this industry. This photograph, taken in about 1933, shows the Clayton firm of Clayton Aniline, which had been founded by Charles Dreyfus in 1876 to manufacture dyes from coke oven benzole. Gradually the range of products increased as did the size of the firm, which became part of CIBA in 1911. Note the extensive use of wood in the building, as this would absorb the chemicals, and the clogs the workmen are wearing.

In the nineteenth century Manchester was also an important engineering centre with many companies making a wide range of products which were exported to various parts of the world. One such company was the locomotive manufacturing firm of Beyer Peacock and Co., which was established in Gorton in 1854. The site was chosen because it was outside the borough of Manchester and hence had lower rates, yet close enough to attract the skilled workers it required. The locomotives it built were of all sizes from small tank engines to massive articulated Beyer Garratt locomotives. This photograph shows a small saddle tank built in 1861 for the Knighton Railway, appropriately enough called 'Knighton'. When it was built it cost £1,300, on which the company made a reasonable profit.

The manufacture of cameras and the taking of photographs required a great deal of precision and care. Manchester developed a reputation for having some very high quality makers of scientific instruments. The most famous was probably J.B. Dancer, who made scientific instruments for scientists like John Dalton and J.P. Joule. He was also something of a photographer, developing the lantern slide and micro-photograph. There were other firms who made scientific instruments for the scientists, hospitals and academic institutions. Among these was the firm shown in this photograph taken in the 1890s, Ronchettl's, later Casartelli's, which was said to be the largest establishment of its type outside London. The firm's involvement in scientific instruments was a sideline as their main business was optical work.

The period between 1918 and 1939 was one when new industry began to replace the old heavy industries. One of the firms which benefited from this was Ferranti's. Originally Ferranti's was involved in the manufacture of equipment for large generating stations, but Sebastian de Ferranti was also interested in the application of electricity for domestic purposes and for domestic equipment, such as electric irons and fires. As well as manufacturing household products, Ferranti also manufactured radio valves, cathode ray tubes and other specialist electrical devices. In 1934 the company moved into the manufacture of radios, but this was not a great commercial success. This particular illustration shows women assembling radio valves in November 1934 at the company's factory at Moston, which had recently opened.

Opposite: At the end of the nineteenth century the engineering firm of Brooks and Doxey employed about 2,000 men at factories in Miles Platting and Gorton. The firm had been founded by Samuel Brooks in 1859 in Union Mill, Minshull Street in central Manchester to manufacture loom temples and small accessories and tools for the textile industry. Demand for the company's products increased rapidly so that within four years of establishment Brooks was employing over sixty people. As demand grew so did the labour force, with the result that the firm outgrew its original premises and in 1865 moved to Gorton, which is the factory shown here. Presumably the men are leaving work after a hard day in the factory. Twenty-five years later, in 1888, the firm took over the Junction Iron Works in Miles Platting to expand production further.

In an industrialized society one of the problems has been unemployment which has varied according to the state of trade. In 1908 the Manchester area suffered from one of its cyclical periods of high unemployment. Attempts were made to find employment for those out of work, such as landscaping a new park in Rusholme, now known as Platt Fields. Meetings were also held in the town hall to discuss the problem. In 1908 the Dean of Manchester made some comments about the unemployed which were regarded as derogatory – this led to a large crowd gathering outside the Cathedral, shown here. There was also trouble in Albert Square, where a force of 800 police were unable to keep order and arrest the ringleaders. There was a fear on this occasion that the crowd of unemployed might storm the Town Hall and do serious damage to the building.

Opposite: Like all large towns and cities Manchester was affected by the General Strike in 1926. Transport and the distribution of food supplies was severely hit. There were also spasmodic outbreaks of violence with lorries being attacked in areas like Oldham Road. Local newspapers published a small edition. This view shows the crowds outside the *Manchester Evening News* offices in Cross Street shortly after the latest news bulletin had been issued.

Industrial relations in industry varied between firms. In the case of the wire-makers Richard Johnson & Nephew in the Bradford district of Manchester, industrial relations were reasonable until the company began to look for economies and brought in a firm of time and motion experts to advise them. One suggestion was to stop the men in the cleaning department working continuous overtime. The men objected to being regarded as machines and walked out on strike. The strike lasted ten months and ended when the firm said that all the posts held by the striking workers had been filled. Here the strikers are seen walking to the factory to collect their tool boxes.

When the Borough of Manchester was created in 1838 a watch committee was established, but the Court Leet and the Police Commissioners, who had governed Manchester up to that time, refused to acknowledge the legality of the borough council or any of its committee. It was not until 1842 that Manchester was able to appoint its first Chief Constable, Captain Edward Willis. Over the next century the duties of the police were increased, including point duty at busy junctions such as Cross Street, Corporation Street and Market Street. It was claimed in the early twentieth century that the presence of police on point duty there speeded up the flow of traffic, although some people had other ideas. This photograph, taken in the 1890s, shows a Manchester police officer walking down Market Street, possibly near the Royal Exchange. Whether he is on traffic duty or just patrolling is not clear.

Fire was regarded as a major hazard in towns and villages so precautions were often taken to prevent it either breaking out or spreading. The duty of the night watches which were appointed was to look out for fire rather than law breakers. The earliest recorded fire precautions in Manchester date from 1566, while the earliest record of fire fighting equipment is to be found in the Court Leet records of 1613. Until the arrival of piped water with sufficient pressure there were always difficulties when fighting fires, especially those involving industrial premises where grease and oil added to the problems. Improvements to the fire service were only brought about gradually. In 1899 the watch committee, who were responsible for the fire service in Manchester as well as the police, purchased the horse-drawn fire escape shown in this picture. It was built by William Rose of Salford at a cost of £145. It was the beginning of a series of improvements which culminated in the construction of a new fire service headquarters at the junction of London Road and Whitworth Street and the development of street alarms linked directly to the central fire station, which speeded up response times and reduced the damage fires could cause to buildings.

The York Stone flags which were used for paving the streets of Manchester and other towns provided street artists with an ideal surface on which they could show their artistic talent. This pavement artist is chalking on the flags in Albert Square, in front of the town hall, oblivious to pedestrians going about their normal business. On occasions such pavement artists would attract small crowds to admire their work. Note the bag or cap to the artist's left into which members of the public could throw a coin. This was a hard way to earn a living and in all probability did not earn the artist very much at all.

Although many thousands of people used to travel into Manchester by bus and tram there were also a large number of people who travelled by train into central Manchester. In the early years of the twentieth century, it was claimed that 93,000 people used Victoria station every day, although not all these would have been commuters. The people who travelled into Victoria station would have come from east Lancashire, places like Blackburn, Burnley, Nelson and Colne, Bolton, Bury and Rochdale as well as from Liverpool, Southport, Blackpool and Yorkshire. This photograph, dating from the 1940s or 1950s, shows platform thirteen at Victoria station as a train arrives, but there is no indication where from. Between the wars this platform was used by trains from Liverpool and Southport. The type of carriage gives the impression that it might have been a local train as the stock appears to be compartment as opposed to corridor stock, used on trains going longer distances.

Opposite: Remove the tarmac from many of the roads of central Manchester and underneath will be found the original road surface, granite or sandstone setts. These were laid by hand on a sand base held in place by tar being poured into the joints. The difference between setts and cobbles is that cobbles are irregular in shape, while setts are regular, being either rectangular or square. In some places, especially around the infirmary in Piccadilly, where quietness was important, wooden setts were used instead of the more traditional stone ones, which these men are laying at an unidentified location in central Manchester between the wars.

Drinking fountains and horse troughs were features which were introduced in the latter half of the nineteenth century. The one shown above appears to have been the gathering point for a group of men. Whether these people were taking a break from their normal work, seeking employment or just watching the world go by is not known, neither is the location of the drinking fountain. However, the photograph does provide the fashion historian with information on the dress of working men at the end of the nineteenth century. Notice that everyone is wearing a hat of some description, often an indication of their status or occupation. At least one of the men is wearing clogs and two have clay pipes, the manufacture of which employed many people in small workshops. Left: In contrast to the men at the drinking fountain these two businessmen caught on camera in the late 1930s stand discussing the day's financial news on the steps of the Royal Exchange.

CHAPTER FOUR

GETTING ABOUT

Since Roman times Manchester has been an important centre for communications and transport. Passing close to the Roman fort was the main route between the legionary bases at Chester and York from which branch roads lead to other forts and settlements in the area. It was these roads which formed the basis of the road system in the area for almost 1,400 years, until the first turnpike roads were built in the area in the eighteenth century. Although there were several turnpike roads leading to Manchester, they all started or stopped short of the centre of the town, with the result that anyone wanting to travel north to south had to pass through Manchester.

Although Manchester is situated on the River Irwell this was not suitable for transporting goods to and from the coast or other parts of the country. Although small vessels were able to reach Manchester it was not until major improvements undertaken by Thomas Steers were completed in 1735 that vessels of up to 50 tons could reach the edge of Manchester. Within thirty years of the improvements being made to the River Irwell the opening of the first canal, between Worsley and Manchester in 1764, and its extension to Runcorn a decade later, ushered in a new era of transport which was reliable and cheap and allowed the bulk carriage of goods over long distances. Not only did industrialists benefit from the canal, but also farmers as their products could be carried cheaply to the expanding towns of the area, enabling these towns to grow without the fear of food shortages. By 1805 Manchester was the centre of a network of canals linking the town with other parts of the country. The ultimate development in the field of water transport was the construction and opening of the Manchester Ship Canal in 1894, which provided Manchester with a direct link to the sea. Although canals were ideal for the bulk carriage of goods they were slow and could be affected by adverse weather conditions. In 1825 a new form of transport had been introduced in the north-east to carry freight and now it was decided to apply the steam engine not only to pulling freight trains, but also passenger trains. In 1830 the opening of the Liverpool and Manchester Railway ushered in the railway age, when the time taken to get between towns was dramatically reduced. Within about twenty years the basic railway network around Manchester was completed, linking the city with other industrial areas, the ports as well as smaller towns and villages. Not only was the train used for freight and long distance travel, but it also encouraged the growth of the commuter and the outward expansion of towns. One difficulty travellers encountered on the railways around Manchester was that it was not possible to cross from one side of the city to the other by rail, except by a circuitous route and hence the full potential of north-south traffic was never developed. Several schemes were proposed, but it was not until Metrolink was opened that this difficulty was alleviated.

Bus services in the Manchester area can be traced back to 1824 when John Greenwood introduced a horse bus service from Pendleton to the Exchange. Within a short time others had taken up the idea and a network of horse bus services developed linking Manchester with the surrounding areas. The horse buses, although not cheap to travel on, gave an impetus to the development of residential suburbs such as Victoria Park and Greenheys. Gradually fares did fall, helped by the introduction of cheap workmen's fares after 1877 when the horse tram network was constructed. The introduction of low fares encouraged working people to consider moving from the over-crowded areas of the central and inner suburbs to more pleasant areas with better quality housing. In 1901 the electronic tram began to replace the horse tram, ushering in a mode of transport which survived until 1949, when the last trams were withdrawn. However, as the trams faded away so motor bus services replaced them, being regarded as more flexible in the routes they could take. Finally in 1929 the granting of a licence for Manchester to operate an airport and the opening of Barton airport in 1930 signalled the arrival of air transport. Barton was replaced by Ringway in 1938 and, although war delayed the growth of air travel, this aspect of travel and transport has mushroomed since the 1960s. Today Manchester Airport is one of the busiest and fastest growing in the country.

In 1830 the Liverpool and Manchester Railway was opened, reducing the time it took to get between these two great Lancashire towns from a day to an hour. There were objections to the railway from some of the landowners in the Liverpool Road/Water Street area as well as from the Mersey Irwell Navigation and the Police Commissioners. The Mersey Irwell Navigation insisted that the railway bridge over the river provided sufficient headroom for vessels to continue using the river to reach its warehouses on Water Street. As a result the railway entered Manchester on a viaduct, which included a bridge across Water Street. Water Street bridge, shown here in 1905 just before it was demolished, was manufactured by William Fairbairn in Ancoats, using calculations made by Eaton Hodgkinson to reduce the amount of iron required. The cast-iron sides were added at the insistence of the Police Commissioners in case a train should fall off and damage the road! Note the separation of pedestrians from the road by a line of Doric columns.

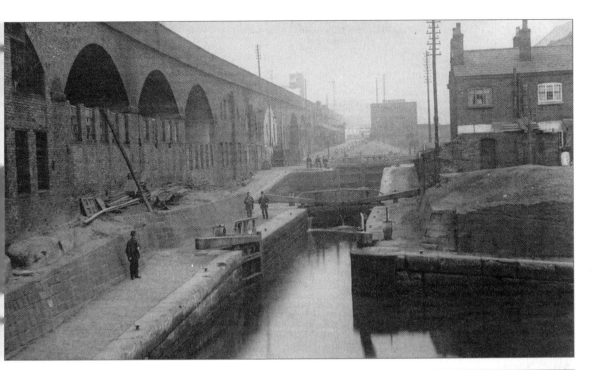

When the Bridgewater Canal was completed there was no direct link between it and the River Irwell. The only way vessels could get on to the river from the canal was to travel to Runcorn and then back along the River Mersey. In 1836 this changed when a clause was included in the Manchester and Salford Junction Canal Act which allowed the Bridgewater Canal to build a lock to provide access to the river. The Manchester and Salford Junction Canal was 5 furlongs in length and was intended to link the Rochdale Canal with the River Irwell at Water Street and reduce the amount of traffic having to be transferred between the two waterway systems by road. The photograph above, taken in about 1892, shows Hulme locks with the lock keepers cottage on the island in the centre. In all, three locks were required to get boats down from the Bridgewater Canal to the River Irwell. The viaduct is that which carries the Manchester to Altrincham railway line. Hulme lock has now been replaced by a new lock providing easier access to the river and Salford Quays. The rather attractive view on the left shows one of Manchester's rivers, the River Medlock, a tributary of the River Irwell, flowing at the back of the Refuge Insurance building in the 1930s. This river was the southern boundary of the township of Manchester. Like all Manchester's rivers and streams it was highly polluted from the various industrial premises on its banks and liable to flooding after heavy rain. The bridge across the river was built in the 1930s to link the Refuge Insurance offices with its car park on the other side of the river.

When the Liverpool and Manchester Railway commenced its services the only station on the line was at Manchester, and even here it was on the outskirts of the town. This photograph shows that station at the beginning of the twentieth century when it was a goods depot. The house on the left had been built early in the nineteenth century by Mr Rothwell, who had industrial premises in the area, and was already in existence when the station was built and was incorporated into the station. The original station consisted of the rendered section in the centre of the picture. The entrance to the left of the horse and cart was for passengers travelling first class while the second and third class entrances are to be seen behind the horse and cart. On entering the building passengers ascended a staircase to track level, where they boarded the train, there being no platforms in the early days. The remaining part of the building shown in the photograph was constructed in 1831–2 with the intention of providing some shops at street level. However, the shops did not materialize and the whole of this area was appropriated for goods and office accommodation. Liverpool Road station closed as a passenger station in 1844 when services were transferred to Victoria station. It then became a goods depot for the next 130 years until its closure in 1975. Since that time, the buildings have been converted into the Museum of Science and Industry in Manchester.

Opposite: The final enlargement of Victoria station took place in the early years of the twentieth century when the number of platforms was increased from eight to seventeen. Not all the platforms allowed trains to run through. Platforms one to ten were terminal platforms for trains from places like Oldham, Rochdale and Bury while platform eleven joined platform four of Exchange station to create the longest platform in Europe. This photograph shows one of the through platforms at Victoria in the 1950s as the class '5MT' locomotive awaits the green flag to depart. Although some passengers appear to be catching this train, others seem to be waiting for another one, possibly a local train to one of the surrounding towns.

Victoria station was opened by the Manchester and Leeds Railway (later the Lancashire and Yorkshire Railway) in 1844, replacing its original Manchester terminus on Oldham Road. The new station was also used by the London and North Western Railway, which had taken over the Liverpool and Manchester Railway. Until the mid-1870s the main approach to Victoria station was by way of Hunt's Bank, past the offices of the Lancashire and Yorkshire Railway on the right. The Lancashire and Yorkshire Railway, although one of the smallest in terms of mileage, was one of the major railway companies in the country as it served not only the Lancashire cotton towns but also the industrial towns and coalfields of Yorkshire. During the latter half of the nineteenth century Victoria station was extended several times, and on each occasion the number of platforms was doubled. This view of the approach to the station dates from the 1870s, about the time the number of platforms was being increased from two to four.

Train services to the south of Manchester started and terminated at London Road station (now Piccadilly station). Although owned by the London and North Western Railway, London Road station was shared with the Manchester, Sheffield and Lincolnshire Railway (later the Great Central Railway) in an uneasy relationship. The original station was opened in 1842, but by the 1860s traffic had increased to levels whereby a new station was required. This was completed in 1866 when great care was taken to ensure that the rival railway companies were kept separate and that passengers could easily identify each company's part of the station. The approach to London Road station was up a slope, whose appearance was made even steeper by the fact that London Road dropped away to cross the River Medlock. This view, taken in the years before the First World War, shows that station and its approach from Piccadilly with trams and taxis adding to the transport scene here. The warehouses on the left were built by the Manchester, Sheffield and Lincolnshire Railway and backed on to the terminus of the Ashton Canal, which was owned by the railway.

The arrival of the electric trams in 1901 and the extension of their services to surrounding towns posed a threat to the commuter traffic carried by the railways. In order to combat this competition, the railway companies looked at the possibility of electrifying their lines and speeding up trains. In 1916 the Lancashire and Yorkshire Railway had electrified the line from Manchester to Bury which resulted in an increase in traffic. On the southern side of Manchester, the Manchester South Junction and Altrincham Railway saw their commuter service threatened by trams and responded in 1928 by deciding to electrify the route to Altrincham. Work started in 1929 and was completed by 1931, at a cost of £500,000. The new trains, one of which is shown here, were described as 'big, comfortable and roomy, with a steadiness and smoothness that makes the journey a pleasant break between the offices and the home'. The new electric trains cut five minutes off the journey time between Manchester and Altrincham.

The last of Manchester's mainline stations to be opened was Central station on 1 July 1880. Central station was built by the Cheshire Lines Committee, which was an amalgamation of three companies which did not have their own stations in Manchester, over a section of the Manchester and Salford Junction Canal which had to be closed and filled in. The main feature of the station was the 210 ft span of the arch over the platforms. If the original plan for the station had been adhered to, this arch would not have been visible as there were plans to erect an office block in front of it, but it is said that there were not sufficient funds to do this. This postcard shows the front of the station together with the covered way which was erected when the Midland Hotel was built on a site bounded by Mount Street, Peter Street, Lower Mosley Street and Windmill Street. The aim of the covered way was to ensure guests arriving at the hotel by train did not get wet in the short walk between the hotel and station. Central station closed in May 1969 and after a long uncertain future it was saved and converted into the G-Mex Centre where exhibitions, concerts and events are held. Visitors arriving at G-Mex and parking under the building do so over part of the former canal.

he Cheshire Lines Committee did not have any stock or engines of its own. Those services it ran were done so
sing equipment leased from its constituent companies. Among the innovations which the Cheshire Lines
itroduced was a fast, punctual service between Manchester and Liverpool, leaving at half past the hour
hroughout the day. There were also services to Southport, Chester and through coaches to many parts of the
ountry. The Midland Railway ran services to London St Pancras via the Peak District from Central station, and
lthough the journey time was longer the scenery was very attractive. As well as long distance traffic Central
tation also had important commuter traffic from the south Manchester area such as Didsbury and Chorlton-cum-
ardy. In many cases it was quicker to travel into Manchester by rail than on the tram, the journey by train only
king ten minutes or so. This atmospheric photograph was taken in 1930 and shows a train arriving while a
nk engine, possibly from the London and North Eastern Railway, awaits the all clear to depart with one of the
00 trains which used the station each day.

In 1824 the first horse buses were introduced between Manchester and Pendleton in Salford. The cost of travelling on these early horse buses was expensive, a single journey costing 6d. As a result they tended to be used by businessmen travelling to and from their business premises. The early horse bus drivers were kept busy – not only had they to manage the horse, but also to blow a horn to announce the progress of the journey, account for the fares at the end of the journey and help passengers on and off buses. In 1851 larger vehicles were introduced which required three horses and as a result the driver was given an assistant, the guard or conductor, who collected the fares. This horse bus was photographed as it entered Mosley Street from Piccadilly. Although all the passengers on this bus are facing the front, in the early buses those on the upper deck sat facing outwards with their feet resting on a board, so that passengers on the lower deck saw an array of boots and shoes of all shapes and sizes and in various states of repair and cleanness. The smell in the interior of these horse buses were said to resemble that of a stable, especially in wet weather when straw was strewn on the floor.

In 1877 a change took place when horse-drawn trams were introduced. The horse-drawn trams could carry up to forty-two passengers at 7 mph. The tracks were laid by Manchester City Council and rented to the tramway operators at a rate of ten per cent of the cost of construction per annum. The horse trams were more efficient when it came to the use of horse power, but still required a large number of horses to be kept in reserve to ensure that they were changed regularly and not tired out. This photograph shows one of the horse trams operated by the Manchester Tramways and Carriage Company in Manchester. By the time horse-drawn trams were introduced, fares had fallen considerably from the 6*d* per journey of 1824 and fell even further when the cheap workmen's fares were introduced. There was also a distinction in fares depending on where you sat, with higher fares being charged for those who travelled inside the tramcar.

When the original tram tracks were laid the leases to the operating companies were for twenty-one years. In 1898, when the first leases were due for renewal, the city council had to decide whether to replace the track and electrify the system, and whether it should continue to be operated by private companies or run by the local authority itself. In the end it was decided that the local authority would take over the operation of the system so that profits would be used to subside new routes. The laying of the new tram track appears to have attracted a great deal of attention if this photograph of the junction of Deansgate and St Mary's Gate is any guide. It also appears to have caused a major disruption of traffic circulation in the town with roads having to be dug up.

This photograph of 1902 shows electric trams at the junction of Cross Street, Corporation Street and Market Street. By the end of 1902 about twenty-six electric tram routes were in operation serving, among other places, Cheetham Hill, Blackley, Queen's Park, Gorton, Belle Vue, Middleton, Stockport and West Didsbury. The new electric trams still had open tops, but in about 1905 the first covered cars were introduced. Also visible in the picture is a horse tram; they still operated on some routes for a further two years. The new electric trams provided competition for the railways, especially on services to Bury, where a significant number of passengers were lost to the new form of road transport.

As the electric tramways developed so the tramcars were improved, and the old system of having no roof and open ends on the upper deck gave way to fully enclosed cars as shown in this picture. The tram in the photograph is on the No. 32 route from Victoria Street to Reddish via Market Street, which was converted to bus operation in 1946. This photograph of the 1930s also shows one of the problems which trams created as the amount of road traffic, especially private cars, increased. Trams had to run on fixed tracks so that cars and other road vehicles were forced to one side, and if the street was busy with pedestrians it could be dangerous for those walking at the edge of the pavement.

In 1931 Manchester created a bus station in the city centre, Parker Street bus station, which enabled buses to be kept off the road when waiting for their time to depart. This view shows Parker Street bus station in the 1930s with bus stands, although covered, still open at the sides to the weather.

Before the First World War Manchester suffered from chronic traffic congestion, but the war delayed the implementation of improvement schemes. During the 1920s attempts were made to reduce the congestion with the introduction of one-way systems and parking restrictions. This photograph shows the junction of Portland Street and Oxford Street in 1933 when Portland Street was made one-way. Tram No. 315 in the photograph was introduced in 1929/30 and was photographed here on the no. 41 route from Victoria Street to West Didsbury. Also in the picture are an Austin 7 car and two Crossley bodied buses: the right hand one is bound for Sale Moor while the left hand one is numbered 28 although it is not possible to identify which route it is on. Further attempts were made to reduce congestion five years later in 1938, when a bold scheme was introduced involving a one-way system from All Saints into Manchester and along Princess Street out of the city centre. The full scheme only lasted six months owing to complaints from shopkeepers that it resulted in a loss of business.

Opposite: Until the arrival of the internal combustion engine goods were taken to and from factories and warehouses by horse-drawn waggons and lurries. Reach, writing in 1849, commented about the waggons 'high piled with goods, hauling loads which horses must shudder to contemplate'. Even between the wars horse-drawn carts were still in regular usage around the streets of Manchester as this photograph shows.

The Manchester blitz of Christmas 1940 changed the face of Piccadilly. All the warehouses facing Parker Street bus station were destroyed. After the war, the vacant sites were converted into temporary car parks as the number of private cars coming into the city centre increased. The post-war development enabled the bus station, which had been badly damaged in the blitz, to be planned and upgraded. This 1957 photograph shows work beginning to be done on the new Parker Street bus station together with the car parks where Piccadilly Plaze now stands.

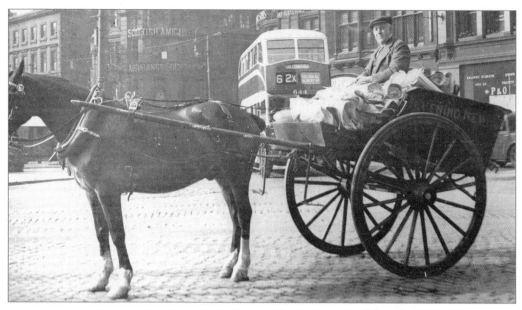

Waggons and lurries were slow, but suitable for carrying bulk goods. However, there were occasions when a faster form of road transport was required, such as for the delivery of newspapers to newsagents and news vendors in the city centre. This photograph, taken in the 1930s, shows a typical two-wheeled cart used to take small loads quickly around town. It is possible that this cart was delivering the *Manchester Evening News* as it appears to be carrying bundles of newspaper in front of the driver.

The scene as goods vehicles negotiate their way along Portland Street in the inter-war years. Not only are there horse-drawn vehicles and a few private cars, but also a steam lorry, a form of road traction which never really caught on. The buildings which lined Portland Street at this time were mainly textile warehouses. The one on the right was built in the 1860s to the designs of P. Nunn and occupied by the Behrens family.

These police officers appear to be checking the documents of this motorist in a central Manchester street between the wars.

During the inter-war years traffic, particularly that powered by the internal combustion engine, rapidly increased giving rise to congestion in city centre streets. This photograph shows the scene in St Peter's Square as traffic makes its way from Peter Street towards Mosley Street and Piccadilly. Horse-drawn vehicles, cars, lorries and even buses are all mixed up, although it does appear that the horse-drawn cart and the bus are segregated from the motor traffic.

Although aircraft had been in existence since the early years of the twentieth century and planes were being built by A.V. Roe in Manchester in 1910, it was the use of aircraft in the First World War which resulted in developments in aircraft design which ultimately led to the development of passenger-carrying aircraft and the race by local authorities to build airports. On 22 April 1929 Manchester was granted the first licence to operate a municipal airport. The earliest Manchester airport was Rackhouse in Wythenshaw. In 1930 Barton airport opened and services were transferred to the new site, but by 1938 the difficulties of expanding on the site had become apparent and a new site was chosen for Manchester Airport, at Ringway on the edge of Wythenshawe, where there was room for expansion. This photograph shows the Lord Mayor, Alderman George Westcott, and a deputation from Manchester in London to receive the licence for the Manchester airport in 1929. The plane in the background was operated by Northern Air Services (Manchester) Ltd, who claimed to have a fleet of 'modern aircraft'.

In 1938 Manchester moved its municipal airport from Barton to Ringway following criticism of Barton by Captain Smirnoff of KLM. The site for the new airport had been acquired in 1935 at a cost of £53,000 and covered over 600 acres. When the airport was opened in 1938 by Sir Kingsley Wood, Secretary of State for Air, the total investment in the project had already amounted to £175,000. The original plan was to construct the terminal buildings once the airport was open, but with increased traffic and the possibility of international flights it was decided to complete the development of the site as soon as possible. The first international airline to start regular flights was KLM, one of whose planes is shown in this 1938 photograph of Manchester Airport.

CHAPTER FIVE

A BREAK IN THE DAILY GRIND

In 1857 Charles Beyer complained that the royal visit to Manchester had resulted in a considerable loss of production and pleaded with Henry Robertson, one of the partners, to come to Manchester to help stir things up. Not only did industry close down for royal visits so did the schools and, as in industry, single days off often extended into two or three more days. During the century after Queen Victoria's first visit to Manchester in 1851 the reigning monarch visited Manchester on several occasions. In all Queen Victoria made three visits to Manchester, Edward VII made two visits, four visits were made by George V and at least two by George VI. By the mid-twentieth century, although royal visits attracted large crowds, they tended not to be the major event they were a century earlier.

As well as royal visits there were local events which were significant. For example, events associated with the opening of Manchester Town Hall in 1877, the Royal Jubilee Exhibition of 1887, not in Manchester but staged very close to its boundaries in Old Trafford, the opening of the Manchester ship canal, which although involving a royal visit in May 1894 had been 'unofficially' open on 1 January 1894, events surrounding Civic Week in 1926 and the centenary of the borough in 1938. Neither should special events which took place in individual communities be overlooked, such as the opening of a new school, town hall or library as these also attracted crowds, just as in the years following the First World War the unveiling of local war memorials were attended by many people from the community.

As well as one-off events, the calendar was also full of events which took place annually and which attracted large crowds of onlookers. Events such at the Shrove Tuesday antics of the students at Manchester University from the late nineteenth century onwards, Whit Walks, Lifeboat Saturday and a host of local events such as the Didsbury Show, started in 1901. Events like these were part of life for people in the nineteenth and early twentieth centuries.

Until the arrival of radio and television the only other means of learning what happened at an event or seeing a personality was to be part of the crowd. There was no switching on television and watching it, you had to be there in person. The development of instant news through radio and television may account for the gradual fall in the size of crowds at some events, although there are some that still attract huge numbers as people want to say they were there when a certain event took place.

Not only are there events which involve towns or cities, but there are also smaller events which are of importance to families, specific organizations or streets, such as weddings, funerals, church events and street parties at coronations. These too much be classed as events as they are not part of the normal leisure and pleasure round. All too often the recording of these local events tends either to be overlooked or pictorial information does not survive in the public domain. Hence the reason for including one or two of these at the end of this section.

In 1887 Manchester organized a grand exhibition to celebrate the golden jubilee of Queen Victoria's accession to the throne. When Manchester had organized an exhibition in 1857 it was of works of art whereas this exhibition was to stress and publicize the industries of the north-west. However, the exhibition, which lasted throughout the summer of 1887, did include a historical element in that there was a tableau of medieval Manchester. This photograph shows the Market Place as Alfred Darbishire thought it might have looked with the market cross in the centre. The costumes of those on the set exhibit some incongruity in that not only are there medieval costumes but also men in Highland dress, presumably a connection with Bonnie Prince Charlie's passage through Manchester in 1745, and men in Victorian dress. It is to be supposed that this tableau provided a welcome break from the displays of machinery and equipment which made up most of the exhibition.

Between 1887 and 1893 Manchester and its citizens were following the construction of the Manchester Ship Canal, intended to link the centre of the English cotton industry with the sea. Although the canal came into full use on 1 January 1894, it was not until 21 May 1894 that it was officially opened by Queen Victoria. The streets were decorated for the occasion and many thousands of people came into the city to see the Queen and admire the decorations. This photograph shows one of several triumphal arches which were erected along the Queen's route from London Road station to No. 1 Dock. It is located at the junction of Albert Square and Mount Street and was similar to one erected at the junction of Cross Street and Albert Square, which can just be seen in the background. Across Deansgate the fire service erected two ladders to form an arch, which was lined with firemen when the Queen passed under it.

It had been hoped that a member of the royal family would have cut the first sod to mark the start of the construction of the Manchester Ship Canal, but this was not to be. When the work was completed Queen Victoria was invited to officially open the Ship Canal. The day set for the official opening was 21 May 1894. The Queen arrived at London Road station at 4.30 p.m. and made her way to Manchester Docks along Market Street, Cross Street, Albert Square, Oxford Street and Stretford Road. On her arrival in Albert Square she was presented with an address of loyalty by the Lord Mayor. This photograph shows the royal carriage in front of the Town Hall with Queen Victoria's head just visible. She appears to be looking at the Albert Memorial, which had been especially restored for the occasion and, at her specific request, left undecorated.

In order that the general public might see the decorations erected for the royal visit in 1894 and celebrate the official opening of the Manchester Ship Canal, the city council decided to ban all but essential traffic from the centre of Manchester on 21 May. It was probably a wise decision as many thousands of people flocked into the centre of Manchester to line the route of the royal procession. This photograph shows a couple in their Sunday best walking through Albert Square during the day, obviously enjoying the day off work and seeing the sights and decorations.

Queen Victoria died on 26 January 1901 and although it had been expected it still sent shock waves through towns and villages. For the first time since 1837 the Lord Mayor had to proclaim a new monarch, Edward VII. On the Sunday after Queen Victoria's funeral memorial services were held in cathedrals and churches throughout the country. In Manchester the Lord Mayor led the official mourning at the service. In this photograph the Lord Mayor, Thomas Briggs, is seen in procession leaving the Town Hall for the Cathedral accompanied by members of the council and other civic dignitaries. The mace, which preceded the Lord Mayor, has black ribbon attached to it.

When Queen Victoria celebrated her diamond jubilee in 1897 Manchester decided to mark the occasion by the erection of a statue in Piccadilly, but before the work could be completed the Queen had died. The statue, designed by Onslow Ford, was paid for by donations from the general public. Lord Roberts was invited to unveil the statue, which was placed in the centre of Piccadilly Esplanade. The unveiling took place on 10 October 1901, exactly fifty years after Queen Victoria had first visited Manchester. The unveiling ceremony, shown here, was attended by large crowds who used every possible angle to get a good view of events. Unfortunately the ceremony was marred by public disorder as grandstands erected for the privileged blocked the view of the general public, with the result that there was much pushing to try and obtain a good view. After the ceremony was over the invited guests had difficulty in getting away so great was the crush.

In 1905 the Manchester Ship Canal Company completed a new dock, No. 9 Dock, intended to accommodate the largest vessels then afloat. Edward VII was invited to open the new dock on 13 July 1905. He arrived at London Road station and travelled through the streets of Manchester to the site of the new dock to officially open it. This photograph shows the royal procession as it passes through Piccadilly on its way to the docks.

In July 1913 George V visited Manchester. On his arrival at London Road station the King was welcomed to Manchester by the Lord Mayor, Alderman Samuel Royse, after which the King travelled to Platt Fields where he was greeted by Manchester's schoolchildren. From Platt Fields he went to the Town Hall, where, after inspecting an honour guard drawn from 2nd Battalion, the Manchester Regiment, he knighted the Lord Mayor on the steps.

Opposite: Edward VII made a second visit to Manchester in 1909 to officially open the new Manchester Royal Infirmary. The streets were decorated for the occasion and on the actual day of the visit, 6 July 1909, large crowds gathered to cheer him on his way. This photograph shows part of the route with buildings decorated with flags and barriers erected at the edge of the pavements to keep the crowds of spectators back.

Although the death of George V was expected it still came as a surprise to people and the news only spread slowly among the population. The uncertainty about the proclamation of the Prince of Wales as Edward VIII only served to heighten the confusion. Eventually on 22 January 1936 the Lord Mayor proclaimed Edward VIII as the new king from the steps of the Town Hall in front of a crowd estimated to be between 2,000 and 3,000 people. This photograph shows the crowd listening to the proclamation, which was also read in Piccadilly, at New Cross and at All Saints.

Opposite: In 1952 George VI died and was succeeded by his daughter, Elizabeth II. Just as at other coronations public transport vehicles were decorated and toured the streets of the city. Whereas for previous coronations tramcars had been used the chassis of a bus was decorated for the coronation of Elizabeth II in 1953. As with other coronations in the twentieth century street parties were held as well as officially sponsored events, but one thing made all the difference, the television. For the first time people at home could see events as they happened.

After his abdication Edward VIII was succeeded by his brother George VI, whose coronation took place in 1937. Not only were the streets decorated for the occasion as this picture shows, but public buildings were floodlit by night. On the day of the coronation the service was broadcast, but this did not stop events being organized in the city. A special service was held in the cathedral and open air services were organized for Heaton Park, Platt Fields and Wythenshawe Park. Bands also played in the various parks and in central Manchester. Special events were organized for ex-servicemen, children and pensioners. The children of Manchester each received a decorated tin of chocolates, a fountain pen or a souvenir book. At night an illuminated tramcar toured the city and firework displays were held in Heaton Park and Platt Fields. As well as the official events there were also many local events, such as street parties in which all the residents participated.

On 24 May 1901 the Manchester Volunteers returned home from active service in the Boer War. Each man received a bounty of £5 for his efforts and, after a parade at Ashton Barracks, travelled to Manchester for a civic reception. The company arrived at London Road station where they were welcomed by the Lord Mayor, Sir James Hoy, and then they marched through the densely packed streets to Manchester Cathedral, where a service was held. The final event of the day was lunch at the Town Hall. The men, who were described as 'grave thin and ill-looking', were apparently wearing khaki rather than the traditional red coats which had been associated with the British army. The *Manchester Guardian* commented that it was a short procession and 'had practically nothing of that bright colour which all healthy Englishmen like to see'. This picture shows the men lined up outside the Town Hall, presumably after returning from the Cathedral.

David Lloyd George was born in 1863 in a house in New York Place, Chorlton-on-Medlock. He was destined to become Britain's prime minister for the last two years of the First World War. Lloyd George only lived in Manchester for six weeks before his parents moved from the city. However, Manchester did not forget the connection when they honoured him in September 1918 by bestowing on him the Freedom of the City of Manchester. The ceremony took place not in the Town Hall as normal, but in the Hippodrome on Oxford Street as this could seat a larger audience. This photograph shows the platform party – Lloyd George is the person standing on the left. After the ceremony a civic lunch was held at the Midland Hotel which was followed by an inspection of a guard of honour in Albert Square. Lloyd George's visit to Manchester had to be curtailed because during the day he developed a severe cold.

Opposite: In 1938 Manchester celebrated the centenary of its incorporation with an exhibition at City Hall on Liverpool Road, which showed different aspects of local government work, a civic banquet and a service at Manchester Cathedral. The celebrations also included a royal visit in that George VI visited the city to officially open the Town Hall Extension. As its contribution to the celebrations Allied Newspapers organized a banquet at the Midland Hotel, shown here, which was attended by distinguished Mancunians and others, including Lord Kelmley and David Lloyd George, who was born in Manchester.

Britain's second wartime leader of the twentieth century, Winston Churchill, was also honoured with the Freedom of Manchester in 1943. Like Lloyd George, he had connections with the city in that he was the Liberal MP for Manchester North West between 1906 and 1908. During the Second World War Churchill was the last politician to make a speech from the platform of the Free Trade Hall before it was destroyed in the blitz. In 1945 Churchill launched his general election campaign during a visit to Manchester at which it was estimated he was seen by crowds in the region of 80,000. This photograph shows Churchill speaking to the crowds from his car in Piccadilly, together with his wife. In the background is Lewis's shop.

In 1917 Manchester bestowed the Freedom of the City on General Smuts of South Africa. At the same time the Canadian and New Zealand prime ministers were granted the same honour. Two years later General Smuts returned to Manchester where he saw some of the city's historic sites, including Chetham's Hospital. Chetham's had been established as the result of a bequest from a textile merchant, Humphrey Chetham, who died in 1653. The school did not set its sights on sending the boys to Oxford or Cambridge as Manchester Grammar School did, but to provide them with a practical education up to the age of fourteen and then apprentice them to a master who would train them in a useful trade. A visit to the school was on the itinerary of most distinguished visitors to Manchester. General Smuts was no exception, and is seen here being shown round by one of the boys in the school's traditional costume. Today, Chetham's School still occupies the same buildings as it did when it was founded and specializes in music education. It should not be forgotten that as well as the school Humphrey Chetham left money to establish Europe's first free library, Chetham's Library, which occupies premises within the school. It was in this library that Karl Marx and Frederick Engels first met in the 1840s.

Some events are more personal than others. For example, a wedding only directly involves the family and friends of the bride and groom, but often local people would turn out to watch if it was someone with whom they were acquainted. As with visits of royalty and other dignitaries, it broke the daily round. This photograph shows a wedding at Wellington Street Baptist Chapel in June 1914. All that is known about the families involved is that one of them is named Wainwright. It is possible that the gentleman sitting on the right is Joel Wainwright, who died in 1916 aged eighty-five. Wainwright was the author and illustrator of *Memories of Marple* as well as being a prominent accountant, member of the Manchester Field Naturalists, member of the Manchester Geographic Society and a member of the International Decimal Society. The dress in this wedding photograph certainly gives the impression of a society wedding.

Opposite: Another view of the Whit Walks, taken by Banks from a similar position. Whether it was the same year is not clear as the weather here appears to be wet with one participant carrying a rain coat. This time Banks has captured some of the adults who took part: clergy, wardens and sidesmen as well as Sunday school teachers and probably some parents as well.

One of the most important events in the calendar for Mancunians was the annual Whit Walks. The first Whit Walk was held in 1801 when it was felt that the children attending the Sunday schools organized by the Church of England should attend the parish church at least once a year. The early processions started from St Ann's Square and walked to the Collegiate Church, which was the parish church of Manchester, to hear divine service and afterwards to have a glass of milk and a bun. When the first walk was held 1,800 Sunday school scholars took part, but gradually the number rose. By 1834 it had reached 4,000 and by 1901 there were 25,661 children from forty-five Sunday schools taking part. As the numbers grew it was necessary to find a new starting spot. In 1877 the Whit Walks started for the first time from Albert Square and made their way along Princess Street, Mosley Street and Market Street to the Cathedral. The Whit Walks were the one occasion when all the children taking part had new clothes; it was considered to be a disgrace if a child did not have new clothes for the walks. This photograph shows some of the small girls taking part in the walk early in the twentieth century. It was taken by Mr Banks, a well-known local photographer, near the junction of Princess Street and Mosley Street.

A major landmark in the life of all Roman Catholics is their confirmation. This photograph was taken outside St Edmund's Church, Miles Platting on the occasion of a visit by Bishop John Vaughan, Auxiliary Bishop of Salford for a confirmation service in 1909. John Vaughan was the brother of Herbert Vaughan who was the Bishop of Salford from 1871 to 1892 before becoming Archbishop of Westminster. St Edmund's Church was established as a chapel of ease in 1871 and became a full parish in 1877, the church being completed in 1896. It was situated in one of the poorer parts of Manchester, surrounded by rows of terraced houses. The procession approaching the church has certainly attracted a crowd, but how many of them actually went to the service is not recorded.

In 1876 the annual Manchester fair was held for the last time on Liverpool Road. The fair, which had been held since 1222, had been moved to Liverpool Road in 1823 and merged with the Bridgewater fair, which had come into existence in 1764 to celebrate the completion of the Bridgewater Canal through to Manchester. By the 1870s the fair, which was held at Easter, had expanded so that it blocked Liverpool Road for about a week and caused traffic congestion along Deansgate. In 1876 the council decided to abolish it as it had become regarded as a nuisance. When this photograph was taken the fair was being staged at Pomona Gardens, but it lasted there for only one year, 1877.

Opposite: As the population of Ardwick grew the Church of England felt that there was a need for a new church to be built. Through the generosity of the Bennett family a site was donated by the family, who also offered to pay for the building as well. The new church, dedicated to St Benedict, was consecrated in 1880 and from the beginning was associated with the Anglo-Catholic wing of the Church of England. This photograph was taken during the period when the Revd William Kemp was Rector of St Benedict's between 1911 and 1941, probably during the 1920s. The note on the reverse of the card describes it as the 'Patronal Festival' which appears to involve a procession of the members of the church through the parish with the wardens carrying the staves, followed by the clergy and then the banners of various church organizations behind. The procession appears to have attracted a large crowd of onlookers, many of whom would have come into contact with Kemp, who worked constantly for those who lived in the parish.

A group of morris dancers entertain shoppers in Piccadilly. In the background is Woolworths store, opened in 1926 on the site of the Albion Hotel.

These rather spectacular floral arches have been erected across Hunt's Bank in readiness for the visit of Edward VII in 1909 to open the new Manchester Royal Infirmary. The building on the right is the office block which formed the headquarters of the Lancashire and Yorkshire Railway.

LEISURE & PLEASURE

In 1833 J.P. Kay commented that 'At present the whole population of Manchester is without any season of recreation, and is ignorant of all amusements, except that very small proportion which frequent the theatre. Healthful exercise in the open air is seldom or never taken by the citizens of this town . . . one reason for this state of the people is that all scenes of interest are remote from this town. . . .' Two years later de Tocqueville commented that in Manchester 'you will never hear the clatter of hoofs when the rich drive back home or are out on pleasure; never the happy shouts of people enjoying themselves nor the harmonious sounds of musical instruments heralding a holiday. You will never see well-dressed people strolling out at leisure . . . or going to the surrounding countryside.'

These two quotations paint a bleak picture of the facilities which were available to Mancunians who wanted to enjoy themselves in the first half of the nineteenth century. Events like royal visits were one thing, but these were infrequent. Working people required other facilities where they could spend their leisure time when they were not working other than in the beer house or the pub. This became all the more pressing when Saturday half-holiday was introduced in the mid-nineteenth century. Some railway companies responded to the closure of warehouses on Saturday afternoons by offering special trips into the surrounding countryside while closer to the centre of Manchester parks began to be established, which provided the opportunity to walk in the 'fresh' air, although until the 1870s many of the parks lacked recreational facilities such as tennis courts, bowling greens and so on, and certainly did not include facilities for children.

Entertainment was also an important part of the leisure-time activities of Mancunians. There were many theatres and music halls in the city which offered a wide range of entertainment from song and dance routines to 'heavy drama'. As well as theatres and music halls there were also musical events in the city. The Gentlemen's Concert Society was the oldest of the organizations which gave concerts, but after 1858 there was the Hallé Orchestra providing regular concerts of classical music while Mr de Jong's concerts tended to concentrate on 'lighter' music. Concerts in the parks attracted large crowds and were popular with brass and military bands.

Another feature of the nineteenth century was the advent of trips to the seaside. It was the development of the railway which helped to popularize the coast, especially places like Blackpool. Factory owners also began to realize that it was better to close the works for a week and undertake the maintenance and repair work than to try and do it with the employees at work. Unlike many of the cotton towns Manchester did not have a specific week when almost everyone left the town. As Manchester was a commercial centre holidays tended to be staggered. In fact, it may be true to say that the Bank Holiday Act of 1870 benefited the workers in the warehouses, shops and offices far more than the man or woman working on the shop floor.

The growth of sporting activities was another feature of the late nineteenth century with Manchester having two football clubs in the Football League by 1900. The playing of football in the streets had been discouraged by the Court Leet as a potential source of disorder. In the 1660s there is even a recorded death of someone by a 'foul' at football. Other sports also made their appearance in the nineteenth century such as cricket, tennis as well as skating, curling and attending the races. These, together with the opening of parks, meant that by 1900 Manchester did have some facilities where people could enjoy themselves after work and on Sundays.

One of the best known places of entertainment in Manchester was Belle Vue. The original pleasure grounds had been established by John Jennison in Adswood, Stockport in 1826, but lack of space for expansion meant that he had to look for an alternative place for his pleasure grounds and small zoo. He chose a thirty-six acre site on Hyde Road, opening there in 1836. After his initial success Jennison ran into financial difficulties, but his creditors gave him time and very quickly he was able to repay his debts well before they fell due. Gradually Belle Vue began to attract a growing number of visitors, helped by the introduction, in 1852, of firework displays based on a theme, such as the Lisbon earthquake or the Afghan wars, which was changed each year. From the beginning Jennison had kept some animals at Belle Vue. As the number of animals increased so did the number of ones from abroad which ultimately resulted in the creation of Belle Vue Zoo. Jennison and his family realized that to be successful, they had to introduce new features each year. For example, the introduction and development of the amusement park fits in with this policy. This photograph, taken after 1908, shows the toboggan run which was introduced in 1908 after James Jennison had seen one at White City in Stretford.

Another feature at Belle Vue was the open-air dance floor, which fronted the firework lake. A wooden dance floor had been introduced in the 1850s and proved to be very popular, a popularity which continued up to the Second World War. Dancing was only one of many activities which were held at Belle Vue. Brass band concerts were introduced in the 1850s, hand bell ringing contests as well as flower shows also featured in the calendar of Belle Vue's annual events. This photograph was taken in the 1930s when Belle Vue was still a popular place for people to visit. Visitors not only came from Manchester, but from many parts of the north of England and the Potteries. There was even a special tram siding constructed at Belle Vue because of the popularity of the place. The largest number ever to visit Belle Vue was on Easter Monday 1944 when around 180,000 crammed into the site. Unfortunately Belle Vue began to decline after the Second World War and was eventually closed; the site was redeveloped in the 1980s.

In 1930 Belle Vue added another event to its calendar – the Christmas circus held in the King's Hall. The circus was organized by the same people who organized the circus at Blackpool during the summer. In many respects they were using their talents to provide entertainment for people who would not have travelled to the seaside in mid-winter, but who would visit something nearer home. Each performance could be seen by 7,000 people, there being two performances a day over Christmas. The first circus at Belle Vue included two teams of liberty horses, eight Shetland ponies, five pygmy elephants and several bears performing different tricks. In addition there were the usual clowns, acrobats and human entertainers. This postcard shows the first of Belle Vue's Christmas circuses in 1930.

Belle Vue was one of the few places in Manchester where big events could be staged as it had several large buildings. The use of Belle Vue for exhibitions and other events had the added advantage that there was something else for those attending to do. This photograph shows the fifth annual flower show of the London and North Western Railway Co. (North Eastern Division) held on 17 August 1912. Entrants from the Manchester area competed for the Founders Cup while for those from Yorkshire there was the Yorkshire Cup. Awards for best station gardening and for flowers grown by signalmen in signal-box window boxes were among those given.

The first public parks in Manchester were not opened until 1845 when Philips Park and Queens Park were handed over to Manchester. The money to purchase the land and to lay them out was raised by public subscription while the borough council obtained approval in the 1844 Police Act to expend money on their maintenance. The intention of those who supported the public parks movement was to try and bring something of the countryside into the urban areas. The parks were laid out in a formal manner with walks, flower beds, lawns and ponds or lakes, but no facilities where games could be played. This picture shows the lake and some of the grounds at Philips Park.

After the opening of Philips Park and Queens Park in 1845 it was another twenty-two years before Manchester added any more public open space to its ownership. In 1867 the council took over the five acre Ardwick Green, which had originally been a private park maintained by the residents of the housing fronting it. When it was a private park the area was surrounded by railings and to gain admission you required a key, one being issued to each resident. The main feature of the green was a large pond or lake in the centre, mentioned by Mrs Banks in her novel *The Manchester Man*. When Manchester took over the green the character of the area was changing, the large houses were being replaced and the green being neglected. When they took it over the corporation improved it and added the bandstand which can be seen in the background.

In terms of area covered, nineteenth-century Manchester was relatively small, with few open spaces which were suitable for providing large parks for its citizens. In 1869 the council looked outside its boundaries for land on which to construct a public park. A site was purchased in Moss Side, but it took almost seven years to resolve the difficulties caused by the fact that Moss Side was not part of Manchester at that time. Eventually in 1876 the problems were overcome and Alexandra Park was laid out at a cost of £60,000. Alfred Darbishire, a prominent Manchester architect, designed the lodges at the entrance to the park. The one which is shown here, on Alexandra Road, not only acted as the park superintendent's home, but also as an administrative office. The broad carriageway was intended to enable carriages to drive through the park although few probably did. As with other parks there was a bandstand which attracted large audiences in the summer when local brass bands and bands from the regiments stationed in Manchester performed.

Opposite: In the inner suburbs of Manchester it was not possible to create parks as the land was too expensive, although these were the areas which needed most public open spaces. In some areas small plots of vacant land were taken over by the council and turned into children's playgrounds with swings, see-saws, roundabouts and slides. Kemp Street playground covered 1¼ acres and cost £12,982 to acquire and lay out. In 1913 the city council embarked on an ambitious scheme to appoint six lady instructors or games leaders to encourage the proper use of the facilities provided. It is possible that one of these instructresses has organized the photographic session as the children look remarkably tidy and organized.

In 1906 the Platt Hall estate was advertised for sale. The original intention was that it should be sold for housing, but it did not find a buyer. A campaign was mounted in Rusholme to encourage the city council to purchase the estate for the public and convert it into a public park. The city council was reluctant to do this, but after a town poll showed there was support for the idea they purchased the estate for £59,875. Much of the land was poorly drained and required major civil engineering works. As there was much unemployment in Manchester at the time it was decided that the unemployed should be given the task of putting in the drains and landscaping the new park. However the work was not done very well and in the end outside contractors had to be brought in to finish the job. The park was opened in 1910 by the lord mayor with a large crowd of people in attendance. This picture shows the 6½ acre boating lake, which was surrounded by a walk of about a mile and in the centre an artificial island where wildlife could breed.

In 1868 the graveyard surrounding St Michael's Church, Angel Meadow, was converted into a playground and area where people could assemble. This was the first of several such conversions during the next seventy years. In 1890, when St Mary's Church off Deansgate was demolished, the site was also landscaped, providing those who worked in the area with a place to go at lunchtime to eat their sandwiches. The difficulty in allowing building on the sites of former churches was that they were surrounded by graveyards. Before any development could take place the bodies would have to be exhumed and re-interred – an expensive operation. In some cases the number of burials exceeded 20,000 as at St John's churchyard on Byrom Street. St John's Church was demolished in 1931. Part of the site was landscaped, but part of it was converted into a playground, shown here, for many of the children who lived in this part of central Manchester.

Towns and cities have always had their street entertainers. Manchester was no exception to this. One of the most popular street entertainers appears to have been the man with the 'dancing bear'. The bears came from Russia and their handlers were probably east Europeans. Dancing bears on the streets disappeared as a result of the First World War.

Street musicians were also a feature of Manchester's streets. Whether this was a barrel organ or a street piano is uncertain as is the exact location of the scene. These instruments could be hired for a few pence and trundled around the streets of Manchester, playing popular tunes of the day. Members of the public would be encouraged to give money to the person turning the handle, thus enabling him to earn a few coppers to support himself and his family. Some of the barrel organs which would have been heard on the streets of Manchester may have been made locally in a factory on Great Ancoats Street, opened in 1894 by Domenico Antonelli. Whether this instrument was made there is not known.

In September 1852 the Manchester Free Library opened in the former Hall of Science in Castlefield. As well as a reference section there was also a lending library, which was well used from the beginning. Gradually the benefits of public libraries became acknowledged and the council began to open branches, often as a result of local demands in areas which would today be regarded as inner city. In some cases these libraries were little more than converted houses, as the one in Hulme was for a number of years. When Manchester absorbed surrounding areas among the services they introduced were lending libraries, but where the authority had introduced a library service it was merged with Manchester's libraries. One district which did not have a library when it became part of Manchester was Chorlton-cum-Hardy, which had been part of Withington Urban District Council. Manchester opened its first library in Chorlton in November 1908 in a converted house, but this was only a temporary measure. A new library was opened in 1914 with a more extensive stock and better facilities. This photograph shows the lending library in Chorlton Library probably in the 1920s. The neatly arranged rows of books and the card catalogue in the background were typical of libraries at this time. The person on the left may be a library assistant carefully straightening the books to ensure they are in the correct order. It is interesting to note that ladies were employed as library assistants in the 1870s as the library could not recruit enough men, especially in the branches. According to one commentator the young ladies were far more helpful and attentive to their duties than their male counterparts and suggested that they should also be employed in the reference library in Manchester as it would improve the service.

Another service which local government provided was that of bath- and wash-houses. Swimming baths were also introduced where members of the public could engage in healthful exercise and children could be taught to swim. This photograph shows the Victoria Baths on Hathersage Road (formerly High Street), which were opened in 1906 at a cost of £59,000. The baths were intended to serve the populations of Rusholme, part of Chorlton Medlock and Longsight, which were among the most built-up parts of the city and lacking the facilities found at the public baths. As well as a swimming pool, the building included a laundry and a Turkish bath. Around the side of the pool galleries were erected so that swimmers could be watched or events staged whereby spectators could have a good view of what was going on. These baths are now closed although attempts are being made to save them and bring them.

Towards the end of the nineteenth century several new theatres were built including two which staged variety shows, the Palace and the Manchester Hippodrome. Both were located in Oxford Street, only a few yards from each other. This photograph shows the Hippodrome, which was designed by Frank Matcham for Oswald Stoll. The theatre was capable of staging music hall, circus or water spectaculars. It cost about £45,000 and could seat 3,000 people. Under the stage there were stables for horses and livestock while over the auditorium part of the roof could slide back to increase ventilation. The theatre opened on Boxing Day 1904 with a show which made use of all the facilities that the theatre had at its disposal. This photograph was taken in 1934 shortly before it closed and was demolished. The replacement was the Gaumont Cinemas, which opened in 1936. The name 'Hippodrome' was not lost to Manchester, but was transferred to the Ardwick Green Empire, which closed in 1961.

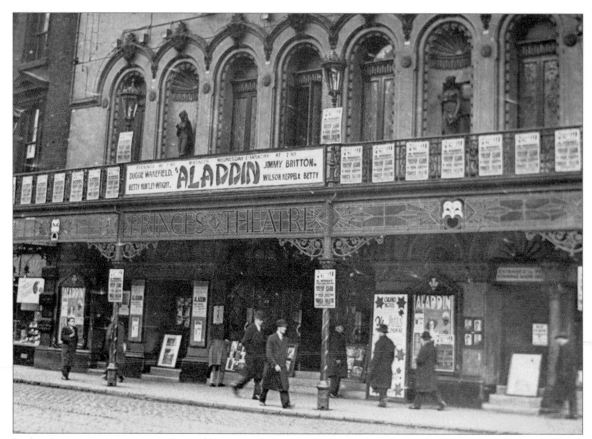

Oxford Street/Peter Street has sometimes been likened to the West End of London as many of Manchester's theatres and places of entertainment were to be found along the two streets or on roads leading from them. Among the theatres which could be found on Oxford Street was the Princes Theatre, a rival to the older Theatre Royal on Peter Street. The Princes Theatre, designed by Edward Salomons, was opened in 1864 by Charles Calvert, a well-known actor-manager. This photograph was taken in 1936 when the Princes Theatre was staging its annual pantomime. During the latter decades of the nineteenth century there was much rivalry between the Princes and the Theatre Royal as to who could stage the most elaborate pantomime, a rivalry which some critics did not like as they claimed that the story was subordinated to the special effects, resulting in the loss of the original idea behind pantomime. The Princes Theatre closed in 1940 and was demolished shortly afterwards.

In November 1922 the first broadcast was made by 2ZY from a small studio in the Metropolitan Vickers Works in Trafford Park. This was the beginning of public service broadcasting in Manchester. The Trafford Park studio was far from adequate and so it was decided to move to the top floor of a warehouse on Dickenson Street and use the chimney of the nearby power station for its aerials. Later the radio station moved to a building off Deansgate, where it had two studios and was able to expand both its output and the type of programmes it could broadcast. In 1928 the BBC, as it now was, moved once more to a newly erected building in Piccadilly, where it stayed until the 1970s, when it moved to New Broadcasting House on Oxford Road. This photograph shows Isobel Baillie (right) and other musicians broadcasting from one of Manchester's studios. Other programmes which were broadcasting in the early days included *Kiddies Corner*, election results and the first full-length drama production, *The Butterfly on the Wheel*.

During the nineteenth century there was a very strong temperance movement centred in Manchester which organized lectures and meetings to try and encourage members of the public to abstain from alcoholic drink. This photograph shows a lunchtime meeting outside a factory gate at which the evils of alcohol were expounded by a speaker. Not all the audience were adults as this photograph shows. There are some at the back of the crowd who are obviously children, but whether they were in employment or not is uncertain. The table in the foreground may have been used when anyone wanted to sign the pledge to give up alcoholic drink.

Manchester City Football Club was started two years after Newton Heath, in 1880, as West Gorton St Marks, a team attached to a church. In 1887 the West Gorton Club merged with Gorton Athletic to form Ardwick FC which in 1894 became Manchester City FC. In their early years the club had several grounds before settling at Hyde Road in 1887. Manchester City stayed at the Hyde Road ground until 1923 when it moved to its present ground, Maine Road. This photograph shows the team sitting down for lunch sometime during the 1930s.

Opposite: Two major football clubs have their origins in Manchester – Manchester United and Manchester City. This illustration shows the Manchester United team which won the FA Cup in 1909 when they beat Bristol City 1–0 at Crystal Palace. This was their first major success since their foundation as Newton Heath Lancashire and Yorkshire Railway in 1878. In 1885 the name was shortened to Newton Heath and became Manchester United in 1902. The team played their early matches at North Road, Monsall, before moving in 1893 to Bank Street at Clayton and finally in 1910 to Old Trafford, which is part of Stretford, not Manchester.

A large family house in Manchester which is fortunate to have its own tennis court. It is probable that the children would not have been allowed to play on the court, it being reserved for their parents and their guests.

Snow brings the child out in everyone, as these men show by having a snowball fight in the back garden.

CHAPTER SEVEN

SOCIAL CONDITIONS

Between 1772 and 1788 the population of Manchester doubled, reaching over 70,000 by the time the first census was held in 1801. This dramatic increase in population resulted in a huge demand for new housing which was difficult to meet. Houses were erected very quickly with little regard for the sanitary conditions or the density of people per acre. Many of the new houses lacked proper foundations and sanitary facilities. Back-to-back houses abounded in places like Angel Meadow, Ancoats, Hulme and Chorlton-on-Medlock as well as in parts of central Manchester. Cellar dwellings and multi-occupation were also common as the population grew. The problem was that the authorities had no powers to deal with the growing slums, not even adequate building regulations. Clean water was a rarity as was the existence of proper sewers. Sewage was tipped into the rivers and streams as was industrial effluent. In the mid-nineteenth century it was a moot point if you fell into the River Irwell whether you were drowned, poisoned or suffocated. An analysis of the River Medlock in 1845 revealed the presence of chemicals such as chlorine in such large amounts that if they were present in those quantities today the city centre would be evacuated.

The 1844 Police Act made an attempt to improve the situation by insisting that all new property had adequate sanitary facilities, but the act did nothing to tackle the legacy of the previous four decades of bad housing construction. It was not until the council appreciated the need for clean, running water, and the construction of the Longdendale reservoirs to supply this in the 1850s, that steps could be taken to improve things.

By the middle of the nineteenth century the population of central Manchester reached its zenith, over 186,000 people, after which it began to decline. Bodies like the Manchester and Salford Sanitary Association began to draw attention to the slums and the condition of those who lived in them. The removal of some of the slums began, not as a result of sanitary legislation but as a result of the demands of commerce, industry and transport for land on which to expand. For instance, the construction of Central station in the 1870s resulted in removal of several thousand people from the area, many of whom lived in poor quality housing.

It was not until after the First World War that local authorities were able to start programmes of slum clearance. At first the levels of council housing were restricted, but gradually the number of houses they were allowed to build was increased. The new house building programme, however, resulted in an increase in the outward growth of the town and the development of what would be called 'green field sites'. Often these sites were to be found between major routes into the city which had been ignored by private developers. The programme of slum clearance continued into the 1950s and 1960s with overspill estates, the expansion of Wythenshawe and the building of system-built houses and flats, the latter proving so disastrous that they have now been demolished and replaced by traditional housing.

For those who lived in the slums of Victorian and Edwardian Manchester there were organizations devoted to help them. Organizations like the Manchester and Salford Methodist Mission, the Manchester City Mission and Wood Street Mission were successful in helping many of those who were in difficulties. For those who could not, or would not, seek help from the voluntary bodies there was always the 'parish' or the workhouse, which was really the last resort.

For those who fell ill there were hospitals and dispensaries. The main hospital was the Manchester Royal Infirmary, but there were several specialist hospitals in nineteenth-century Manchester such as the eye hospital, the skin hospital and St Mary's Lying-in Hospital. In the poorer parts there were organizations like the Chorlton Dispensary at All Saints and the Ancoats and Ardwick Dispensary. Sometimes the charitable organizations provided help, such as the nurses employed by the Manchester and Salford Methodist Mission, who were said to be very highly regarded by the residents of Ancoats and trusted far more than doctors.

Until the late nineteenth century this court, known as Bakehouse Court, stood behind the buildings on Long Millgate facing Manchester Grammar School. The properties were probably built in the fifteenth or sixteenth centuries when Long Millgate was a main route out of the town. Originally the houses would have fronted the road, but as the population expanded so the gardens were built over and cottages erected. Gradually the standard of the area declined so that by the late nineteenth century many of the buildings required urgent structural work as well as other improvements to make them habitable. This is clearly obvious from the building on the right which is held up by timber beams not only at the gable end, but also to adjacent properties. These cottages were timber-framed and at least one of the buildings on the site was cruck-framed. As a result of redevelopment in the late nineteenth century these buildings were demolished. Within a hundred years even their replacements have disappeared and the site is now a car park.

Further along Long Millgate, in a bend in the River Irk, stood Gibraltar which was in a very poor state by the time this photograph was taken. The timber-framed house in the centre was built, according to the date over the door, in 1654 when the area would have been surrounded by open country and the river full of fish. By 1852/3 those inspecting the area for the Manchester and Salford Sanitary Association were recommending that the buildings be demolished. Many were in multi-occupation and in need of urgent works. In some cases there were five or six people living in a room. It was not until the end of the century that something was done and the buildings cleared away.

One of the worst areas of poor quality housing was Angel Meadow which lay between Rochdale Road and the River Irk. The area had started to develop in the late eighteenth century as Manchester expanded, and by the mid-nineteenth century back-to-back houses and courts abounded. The main road leading into Angel Meadow was Angel Street, photographed here in the 1890s. This was the widest street in the district with three-storeyed houses lining it. These houses may have started out as houses with workshops on the top floor, but by the time this photograph was taken some of them had been converted into lodging houses. These houses were probably built in about 1800, each having a cellar which, although railed off, probably housed a family. Note the rather nice Georgian door cases which were to be found in many parts of Manchester. It was said that the only person who did not live in the area who could enter safely was the midwife, while the police were said to patrol in twos and threes.

This rather tumble-down block of buildings was known as Parsonage Buildings and located at St Mary's Parsonage, behind Deansgate and close to St Mary's Church. Although today it is an area of offices, in the nineteenth century there were several hat manufactories, a brass and copper works and a mill backing on to the river. Other industrial sites in the area including a fustian and cotton stiffening works, a coach manufactory and a cotton finishing works. Gradually these factories disappeared as did the church in 1890, the site of the church and the churchyard being landscaped.

During the 1890s there were several schemes to try and improve living conditions for the residents of Ancoats. One of the more ingenious schemes was the conversion of a former cotton mill on Jersey Street. The work involved dividing the building cross-ways so that each flat or tenement had three rooms, two with outside walls and natural light while the third room, in the centre, had no natural light at all. Each flat was provided with running water in the living room, but there were no individual toilets, each floor having its own. During the years between the wars it was reported that Jersey Street dwellings became the home of several of the gangs which were to be found in the Ancoats area. During the Second World War it was said that the elderly people who lived there felt safter in the inner rooms of their flats than in an air-raid shelter. Eventually they were evacuated because the size of the mill made it an obvious target. The mill was demolished after the war.

In 1892 Manchester sponsored a competition to design a tenement block in which to rehouse some of the people who lived in the New Cross area. One of the entrants was Thomas Worthington who included bathrooms in his scheme, a proposal which was greeted with scepticism by some who said the residents would use the baths to keep coal in. The winners were Spalding and Cross, who designed the building shown here. Each flat had its own water supply and toilet with a balcony which overlooked a court yard. A contemporary account described the block as 'of fair, average character, light and airy'. At street level shops were provided to replace some of those which had been demolished when the area was cleared for Victoria Square. The block has recently been refurbished and is used as sheltered housing for elderly people.

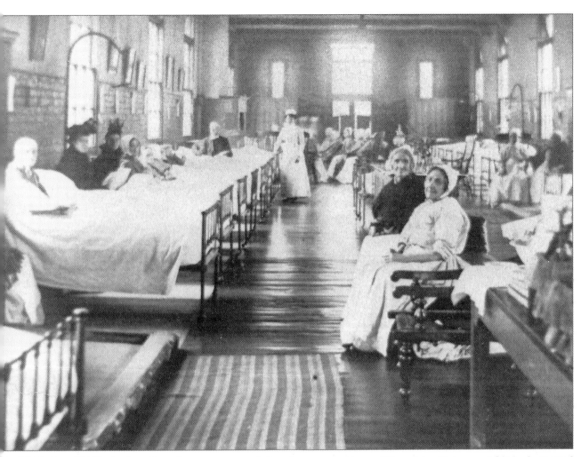

In 1834 the old Elizabethan Poor Law was amended and a new system of Poor Law Unions established. Central Manchester together with Cheetham and Ancoats constituted the Manchester Union while all the districts between the rivers Medlock and Mersey became part of the Chorlton Union. Districts to the north of Manchester which eventually became part of the city were included in the Prestwich Union. Each union had its own workhouse and officials. The Manchester workhouse was originally located on New Bridge Street, on a site which was later to be absorbed by Victoria station. The Chorlton Union initially used a workhouse in Hulme, but this soon proved to be inadequate and so was moved to a new site in Withington, which cost £180 per acre and where there was sufficient room for expansion. The workhouse opened in 1855 and hospital wards were added between 1860 and 1868, designed by Thomas Worthington and based on the recommendations of Florence Nightingale. This photograph taken in about 1900 shows one of the female wards in the hospital part of Withington Workhouse.

When the census for the workhouse is examined it is surprising how few staff are recorded as being present on census night. Some of those were what could be called today members of the management team, including the master and matron as well as the porter and teaching staff. Although the workhouse had around 1,300 inmates there were still only about twenty nurses. It is possible that a number of staff went into the workhouse each day and lived in the surrounding area, although the census does not reveal who they were. It is possible that a lot of the work around the workhouse was done by the inmates themselves as a wide range of occupations was represented from labourers to laundresses and, in 1871, a curate of the established church. Although workhouses were detested, as they separated husbands and wives and children, it has also to be borne in mind that the conditions they might have been living in outside the workhouse would have been terrible. The children did receive some education and may have been better educated than their counterparts outside. By the beginning of the twentieth century, diets for the inmates were published in the Union's yearbook. It was not very exciting with breakfast and tea being the same, although dinner did vary each day. The most interesting fact that can be gleaned from these dietary tables is that one group had ½lb of rice pudding, sago pudding or bread pudding just before going to bed! This photograph, taken at the same time as the previous one, shows some of the male inmates in what appears to be a workshop.

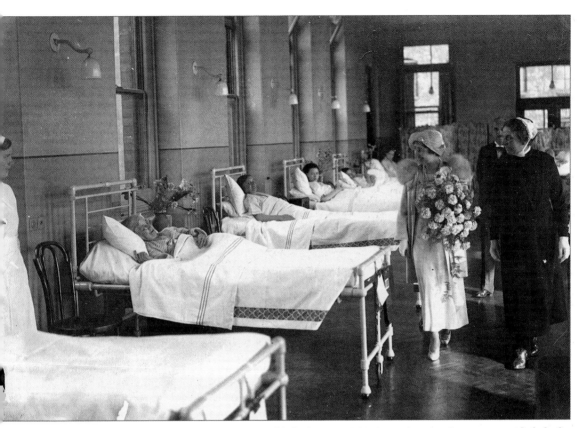

n 1828 the Ardwick and Ancoats Dispensary was established at No. 181 Great Ancoats Street to provide help for hose who lived in this densely populated part of Manchester. In the first years the dispensary dealt with 1,108 nome patients and outpatients together with 169 accident cases. As the demands made on the dispensary grew so t was necessary to find larger premises, which it did at Ancoats Cresent, opposite Every Street. However in 1870 his site was purchased by the Midland Railway and the dispensary had to move again. This time a site was found on Mill Street and the nucleus of Ancoats Hospital was built and opened as a proper hospital in 1879. Demand for beds always outstripped availability because of the area it was located in and the large number of factory accidents. By the 1880s these exceeded 3,500 per annum and continued to grow. This photograph shows the Duchess of York (later to be Queen Elizabeth when her husband, George VI, became king) visiting in 1932. Note he lack of privacy with no curtains, or even provision for curtains, around each bed.

In 1916 the British Red Cross acquired Grangethorpe House on the borders of Rusholme and Fallowfield and converted it into an orthopaedic hospital for men who had been injured during the fighting in France and elsewhere. The house was built in 1882, probably for a merchant and his family. This photograph is captioned and gives the date of Christmas 1917. It shows the wards decorated for the event together with some of the nurses. In 1929 the building was acquired first by the Manchester Royal Infirmary and then by Manchester High School for Girls in 1929.

In September 1910 Manchester opened a hostel for women on a site at Red Bank. Mary Ashton House, as it was called, was a continuation of Sir William Crossley's housing experiment which had already resulted in a men's lodging house being erected. This new hostel, designed by the city architect, cost £13,000 and was open for inspection by the police at any time of the day or night. It was said that the hostel combined a firm but humane management of the 222 women who could be accommodated in their own cubicles. In addition to sleeping accommodation the building also included a recreation room, kitchen on the ground floor and a wash-house, shown here, with baths and lockers in the basement.

Wood Street Mission was founded by Alfred Alsop in 1869 in premises on Lombard Street, moving to Wood Street in 1873. The area where Alsop worked was described by a police officer as 'the rendezvous of thieves and a very hot bed of social iniquity and vice'. Alsop's original aim was to relieve need 'whether spiritual, physical or mental'. Meals were served to the hungry and clogs and clothing given away to those who needed them. Seaside trips for children and Christmas treats became a feature of Wood Street. As social attitudes and requirements changed the Wood Street Mission adapted its activities to meet the changing demand. As well as relieving the needy the Mission took on an educative role, such as the one shown here where girls are being taught first aid.

In the slums of Manchester much work was done by various charitable and religious organizations. For example, the Manchester City Mission was associated with the Church of England while the Methodists established the Manchester and Salford Methodist Mission to work in the slums of the city. The Methodist Mission was started in 1886 when the Methodist Central Hall on Oldham Street was rebuilt. This photograph, taken between the wars, shows coal being delivered to a resident of poor quality housing in Manchester. In the background washing can be seen hanging across the road, indicating that the delivery is taking place in an area of back-to-back housing. The hanging of washing across the road was forbidden in the 1844 Police Act and those breaking the law could be fined up to 40s.

The Manchester and Salford Methodist Mission was very much a 'doing' organization. Its staff were prepared to go out into the streets of Ancoats and Hulme to being help and assistance to all who needed it irrespective of their religious persuasion. They met prisoners being discharged from Strangeways Prison and offered them assistance. They also provided accommodation for men coming into Manchester seeking work who did not want to stay in one of the many lodging houses in the city centre. In order to pay for their accommodation those men who did not have work would chop firewood, sell it, whitewash buildings and do other work arranged by the Mission. For women who sought assistance help was also available from the Mission in the form of a refuge as well as a coffee tavern, shown here, and a servants' registry was even maintained. In addition to services the Mission also provided some basic medical help for the residents of the poorer parts of Manchester, those using it often preferring the advice of the sisters to that of doctors.

Another organization involved in helping the needy was the Salvation Army. During the Depression in the 1930s the Salvation Army ran soup kitchens to provide some food for those in need. This photograph shows one such soup kitchen where those recipients are being fed. According to the labels on the canisters and on the van, rice, peas, beans and potatoes form the basic diet. It may not have been a scientifically balanced diet, but for hungry people it was sustenance which they gratefully accepted.

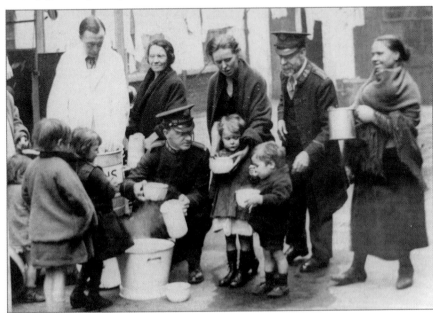

Another picture of the Salvation Army in the 1930s providing food for the needy of Manchester. What is in the bucket is not clear, but it is certainly hot as steam can be seen rising from it. It appears as if priority is being given to the children with their small basins while the adults are holding jugs.

In complete contrast to the conditions which were found in central Manchester, where population densities could be as high as 400 or 500 people per acre, this family lived in the leafy suburbs, away from the overcrowding and unhygienic conditions of areas like Ancoats. This photograph was taken in the front garden, as houses on the opposite side of the road can just be seen in the background.

Another family group showing the ladies of the house and the children. Their dress contrasts with that of the children shown in other pictures in this section, and the ones in Chapter Eight.

CHILDREN

According to the Concise Oxford Dictionary childhood is the 'time from childbirth to puberty', one of the few events in life that everyone experiences. Although this definition appears to be satisfactory it must be remembered that there have been and still are cultures, and periods of history, where childhood ends before puberty, and others where it technically carries on for a number of years afterwards. In this section childhood has been assumed to end when the child leaves school.

What is known about childhood, especially that of last generations, depends on people's recollections being recorded in some form or other. Much is only known from hearsay or legend. Everyone has had a different experience of childhood, and there will even be variations depending on which part of the country a child grew up in.

Although people recall their childhood memories, often it is through 'rose-coloured spectacles' – 'the summers seemed longer and sunnier and winters snowier'. Photographs are one way of helping to recall childhood in some cases and enhance a person's sketchy recollections. Sometimes people in old age will see a photograph which will remind them of something they have done or been involved with and pass the information on. Sometimes they can add information relating to a picture which brings it to life. Often people do not think anyone will be interested in what they did as children and are pleasantly surprised when someone does express interest.

This final section of the book is devoted entirely to photographs of children from Manchester. If some could speak they would reveal that they have seen a great many changes not only in the face of the city, but also in the way we live and do things. When these children were photographed radio and television had not made their appearance, while moving pictures were just beginning to flicker across the screen. Again in the field of transport, railways and trams were supreme while cars were noisy and unreliable.

Children are the future generation and lifeblood of any settlement. If there are no children the community dies out. What these children did in their lives will have helped to shape the succeeding and future generations, not only of their own families but of life in Manchester generally. The more recollections that we have from children the better our understanding of what life was like in the past, and 'flesh and bones' are added to the skeleton of facts.

Manchester High School for Girls was founded in 1874 'to provide for Manchester's daughters what has been provided without stint for Manchester's sons'. When it was founded in Portland Place it was regarded as a pioneer in the education of girls. In 1880 the school moved to Dover Street where it remained until 1929 when it moved to Grangethorpe House. The old house was replaced by a new school building which was destroyed in 1940. In 1951 a new school building was opened on the site. This photograph shows the girls packing parcels, but the note at the back does not explain for whom they are intended. The building in which the photograph was taken was the one at Dover Street, now part of Manchester University.

Ardwick Higher Grade School was opened in 1894 on Devonshire Street. Later, in 1909, Manchester Education Committee introduced a new policy whereby facilities were made available for children who could stay on at school above the minimum leaving age. The schools which were to cater for these children were to be called central schools. Rather than build new schools several existing schools were renamed, including Ardwick Higher Grade School which was sometimes referred to as Devonshire Higher Grade School. One well-known pupil who attended Ardwick Higher Grade School was Ellen Wilkinson, also known as Red Ellen. She went on to become a Manchester city councillor and later MP for Middlesbrough East and Minister of Education in the first Atlee government in 1945. Another well-known person who attended the same school was Frederick James Marquis, later Lord Woolton, who was not only a pupil at the school but also a pupil-teacher there as well. Unfortunately this picture of one of the classes at the school in the inter-war years gives no indication of which class it was or the date, only the name of the school.

This group of children came from St Andrew's School on Homer Street in Ancoats and was probably taken at Mayfield baths. St Andrew's School was founded in 1836 as St Andrew's Infant and Sunday School and gradually extended over the next two decades until by 1860 it was a two-storeyed building with three entrances. The school lost many pupils in the 1870s when Ancoats Goods Depot was built, a problem which was to occur again in the twentieth century. It is interesting to note that as early as 1871 the school was having photographs of its pupils taken, so this one is one of a long series of school photographs from St Andrew's School. However, only a few appear to have survived. The school buildings were eventually demolished at the same time as the church, in about 1961.

In 1790 a disagreement developed between the medical staff at the infirmary about the treatment of children and women with gynaecological problems. Several doctors, led by Dr Charles White, left the infirmary and established St Mary's Lying-in Hospital in premises on Quay Street. During the next 100 years the hospital occupied several different buildings in the Quay Street and Salford areas. In 1892 St Mary's moved to a new hospital at the corner of Gloucester Street (now Whitworth Street West) and Oxford Street, but in 1904 the hospital merged with the Southern Hospital for Women and Children. In 1911 a new hospital was opened on High Street (now Hathersage Road) in Chorlton-on-Medlock, but the one in central Manchester was retained as it was felt that there was a need for such facilities in the area. This photograph shows one of the wards at the High Street Hospital where the staff concentrated on babies and gynaecological problems. At the side of each bed there is a cot while the staff, in their starched uniforms, stand by a cabinet containing medicines.

Opposite: From its earliest days Manchester free libraries appreciated the importance of providing facilities for children in its libraries. Reading rooms for boys and girls were included when new libraries were built. This photograph shows children sitting at tables in the Chester Road Library in Hulme between the wars. Chester Road children's room was established in the late nineteenth century and was very popular from the time it opened.

This group of children was photographed in about 1904 in Rusholme with a leading Rusholme resident, William Royle. Why he had gathered them together is not recorded, but the existence of a garland, held aloft by one of the children, suggests that it might have been a May Day celebration organized by Royle for the people of Rusholme.

At a time when the ambition of every little boy was to be an engine driver, this boy and a girl, presumably his sister, are trying out this motor car for size. It is not possible to identify the make of car, but it is worth noting that Manchester did have a car industry in the early twentieth century. The early Rolls-Royce cars were made in Hulme, while between 1910 and 1929 Ford cars were made in Trafford Park and Belsize cars were made in Clayton.

It is not known who this little boy is or whereabouts in Manchester he was photographed. The photograph, which was almost certainly posed, gives a good indication of the type of dress boys were wearing at the beginning of the twentieth century, including a waistcoat. Despite the fact that he is bare-footed the boy seems cheerful enough.

This is a scene which must have been repeated countless times throughout the north-west, donkey stoning the steps and pavement in front of the house. Donkey stones, obtained from the ironmonger or more likely from rag and bone men, were made on the ground mixed with additives such as dolly blue. The result was a door step which looked white or cream when freshly completed. Although donkey stoning was usually done by the woman of the house on this occasion a boy appears to be doing it, but for what reason it is not known.

One must wonder what these three boys were talking about or what mischief they were planning. These must have been halcyon days for the three before they left school and started work in the local mill or factory. Once they left school the opportunity to sit and exchange stories would have disappeared, and so would their childhood.

Christmas time was always eagerly awaited by the children and adults associated with Wood Street Mission. The provision of Christmas treats was established in the nineteenth century and continued into the twentieth century. Those who benefited were the poor and needy, but by the twentieth century the work of the Mission covered the whole city and not just the small area around Wood Street. This photograph of the inter-war years shows the Lord Mayor of Manchester and the officials of the Mission awaiting the arrival of Father Christmas with a crowd of children, who appear to be oblivious of the gentleman in red, who is probably standing on the fire escape.

Opposite: One of the events of the year for children who were associated with the Wood Street Mission was the annual visit to the seaside for the week. The children were taken by train to Ainsdale where they camped close to the sea and spent a week under canvas. The cost of the visit was met from donations with a small contribution from the parents. Once at Ainsdale the camp was visited by local dignitaries such as the mayor and other leading citizens of the town. This photograph shows the girls, all smartly dressed in smocks for the photographer, lining up outside the mission's premises on Wood Street in central Manchester. If you look on the left hand side of the photograph you can just see the boys waiting for their turn to be photographed.

ACKNOWLEDGEMENTS

Over the years a large number of photographs have been taken of Manchester and its suburbs. Although there were photographers taking them in the decades between 1850 and 1890 it is to members of the Manchester Amateur Photographic Society that historians must be grateful, for it was from that body that the first attempt was made to photographically record Manchester for posterity. From then on, until the 1970s, the Record Section of MAPS recorded, at the behest of the Manchester Local History Library, many of the streets and buildings of Manchester, buildings and streets which have since disappeared. As well as members of MAPS there are many other local photographers who have helped to preserve a photographic image of Manchester, its buildings and its events. Some early ones were James Mudd, W. Fischer and A. Brothers, while others like Samuel Coulthurst and R. Banks were working at the end of the nineteenth and beginning of the twentieth century using newly developed cameras and films. Nor should the work of the City Engineers Department be overlooked for from the late 1890s cameras became part of their equipment. Photographs of many of their major projects were recorded as well as general views of streets when such illustrations were required for reports to council committees. Another important group who deserve thanks are the press photographers and the thousands of photographs they took not only of events, but general scenes like people at work. They too add to our knowledge of what Manchester looked like in the past. We should remember to thank the postcard producers of the late nineteenth and early twentieth century for the vast number of cards they produced, not only of buildings but also of street scenes and scenes in the suburbs of Manchester. Many of these were not nationally known postcard publishers, but small local people, often newsagents. My thanks are due to all these photographers and postcard publishers for their dedication and work. Without them such books would be impossible to compile.

My thanks are also due to Manchester Public Libraries and in particular the Local History Library, now the Local Studies Department, for their work in collecting and preserving so many photographs. My thanks are due to the staff there, in particular David Taylor, for their help over the years when researching for this and other books.

I also wish to thank Ted Gray, Airviews (Manchester), Salford Archives Department, Manchester and Salford Methodist Mission, Wood Street Mission, A.J. Pass and Manchester Public Libraries for permission to reproduce some of the illustrations used in this book. I apologize in advance if I have overlooked anyone who should have been acknowledged and has not been.

I also wish to thank Simon Fletcher of Sutton Publishing for his help and also Sutton Publishing for giving me the opportunity to compile this collection of illustrations on Manchester. Without the work of publishers like Sutton Publishing illustrations of towns would not be so readily available, and many people would not have come to appreciate the historical importance of their own community.

Finally I would like to thank Peter and Anna, for the understanding that when their father is working on a new book he should not be disturbed any more than necessary, and my wife Hilary for her tolerance and encouragement while I have been working on this book, especially as I tend to spread out with books and papers everywhere.

PART TWO

MANCHESTER
A SECOND SELECTION

*To mark the coronation of George V in 1911 the residents of Didsbury
organised a procession through the centre of the village. In this photograph,
the procession is seen passing along Wilmslow Road in front of the
police station.*

In December 1908 the last patients were moved from the Infirmary in Piccadilly to the new hospital on the edge of Chorlton-on-Medlock. The move took about two hours to complete as many patients had already been moved or admitted to the new building. For a period of three weeks the old accident room in the Infirmary was kept open while a central out-patients department was prepared to handle minor casualties. This new department lasted until 1935 when it was closed and demolished. The patients were reported to be very pleased with their new surroundings. The new hospital had provision for 483 patients compared with about 272 in the old building, and included what were then state-of-the-art facilities such as a proper X-ray and radiology department. The cost of the new hospital amounted to £500,000, of which £400,000 was raised by the sale of the Piccadilly site, with the balance from voluntary contributions. The official opening of the hospital was by Edward VII, accompanied by Queen Alexandra and Princess Victoria, on 6 July 1909. The King and his party were welcomed by William Cobbett, the Chairman of the Board of Management, who sought permission to name two of the wards after the King and Queen. After the King's reply, he knighted Cobbett who remained on the board until 1925, when he resigned through ill-health. After the welcome the royal party toured the hospital and unveiled plaques in the wards named after them before leaving from the front entrance, shown in this photograph. Incidentally, the royal visit cost the Infirmary authorities £530!

INTRODUCTION

It has been said that the growth of Manchester during the latter half of the eighteenth and early decades of the nineteenth centuries was due to the Industrial Revolution, that period in English history which affected the lives of every man, woman and child as well as the townscape and landscape of the country. It was a period when production moved from the home to the factory, when water and then rail transport developed and when industrial towns, with their factories and poor housing conditions, grew with a rapidity not seen before. Although Manchester was the most important town in south-east Lancashire and north-east Cheshire before 1750, during the next century its importance and influence greatly increased. Visitors were attracted to Manchester to see these changes, which affected all aspects of life. During the period 1750 to 1850 some of the people who came to Manchester recorded their impressions of the town in their diaries, in articles or even in books. Many of these visitors came from European countries, but there were several from America.

Later in the nineteenth century people came not merely to see the town, but often on business, purchasing cotton, engineering products and anything else that Manchester and the surrounding region produced and was prepared to export. It was said that the Lancashire textile industry, with Manchester at its heart, produced for the home market before breakfast and for export during the rest of the day. Statistics have shown that the north-west generated over one-third of the country's exports in the mid-nineteenth century.

An examination of the census enumerators' returns is a useful way of discovering who was staying in Manchester and their occupations, and although it is not possible to identify where they came from, it is possible to discover their place of birth: as they were staying in a hotel, it is possible that they had come to Manchester from that country. Certainly the occupations given indicate that many were here on business trips, such as the Swedish Railway engineer who was staying in Manchester in 1861, around the time that Beyer Peacock & Co. were manufacturing locomotives for that country's railways. There were also a number who were involved with various aspects of the textile industry, often described as 'buyers' or 'agents'. Many of the hotels that these foreign visitors stayed in were located around Piccadilly, close to the warehouse area. The leading hotels in the late nineteenth century were the Mosley Hotel, the Queen's Hotel and the Albion Hotel (which a French visitor described as having one of the best cuisines in Europe), the Clarence, the Waterloo and the Hotel Des Etrangers, while just off Piccadilly was the Grand Hotel, which claimed that it was in a quieter part of Manchester although convenient for the warehouses and the station. Several of the hotels claimed that they had staff who, between them, could speak several European languages. According to the 1871 census these hotels had guests who were born in Vera Cruz, West Indies, France, Cuba, Spain, Norway, Santo Domingo, Italy and Brazil. Ten years later the list included Canada, Germany, Bavaria, Australia, Spain, Portugal, Italy, France, Denmark and the United States (including W.F. Carver, who described his occupation as 'champion shot putter of the world' and was staying at the Queen's Hotel). Manchester was certainly a magnet for foreign visitors, but it should also be remembered that there was a sizeable foreign community already living in Manchester by the middle of the nineteenth century, many of whom had come from Germany, while there were others who had come from parts of the Ottoman Empire. Many of these foreigners had come to Manchester for business reasons and established themselves in many walks of life.

Even before the Industrial Revolution visitors came to Manchester and recorded their impressions of the town. These early visitors were English rather than foreign. The earliest surviving description of Manchester comes from John Leland in 1535, who described the town as being 'on the south side of Irwel River' and that it 'stondith in Salfordshire'. He went on to say that it 'is the fairest, best buildid, quickkest and most populous tounne of all Lancastreshire: yet is in it but one parock chirch, but is a college. . . . Ther be divers stoner bridgis . . . the nest is of iii arches is over Irwel, cawllid Salford Bridge . . .'. Leland then goes on to describe the remains of the Roman fort at Castlefield, pointing out that much of the stone had been used for the bridges across the Rivers Irwell, Irk and Dene.

Leland was followed later in the century by William Camden, who commented that the town surpassed the neighbouring towns in 'elegance [and] populousness' and that it was well known for its 'woollen manufactures, markets, church and college'. Like Leland, he commented on the remains of the Roman fort, which he claimed gave Manchester its name, and on the important buildings in the town, but, more importantly, he drew attention to the importance of the woollen textile industry. Similar sentiments were expressed in 1617 by Fynes Moryson who described Manchester as 'an old town, fair and wel inhabited, rich in the trade of woollen cloth', and said that it was 'beautified by the market place, the chirch and the college'.

By the end of the seventeenth century visitors to Manchester were not only reporting regularly on the town and its buildings but also on the goods produced and sold in the town. Celia Fiennes, visiting in 1688, commented that 'Manchester looks exceedingly well at the entrance, very substantial buildings, the houses are not very lofty, but mostly of brick and stone . . . there is a very large church . . . the market is kept for their linen cloth cotton tickings, incles, which is the manufacture of the town . . . this is a thriving place.'

In 1725 William Stukeley visited Manchester, which he described as 'the largest, most rich, populous and busy village in England'. After describing the buildings, he draws attention to Manchester's industry and trade which he says was 'incredibly large . . . fustians, girth web, tickings, tapes etc. which is dispersed all over the Kingdom and to foreign parts: they have looms which work twenty four laces at a time'. Stukeley's comments about the fact that Manchester was not a borough were echoed by Daniel Defoe a decade later when he described Manchester as the 'greatest, if not really the greatest mere village in England', and commented on its growth during the early years of the century. Defoe's comments about it being a village were accurate as Manchester was technically a market town until 1838. The state of the government of the town and its lack of Parliament representation was commented upon in 1730 by Don Manuel Gonzales, who was one of the earliest foreign visitors to Manchester to record his views. In his opinion Manchester 'is so much improved in the last century above its neighbours that though it is not a corporation, nor sends members to Parliament, yet as an inland town, it has perhaps the best trade of any in these northern parts and surpasses all the towns near abouts in building and number of people and manufacturers. . .'.

As the eighteenth century progressed, visitors to Manchester tended to comment less on the buildings and more on the state of the town and its appearance. For example, in 1777 Samuel Curwen, an American, commented that 'the centre consisted principally of old buildings: its streets narrow, irregularly built with many capital houses interspersed'. However, he pointed out that streets were being widened and that King Street was the 'best built . . . busy, sufficiently wide and most of its houses noble'.

However, other things began to attract the attention of visitors. For instance, in 1745 a supporter of Charles Stuart, John Ray, considered that Mancunians were 'very industrious'. Others noticed different facets. In 1777 Johann Busch commented that the 'first thing that strikes you about Manchester is the bustle: a drive rewarded by ample profit and proven by the continuing growth of the town . . .'. He compared Manchester and Salford, pointing out that it appeared that the two adjacent towns had different philosophies about allowing and encouraging industrial development, commenting that 'once the creative ingenuity of our time is achieved, it wants to see everything arranged in its own way. Nothing must stop it from procuring all the conveniences and individual comforts needed.' In his view this did not exist in Salford, which he described as 'an old smoke-ridden town with narrow, crooked alleys and leaning buildings, full of nooks and crannies' where ingenuity is not as thriving as in other places. It rather settles, as I saw it, here in Manchester and not in such a place as Salford.'

This idea of everything geared towards making a profit was also commented on by another visitor, Johann Volkman, in the early 1780s, who wrote that 'it is said that more money flows in this town in a single month than in the county of Huntingdon in half a year'. Twenty years later, in 1803, Johanna Schopenhauer commented that 'Work, profit and greed seem to be the only thoughts here'. Thirty years later, in 1835, a French visitor, Alexis de Tocqueville, suggested that Manchester consisted of a 'populace bent on gain, which seeks to amass gold so as to be able to possess everything else later on all at the same time'.

As the eighteenth century progressed, although visitors set the scene by describing the town, it was the new developments that attracted visitors, especially newspaper reporters. One of the earliest of these was Philip Nemnich of the Tublingen paper *Allgemeine Zeitung*, who visited Manchester in 1799. Not only did he visit and report on the places that he thought visitors ought to see if they were in the town, but he also reported on the changes that were taking place at the time. He drew attention to the effects of the introduction of machinery, and presumably steam power, which would, he believed, lead first to unemployment and then to new products and increased employment opportunities.

In 1814 another visitor to Manchester was Johann May, who may have been a Prussian industrial spy. His reports concentrated on the mills and their equipment. At the time of his visit Manchester and the surrounding area were working to full capacity as the mills were producing cloth for uniforms for the British army fighting Napoleon. May painted a grim picture of the mills which he described as towering 'up to five or six storeys in height. The huge chimneys at the side of these buildings belch forth black coal vapours and this tells us that powerful steam engines are used here. The clouds of coal vapour can be viewed from afar. The houses are blackened by it. The river which flows through Manchester is so filled with waste dye matter that it looks like a dye-vat. The whole scene is one of melancholy.'

About the same time as May visited Manchester a Swiss national named Johann Escher also arrived. He was able to see inside a cotton mill that was under construction, which he claimed as '130 feet long and 50 feet broad and has six floors. Not a stick of wood is being used in the whole building. All the girders are being made of cast iron and are joined together. The pillars are hollow iron columns which can be heated by steam . . . there are 270 such pillars. . . . Nearly all the spinning mills are six or seven floors . . . the attics have windows which are parallel to the roof and are similar to those used in greenhouses'. (Incidentally, Escher also commented that all those who were well off in Manchester had a greenhouse in which they grew fruits like grapes and peaches. He observed that they were of better quality and riper than those grown in Switzerland, but did not last as long.) The steam engines, according to Escher, frequently powered between 40,000 and 50,000 spindles, and he commented that in Manchester there were more spindles in a single street than in the whole of Switzerland.

Steam power was the making of Manchester in the early nineteenth century. It was still a force whose full potential had to be unlocked. As late as 1847 the author of an article in the *People's Journal* commented that 'perhaps still fewer amongst us have an adequate conception of the importance to the future of these gigantic forces which as yet lie undeveloped in the system of which it is the representative. Manchester is the type of one grand idea – machinery – an idea which is new in the world, at least in that large sense in which its vital significance consists. . . .'

It was not only the industrialisation that attracted attention. Developments in transportation were also looked at with interest. Brindley's aqueduct at Barton had attracted visitors from the time it opened in 1761, but the canals also had other features that attracted the attention of foreign visitors. One of these was a German engineer, geographer and cartographer, Johann Hogrewe, who visited Manchester in 1780 to look at the newly completed Bridgewater Canal. The account of his visit was published the same year and provided a detailed account of the Manchester terminus of the basin, including the Giants' Basin, the water-powered hoist to raise the containerised coal from canal level to street level, a height of 25 to 30 ft, and cross sections of the canal itself. However, by the time the railway arrived some of its novelty had disappeared, although train travel was still something of an experience, and even an ordeal, for those who were not accustomed to it.

Although many of the visitors to Manchester in the late eighteenth century were impressed with what they saw, there were those who were not. In 1790 John Byng described the town as a 'great nasty manufacturing town . . . their Exchange is a handsome building, but crowded up in a low situation. Their market place seems to be a bad one . . . the new part of the town . . . is of a better sort.' Six years earlier it had been reported that there was not a good inn in Manchester and that the people were 'insolent beyond description'!

Another visitor at the beginning of the nineteenth century was Don Manuel Alvarez Espriella, better known as Robert Southey (he visited Manchester and apparently travelled through England under the guise of a Spanish man), who wrote that 'a place more destitute of all interesting objects than Manchester is not easy to conceive. In size and population it is the second city in the Kingdom, containing about four score thousand inhabitants. Imagine this multitude crowded together in narrow streets, the houses built of brick and blackened with smoke; frequent buildings among them as large as convents, without antiquity, without their beauty, without their holiness; when you hear from within . . . the everlasting din of machinery: and where, when the bell rings, it is to call wretches to their work instead of their prayers. . . .' As for the interiors of the mills, Southey likened them to one of Dante's hells and said there was 'endless motion' and 'noise'.

It was the noise that also attracted the attention of de Tocqueville in 1835 and Leon Faucher in 1844. Faucher commented that 'Manchester does not present the bustle of London or Liverpool. During the greater part of the day, the town is silent, and almost appears deserted. The heavily laden boats glide noiselessly along the canals . . . between rows of immense factories which divide amongst themselves the air, water and fire. . . . You hear nothing but the breathing of the vast machines, sending forth fire and smoke through their chimneys.'

A similar view of the noise and the effect of the mills on the landscape and townscape was by A.B. Reach in 1849, when he described the 'dull leaden-coloured sky, tainted by thousands of ever smoking chimneys'. He goes on to comment on the 'unsightly mills, with their countless rows of windows, their towering shafts, their jets of waste steam continually puffing in panting gushes from the brown grimy walls'. Although not mentioning the machinery and its noise, the implication of noise is there. Reach visited the poorer parts of the city and wrote about the places that few people ventured into. These were the areas that Engels described as being hidden behind the façades of the shops, public buildings and warehouses, which the merchants knew little about.

During the nineteenth century it was the declining conditions in which people lived and worked that began to attract the attention of visitors to Manchester. The general impression given is that Manchester was a dirty town, albeit an industrious one, where industrialisation had a dehumanising effect on the lives and morals of the population. Southey was horrified by the conditions under which people lived. He wrote that the 'dwellings of the labouring manufacturers are in narrow streets and lanes, blocked up from light and air . . . crowded together because every inch of land is of such great value that room for light and air cannot be afforded them . . . a great proportion of the poor lodge in cellars, damp and dark, where every kind of filth is suffered to accumulate, because no exertions of domestic care can ever make such homes decent. These places are so many hot-beds of infections.'

Another visitor, Johann Meidinger, in 1820, referred to the 'poverty and uncleanliness' that was 'everywhere apparent. Brutality and immorality are rife'. He described those who lived in Manchester as 'pale and poorly dressed' and living on 'buttermilk, oatcakes and potatoes'. He was not impressed with Manchester, which he described as 'a sprawling town with a few beautiful buildings and streets'. 'On Saturdays the shops', he wrote, 'are seldom closed before midnight or 1 o'clock because . . . the workers receive their wages late in the evening and then get the remains of their provisions. Many immediately squander their wages in the taverns.'

During the first half of the nineteenth century it was as if interest in the industrialisation of Manchester had diminished and people were becoming aware of the problems it created. Social conditions became the common theme for many of the visitors, but there were still those who took a general overview. Henry Adams wrote in 1861 that 'The City of Manchester seems to be a collection of enormous warehouses, banks and shops, set in a broad margin of common brick houses, which the lower classes live in. But the best and largest factories lie at a distance varying from one mile to fifty or thereabouts, in little towns of their own, and the houses of the wealthy citizens are all country houses on the outskirts of towns so that for miles about one meets long and very pretty roads with villas and parks which make the environs charming, but which leave the city proper very dull and gloomy. . . .'

In addition to the people mentioned in this introduction who visited Manchester up to the middle of the nineteenth century, which appears to be roughly when the 'excitement' of industrial Manchester died down, there were many more. Some have been quoted in Bradshaw's *Visitors to Manchester*, others in Brooks and Haworth's book *Manchester: this good old town: an illustrated anthology* and in Thomson's *History of Manchester to 1852*. Descriptions of Manchester help to paint a picture of the town and this can be supplemented by illustrations, especially the photograph. Perhaps the advent of the photograph and its development in the nineteenth century reduced the need for verbal descriptions. It has been said that one photograph is worth a thousand words. However, the last word should be left to a visitor, J.G. Kohl, who wrote in 1844 that 'I know of no town in Great Britain, except London, which makes so deep an impression upon the stranger as Manchester. London is alone of its kind, and so is Manchester. Never since the world began was there a town like it, in its outward appearance, its wonderful activity, its mercantile and manufacturing prosperity, and its remarkable moral and political phenomena.' Kohl was impressed with Manchester and rightly so.

This photograph was taken in 1932 to show the traffic island that had been installed at the end of Cross Street in order to make it safer for pedestrians to cross this busy road junction. In the early twentieth century the police regarded it as a problem junction and stationed a policeman there to control the traffic. There were many complaints about the delays experienced by road vehicles, but the City Engineer and the police claimed that average delays were less than two minutes! The building on the left with the Craven A sign was on the corner of Corporation Street, where Marks & Spencer built their shop after the war.

In July 1934 the foundation stone for the Town Hall Extension was laid by George V when he visited Manchester to open the new Central Library. The Town Hall Extension was designed by Vincent Harris as a match to the Central Library, which he had also designed. The estimated cost of the new building was £711,000 and included a new Council Chamber and a large public area known as the Rates Hall, where rates, council house rents and other bills could be paid. The Town Hall Extension was completed in 1938 and opened by George VI on 16 May 1938. This photograph shows the steel framework of the new building in the course of erection, already masking the tower at the Princess Street/Cooper Street end of the original Town Hall, and eventually to mask the lower part of the main tower on the Albert Square frontage of the Town Hall.

CHAPTER NINE

STREET SCENES

Shortly after the pictures for the first *Manchester in Old Photographs* had been selected, part of the centre of Manchester was devastated by a huge terrorist bomb which severely damaged a number of buildings, several of which had to be demolished. Even now reconstruction work is still going on with some buildings still surrounded by scaffolding, denying the public a view of their Victorian grandeur. Although several of the Victorian buildings were damaged, and in particular the former Corn Exchange, it was the modern post-war buildings which were most severely damaged and have had to be demolished.

The area which was worst affected by the bomb blast was close to what might be described as the centre of medieval Manchester, around the Market Place and Cathedral. The damage caused has allowed the local authority to look again at the area and to prepare plans for its re-development, although these plans have aroused controversy. However, if the history of this particular area is examined, over the last two centuries there have been many changes, beginning with the demolition in 1792 of the Exchange, built by the Mosleys in 1729, to the construction of Corporation Street in 1846, the building of Victoria Buildings in the late 1870s and redevelopment resulting from damage caused by the Christmas blitz of 1940.

The Market Place/Corporation Street area is not the only part of central Manchester to have seen changes over the years. Market Street and parts of the Piccadilly area have also been affected by re-development while individual buildings have been refurbished and new uses found for them. Former warehouses have been converted to hotels and residential accommodation, while former railway stations have been converted to exhibition centres, museums or events arenas. Recently Cross Street Chapel has been demolished and replaced by an office block, although incorporating a chapel within the new building.

Change is essential for a town or city centre to remain vibrant and interesting. Change sometimes makes people aware of buildings and places which they have passed many times, but never paid much attention to. Demolition may open up new views while the demolition of an adjacent building will encourage someone to look for the first time at a building taken for granted. It is surprising how many people walk around with their eyes closed or look just in shop windows. They miss much of interest on upper floors.

Photographs of streets not only record the architecture of the street as it was, but also show the traffic, the street furniture, the dress of those who are walking along and even adverts and shop windows. However, what they do not show is the dirt and grime, and the piles of horse manure from the hundreds of horses which passed along the streets in the nineteenth century. On Market Street boys were employed to sweep the road where people crossed. Later, watercarts were used to try to keep the dust down as the horses' hooves pounded their droppings into a fine powder. Congestion was taken seriously. In the mid-1870s, it was suggested that many bus journeys along Market Street took so long that it was quicker to walk, and that the buses should terminate in Piccadilly rather than add to congestion on Market Street. It is hoped that the illustrations used in this section complement those in the previous volume, showing buildings and areas which were not included or areas where change has taken place. They have been arranged in the form of a walk from Deansgate to the markets, returning to Cross Street. Not only have street scenes been included, but also photographs of some of the people who were to be seen in central Manchester during the last 150 years, people who might be called 'characters' and added so much to the variety of life in the city.

In 1849 Angus Bethune Reach described Manchester's streets as bustling with people, hurrying to and from their places of employment. A similar comment was made fourteen years earlier by Alexis de Tocqueville, who added that Mancunians going about their business rarely smiled. This photograph of the bottom end of Market Street, close to the Market Place, in about 1895, shows just this, businessmen hurrying about while horse-drawn trams bring more people into Manchester, possibly to visit the many shops in the area.

Historically, Deansgate is an important east-west route across central Manchester, following roughly the line of a Roman road. This photograph, taken at the beginning of twentieth century, shows Deansgate looking east from its junction with Whitworth Street West. Dominating the scene are the railway bridges leading to Central Station and the Great Northern Railway's warehouse. In front of the Railway Hotel is the Deansgate Tunnel through which the Rochdale Canal which originally ran between Deansgate and Albion Street, but which was removed about 1845, leaving only a short section under Deansgate. Today, the Railway Hotel has been restored as offices while the front railway bridge carries the Metrolink trams. The bridge in the background no longer exists, having been demolished in the 1970s.

In 1909, further redevelopment on Deansgate resulted in the demolition of nos 88–90, which were the premises of Thomas Armstrong, who started as a maker of clocks, watches, optical and scientific instruments in about 1825. The building, said to have sandstone walls and a low ceiling, was divided into two shops, one specializing in clocks, watches and jewellery and the other in optical and scientific instruments. Over the years, the firm built up an extensive optical practice which had a high reputation for the manufacture of optical equipment, including artificial eyes. Armstrong's were also official opticians to the Manchester Royal Infirmary and the Eye Hospital. On the extreme left are the premises of an even older firm of silversmith, clock and watchmakers, Kents, who were established in 1760, and who were in 1904, when this photograph was taken, suppliers of clocks to the Post Office and Excise Offices in Manchester. The building which replaced these shops was the Houldsworth Hall, also known as Diocesan House, which was completed in 1910.

Although a number of central Manchester's roads were improved and widened in the early nineteenth century, there were no improvements made to Deansgate until the 1860s as many of the property owners were not prepared to sell the Council the land they required to widen the road. Eventually agreement was reached and work was started to widen Deansgate in the late 1860s. Consequently there are no very old buildings to be seen along this road: most date from the latter half of the century. The rather uncongested junction is of Deansgate, John Dalton Street and Bridge Street. With the exception of the building on the extreme right with the blind over the shop front, all the buildings on this photograph are still standing. Today it would be impossible to walk down the centre of the road as the man next to the penny-farthing bicycle is doing. The clean-looking building was erected in the early 1880s for one of a number of building societies that existed at that time, the Queen's Building Society.

Opposite: Fronting on to Cross Street were the offices of the *Manchester Guardian* and *Manchester Evening News*. The *Manchester Guardian* had been established in 1821 as the voice of liberalism and free trade in the town, while the *Manchester Evening News* had been started by a candidate in the 1868 General Election to get his views known. When the election was over, the evening paper was purchased by the *Manchester Guardian*, who continued to publish it as an evening paper. As a result, the area just behind Cross Street (where the printing was done) was always very busy, especially when the papers were being dispatched to wholesalers, newsagents and the street newspaper vendors. This photograph, taken in the 1930s, shows not only one of the motor vans which was used, but also the horse-drawn trap which was used for distribution purposes in the centre of Manchester.

Although the name Deansgate may imply the existence of a gate and a walled town, this is not the case. The name probably means the street leading to the River Dene, 'gate' being the Anglo-Saxon word for street, and the River Dene originally flowed down Shudehill and Withy Grove to reach the River Irwell near Victoria Bridge. In the late nineteenth century the section of Deansgate around Kendall's shop was always very busy, not only with shoppers but also with businessmen, as many of the buildings were in multi-occupation with firms renting suites of rooms for offices. This photograph, taken in the 1890s, shows a group of girls or young women wearing what might be described as typical dress of the period for such people – dark clothes, shawls over their heads and clogs. One appears to be a newspaper seller while the others may have been shopping or on their way to or from work. Behind the group a small boy, also in clogs and wearing a cap, is selling newspapers, while horse-drawn buses and delivery vans pass by.

St Ann's Square, known for many centuries as Acres Fields, was originally one of the large open fields on the edge of medieval Manchester and the location for the annual fair granted to Manchester's inhabitants in 1222. When it started, the fair was held for two days in late September when the harvest had been completed, but in 1227 it was extended to three days. The fair continued to be held here until 1821 when it was moved as it was not regarded as a suitable event to hold in a residential and shopping area. This photograph was taken in 1878 and shows St Ann's Church, consecrated in 1712, which was the second Anglican church to be built in the centre of Manchester. In contrast with the Collegiate Church (now the Cathedral), which was regarded as 'high church' with a tendency to support the Jacobite succession, St Ann's was regarded as 'low church' and supported the Hanoverian succession. The cab stand in the centre was one of the earliest official places for hansom cabs to stand and was the place from which distances from Manchester were measured. Some of the buildings on the right are still standing today, although their ground-floor windows have been altered. The most interesting of the names that can be read is that of J. Mudd & Son. James Mudd was a photographer in Manchester who took some of the earliest photographs of the town. Later the building was used by Chapman's, photographic equipment dealers and photographers. The statue in the centre is of Richard Cobden, one of the leaders of the Anti-Corn Law League, who gave the movement the land where the Free Trade Hall was eventually built, and whose house on Quay Street was acquired for the establishment of Owen's College in 1851.

The Manchester Stock Exchange is able to trace its history back to 12 May 1836, when a group of twenty businessmen formed an association to trade in stocks and shares in Manchester. It was not until 1868 that the Manchester Stock Exchange had its first home, at the rear of a building erected on Cross Street. In 1906 the Manchester Stock Exchange moved to a new building on Norfolk Street which had been specially designed as a stock exchange. This new building included 4,000 square feet of 'floor' space as well as facilities for members to meet their clients and discuss business in private. The Stock Exchange claimed that one benefit of the new building was that it was close to the Royal Exchange and the financial heart of Manchester on King Street, as well as to the General Post Office on Brown Street. In an undated booklet published by the Stock Exchange, it claimed that its position at the centre of such an important financial and industrial area gave it a unique position in the north of England, so that it was able to specialise in shares of companies based in the area, especially in the textile industry. This photograph shows the Stock Exchange building in the 1920s, but unlike the outside of the Royal Exchange it appears to be relatively peaceful and calm.

King Street is divided into two halves by Cross Street. The lower half, between Cross Street and Deansgate, is devoted to shopping while the upper half, between Cross Street and Spring Gardens, is Manchester's financial centre. This photograph, taken in the early 1960s, shows the buildings which were demolished to enable the National Westminster Bank and Sun Alliance to build new office blocks. The NatWest tower was built where the District Bank was located while Vulcan Insurance made way for Sun Alliance. This latter building was designed by Alfred Waterhouse and was completed for Royal London Insurance in 1862, but they never occupied the building, leasing it to Vulcan immediately on completion. Vulcan were specialists in the insuring of boilers used for steam engines. Eventually they purchased the building outright and made major internal alterations to bring it up to the standards of the day. The buildings were demolished in the early 1960s. The clean white building on the left is Lloyd's Bank, which stood where the original Manchester Town Hall was located. The Tower and the District Bank, erected in 1889 to the designs of Mills and Murgatroyd, occupied the site of the Albion Hotel where Manchester's first borough council meeting was held, where the Chamber of Commerce had its origins and where the first meeting of the Anti-Corn Law League was also held in 1838.

Albert Square was created especially to house the memorial to Prince Albert, the statue of which was given to Manchester by Alderman Goadsby. It was handed over to Manchester in January 1867 and was restored by the City Council in 1894 in preparation for Queen Victoria's visit to open the Manchester Ship Canal. Although it resembles the Albert Memorial in London, the memorial in Manchester, designed by Thomas Worthington, was completed before the capital's. The photograph, probably taken in the last years of the nineteenth century, also shows the fountain that was erected to mark the completion of the Thirlmere Aqueduct, which brought water from the Lake District to increase supplies available in Manchester. Behind the statue of John Bright a vacant site can be seen. This was the result of the demolition of a block of two-storeyed domestic-type buildings prior to their replacement by a modern office and shop building, which today house the Manchester branch of the HMSO bookshop.

The atmosphere in Manchester was very smoky in the nineteenth century, so new buildings rapidly became grimy and covered with soot. However, cleaning during the late 1960s revealed much of the architectural detail which had been hidden. This photograph shows the contrast between the cleaned and dirty portions of the Gothic Town Hall.

Oxford Street was, and still is, the main route into central Manchester from the residential suburbs to the south. This photograph of about 1914 gives a good indication of the amount of traffic using this important road. As well as horse-drawn vehicles, there are also trams travelling in both directions. The trams in the middle distance, lead by No 502, which had originally been built in 1903 with an open top, appear to be waiting while a team of horses hauls a waggon across the junction from Chepstow Street. The building on the corner of Portland Street and Oxford Street has now been demolished, but it had an impressive array of windows at roof level together with an advertisement for *Nobody's Daughter* at the Princes Theatre.

When Manchester opened its new town hall in Albert Square in 1877, it enabled the authority to bring all its departments together in a single building, but as the functions of local government continued to increase the Town Hall became over-crowded and some departments began to move to other buildings in the centre of Manchester. For instance, the Gas Department had a building especially built on Deansgate, near the John Rylands Library, where bills could be paid, appliances hired and even repaired. During the years after the end of the First World War the position became worse, as local government took on new responsibilities such as slum clearance and the building of council houses. Departments spread throughout the city did not make for efficient local administration, so discussions began about the possibility of erecting an extension for the Town Hall. Initially there was opposition from the business rate payers who felt that, with the depressed state of the economy at the time it would force their rates even higher. However, the City Council was able to remove some of the opposition by agreeing to insert a clause in the contract with the builders that local men were employed, the view being expressed that they would spend their money locally. Work started in 1931 to clear a site between the new Central Library, then under construction, and the Town Hall. This photograph shows the demolition of the former *Manchester Examiner and Times* building. (The *Manchester Examiner and Times* had been published between 1846 and 1897.) The photograph provides an interesting insight to the layout of the old building, and the problems of internal layout when the building has a curved frontage.

Many people do not appreciate that Manchester has developed on the crest of a ridge with land falling away to the north to the Rivers Irwell and Irk and the River Medlock to the south. One street that leads to the crest of the ridge overlooking the River Medlock is Mount Street, which leads to the highest point in this part of Manchester where the G-Mex is now located. This photograph was taken in about 1939 and shows the relationship between Central Library and the recently completed Town Hall extension. Mount Street also has other important buildings along its route: the Friends Meeting House and Lawrence Buildings, formerly the Inland Revenue offices in Manchester, although now used for other purposes. The buildings on the extreme left form part of the Gaiety Theatre, which had been converted to a cinema in 1921.

In 1873 a decision was taken to re-invigorate the almost moribund branch of the Manchester YMCA after many years of inactivity. The revitalised YMCA took premises in Piccadilly with accommodation for its members in various parts of Manchester, but it was felt that a more permanent home was required. In 1875 the YMCA was able to acquire the building that had formerly been occupied by the Manchester Natural History Society on Peter Street. The Society had disposed of the building in 1868 to Owen's College, who had housed their Natural History department there until new buildings in Chorlton-on-Medlock had been completed. The former museum building was converted to provide meeting rooms, refreshment facilities and rooms where recreational activities could be carried out. The old building provided adequate facilities for the YMCA until the early twentieth century when its growing membership and the changing demands made of the facilities rendered the old building less suitable. A decision was taken to demolish the former Museum building and erect a purpose-built headquarters in Manchester. This is the building shown in this photograph; it included meeting rooms, refreshment facilities, a gym and a swimming pool. To the right of the building is the warehouse which the Midland Hotel considered demolishing in the early 1920s to enable an extension to be built, but it never materialised.

As the size and population of Manchester grew during the late eighteenth century, several new churches wer
built including St Peter's, at the junction of Dawson Street (now Mosley Street) with Oxford Street and Pete
Street, which was designed by James Wyatt who had recently completed work on Heaton Hall. The new churcl
was designed in the Classical style, which was very much in vogue. The Classical effect was partially lost whe
the tower was added in 1816, a development which did not meet with the approval of Wyatt. When the churcl
opened in 1794 it was on the edge of Manchester, but within a few years it was engulfed by the rising tide c
redevelopment. During the late nineteenth century, as the character of the area changed and people began t
move away, often as a result of re-development of sites for commercial or transportation purposes, St Peter's lost
large part of its congregation and its up-keep became more difficult. In 1906 an Act of Parliament gav
Manchester Diocese the authority to close and demolish several churches in central Manchester including S
Peter's. The church was demolished in 1907 and the site marked by a white Portland Stone cross. Thi
photograph shows St Peter's Church at the end of the nineteenth century on what appears to be a very quiet day
possibly a Sunday.

Lower Mosley Street came into existence at the end of the eighteenth century and was really a continuation of Mosley Street. The view along Lower Mosley Street towards Piccadilly was closed off by St Peter's Church, as this photograph taken in March 1897 shows. The buildings on the left-hand side of Lower Mosley Street were demolished when the Midland Hotel was built. These buildings included, from left to right, the Lower Mosley Street Schools, which had been built by Mosley Street Unitarian Chapel; the People's Concert Hall, originally called the Casino, which opened in 1852 as a music hall and where the musicians in the orchestra pit were protected from objects thrown on to the stage by the audience by a net; and the Gentlemen's Concert Hall, opened in 1831. On the right, the shop selling tripe dinners and suppers was typical of the mixed commercial and residential property which existed in central Manchester. The railings around the cellars are not to stop people living there, but to prevent people falling down the hole and injuring themselves. Next door to the shop was the Concert Hall Tavern, which presumably took its name from the presence of the two places of entertainment across the road. These buildings eventually disappeared in the 1970s and have been replaced by Georgian-style buildings, which appear to be houses but are actually offices.

Trams, motorised vehicles and horse-drawn wagons mingle in this photograph of Oxford Street close to its junction with St Peter's Square, *c.* 1937. The photograph was taken before this part of Oxford Street became a one-way system. Oxford Street, together with Peter Street and Quay Street, formed the entertainment centre of Manchester with many theatres, and later cinemas, along their combined lengths. The Paramount Cinema (later to become the Odeon) on the left was built in 1932 and was one of a number of cinemas which had opulent interiors where those going to see films could forget the problems of the recession and enter a 'make-believe' world. Next door can be seen the Plaza, which was one of several dance halls in central Manchester. According to some reports, it was more respectable than its sister, the Ritz. The ground floor is used for commercial purposes with Muir's, pawnbrokers, occupying the corner site. Across the road is the News Theatre, while the Paramount Whist Hall occupies part of the Princes Theatre. Further down Oxford Street, but not visible in this photograph, were the Palace Theatre and the Gaumont Cinema, which replaced the Hippodrome in 1935.

In 1906 Manchester opened its Municipal Technical College on Whitworth Street. The college was created by taking over the education institutions that had been run by the Trustees of Sir Joseph Whitworth and had included the former Mechanics Institute, which was at 103 Princess Street. The new building, shown in this postcard, included classrooms as well as lecture theatres, workshops and an observatory. The landscaped area where the children are standing is known as Whitworth Street Park, which was created because the architects of the College wanted their new building to be appreciated by the public. Rather than allow another building to be erected on the site, they persuaded the City Council to purchase the site and landscape it. The children may have come from the nearby Manchester Central Board School, the corner of which can be seen on the extreme left of the picture.

The idea of converting warehouses to hotels may be regarded by some as a modern development, but this is not the case. In 1868 a new warehouse was built for Collie and Co. on the site of the former House of Recovery on Aytoun Street. However, in the early 1880s Collie and Co. collapsed and the warehouse was sold. The architects, Mills and Murgatroyd, were commissioned to convert the building into a hotel, which opened in 1883 as the Grand Hotel. The furnishings for the new hotel were provided by Kendal, Milne and Faulkner, while the hotel boasted it was the first in Manchester to have a passenger lift. The Grand Hotel claimed that it was in a quieter part of central Manchester, although close to the warehouses and shops. It continued to be used as a hotel until the late 1980s when it closed.

Demolition of one of Manchester's landmarks is under way in 1909/10 – the former Manchester Royal Infirmary which had dominated Piccadilly since 1754. When the Infirmary had been built in 1752, there were no other medical facilities in Manchester and Salford except for a few doctors, but by the time the hospital moved to its new site in Chorlton-on-Medlock there was one other general hospital at Ancoats and also several specialist hospitals in the city. During its time at Piccadilly the Infirmary had seen many great advances in the treatment of illness and injuries as well as in the training of doctors, nurses and surgeons. The building had also had its fair share of problems, not all of which were medical or financial. For example, in August 1819 there were reports that several of those injured at Peterloo were refused treatment at the Infirmary because of their presence at the event, while in 1834 the Secretary to the Infirmary absconded with £500. It had also seen many events pass its portals, such as Queen Victoria's visits of 1851 and 1894, the Grand Trades Procession to mark the passing of the Manchester Ship Canal in 1885 and the unveiling of the statues of the Esplanade in front of the building. This photograph shows the Mosley Street wing of the Infirmary at a time when the roof has been taken off the building and demolition is well under way. The Mosley Street wing and the one on Portland Street were similar in appearance, giving the three most prominent sides of the building a symmetry which was common in the early nineteenth century. The dome was added in the 1830s when the front portico was added, designed by Richard Lane. The poster gives details of where the entrance to the Student Room is and the times it was open.

Opposite: The view which a visitor to Manchester would have had across Piccadilly in the mid-1930s, a view which only became possible after the demolition of the Infirmary. In the background are the warehouses which were destroyed in the Christmas blitz of 1940; this is now the site of Piccadilly Plaza. In the foreground is the statue of Queen Victoria, unveiled in October 1901 by Lord Roberts.

The demolition of the former Infirmary appears to have attracted a lot of attention from the public. This photograph must have been taken after the columns of the front portico had been demolished, but who the men were and why they are standing where they are is not known; but it is possible that they were the men responsible for the demolition and the photographer was recording their work. (See page 16 for a photograph of the columns collapsing.) Behind the man on the front column can be seen the rebuilt Mosley Hotel, next door to which is the Ceylon Coffee House which opened in 1906.

In 1912 the former Town Hall on King Street, which had housed Manchester's reference library since 1878, was declared to be structurally unsafe and had to be closed almost immediately. As there was no alternative building where the library could be placed at such short notice, several wooden huts were erected on the edge of the former Infirmary site to accommodate the library until a permanent building could be found. However, with the outbreak of war in 1914 plans to build a new central library were delayed until after hostilities had ceased. Work on the new library did not start until 1929, and it was another five years before the new building was completed and the Reference Library could be moved to its new home in St Peter's Square. This photograph, taken in the late 1920s, shows the library huts in Piccadilly Gardens.

Piccadilly was a major thoroughfare, not only for traffic but also for pedestrians passing between Market Street and London Road station. This photograph, taken in the 1890s in front of the Albion Hotel, which stood on the corner of Piccadilly and Oldham Street until 1926 when it was replaced by Woolworth's store, shows some of the many people who passed through the area during the day.

This photograph was taken in about 1890 close to where Piccadilly, George Street and Mosley Street meet. It shows an ice-cream seller being patronised by several lads, who may have been errand boys or messenger boys employed in the shops, offices and warehouses around. Behind the horse bus is the Mosley Hotel, which had moved to Piccadilly in 1828 when it was displaced from its original location by the widening of Market Street. In 1894 the Mosley Hotel was rebuilt and became one of Manchester's leading hotels.

Stevenson Square, located between Oldham Street and Lever Street, was named after William Stevenson, who purchased 9 acres of land from the Lever family in 1780. When he began to develop it for residential purposes, the building line on the Great Ancoats Street side was set back (right), thus creating a square which it was hoped would rival St Ann's Square, but this did not occur. The Square itself eventually developed a commercial bias with the demolition of St Clement's Church in the 1870s. In the latter part of the nineteenth century Stevenson Square became a popular venue for public meetings in Manchester, with temperance and political gatherings attracting large audiences. This photograph, taken possibly in 1939, shows the bus station which was developed in Stevenson Square. The vehicles on the right are trolley buses, which were introduced on the No. 27 route (re-numbered in 1950 to 215) between Manchester and Audenshawe (Snipe Inn) in July 1938. Behind the trolley bus is the Grotto Café, of which there were four in central Manchester during the 1920s and 1930s.

In 1772 a public meeting in Manchester decided that a track which left Lever's Row (now Piccadilly) in the direction of New Cross should be improved for the benefit of the town. The land was acquired from its owner, Adam Oldham, and a new road laid out. In 1875 a Manchester periodical *The Critic* described Oldham Street as 'decidedly retail', while twelve months later another Manchester periodical, *The Shadow*, commented that Oldham Street had recently become the centre of the drapery trade and that the street came alive on Saturday afternoons and evenings as all the shops were open then. (Those on King Street, Deansgate and Market Street closed at 1 pm on Saturdays.) There were several well-known firms on Oldham Street in the late nineteenth century, including Affleck and Brown, Thomas Peel, Beatty Bros, Robert Lowe and Bateman's. This photograph, taken in about 1892, shows the central section of Oldham Street between Dale Street and Hilton Street and the buildings occupied by Beatty Bros, tailors; the Old Hen and Chickens, established in 1831; Lipton's, provision dealers; Mrs Elizabeth Day, cabinet maker; Robert Mitcheson, mantle warehouse; and Bateman's, drapery and mourning warehouse.

During the nineteenth century Market Street underwent a series of changes which resulted in its character being completed changed. At the beginning of the century it was an irregular line of houses and shops, some built of brick and others with timber frames. In the 1820s and 1830s the old buildings were gradually demolished, the gradient of the road made easier and a building line set back so that the street had a constant width. As the century progressed so other changes took place, as buildings were rebuilt or altered to meet the changing demands of commerce. As the buildings changed, so did their uses. At the beginning of the century Market Street was still residential, but by the middle of the nineteenth century the number of people who lived there had declined considerably, so that by the beginning of the twentieth century there were few people living in the street. The upper floors of the buildings were either workshops or offices, while at street level there was a variety of shops ranging from those selling provisions to gentlemen's outfitters and travel agents. The buildings on this photograph start at no. 27, where J. & R. Brown were trading as hosiers. Next door was one of several shops that Brooke Bond & Co. had in Manchester: they made their name mixing and supplying tea. Their neighbours in about 1891 were Joseph Bohanna, a stationer, whose upper floor was occupied by The General Coffin Furniture Co., whose head office was in Birmingham. Among the other occupiers on this part of Market Street were a belting manufacturer's agent, a firm of mechanical engineers and the Exchange Telegraph Co. The other firm whose sign is clearly visible is that of Kino Bros, court, naval and military tailors. Between Kino's premises and no. 39 was the entrance to Cromford Court, so named because Richard Arkwright, whose main factory was in Cromford in Derbyshire, had premises there in the late eighteenth century. The reason why the photograph was taken appears to be the parade of men along Market Street, but who they were and where they were going is not recorded. The uniform is very similar to that of the police, but it has been suggested that they might have been a volunteer battalion. Whatever the event, the marching men appear to have attracted a large crowd of onlookers, especially on the right-hand side of the photograph, while those on the opposite side of the road appear to be paying less attention to what is going on in the road. Although there are men marching along Market Street, horse-drawn trams and other vehicles appear to be moving along the road as normal. Today the buildings on the left have been demolished and Market Street is pedestrianised.

The impression this 1890s photograph of the junction of Market Street and High Street gives is that the pedestrians are in no particular hurry, possibly because it was dinner time. The tall building in the background is one of four warehouses in the area belonging to the firm of John Rylands, which was started by his father in Wigan in 1819 and moved to Manchester in 1822, opening a warehouse on High Street in 1823. The company not only imported raw cotton, but also manufactured the cloth, which it then dyed and used to produce clothing and other products which were sold to retailers.

Compared with the market-places of other towns, Manchester's Market Place was small and congested even in the seventeenth and eighteenth centuries. The position was made worse when the Mosleys erected a market hall, known as the Exchange, in the centre in 1729. During the eighteenth century, as the population of Manchester and the numbers attending the market rose, the market stalls spread into adjacent areas. Although many of the stalls were eventually moved to a new site off Shudehill in the 1820s, some remained. They lined the pavements and reduced the width of roadway through the area, which, until the completion of Corporation Street in the 1850s, was one of the main routes out to the northern suburbs. In 1891 the City Council decided that it would remove the last of the market stalls from the area to reduce congestion and make the area a safer place. This decision was greeted with approval in the local press. The photograph was taken in about 1890 and shows the problems which faced the authorities. In the background is the firm of Yates, who were well known as seedsmen and florists and whose nursery was on the banks of the Peak Forest Canal in Disley. Most of the Market Place was lost when Marks and Spencer developed a store on the corner of Market Street and Corporation Street.

Opposite: This couple, photographed in the 1890s, is crossing High Street where it joins Market Street. In the background, the Midland Bank is located at the corner of the Rylands Building, shown in the previous picture. Across the road is the Market Street frontage of Lewis's department store, which opened in 1877 in the former premises of Bon Marché. By the time this photograph was taken, Lewis's had been described as 'the greatest show place of Market Street' and a 'huge emporium of everything' with an exterior 'garnished with all the architectural embellishments of a handsome and highly ornate building' whose 'towers and cornices and projections . . . occasionally affords a means of special display in the holiday costume of innumerable flags and brilliant at night with electric light and the reflections of thousands of lamps'. The aim of the company was to supply everyday items as 'advantageous prices', encouraging the rising number of 'white collar' workers to do all their shopping under one roof.

Two of the best-known buildings in the Market Place are the Wellington Inn and Sinclair's Oyster Bar. This photograph shows the Wellington Inn towards the end of the nineteenth century. The building appears to have been built in the sixteenth century as a domestic residence with a shop at street level. It was not until the 1830s that it became a public house, and it did not assume its present name until the 1840s. Although it survived the blitz, modern redevelopment resulted in it having to be raised several feet to fit in. Now it is in the process of being moved again to a new site, as the area was devastated by a terrorist bomb in June 1996 and the whole area has dramatically changed yet again. The taller building at the end of the block is Sinclair's Oyster Bar, which came into existence in the mid-nineteenth century and occupied part of the site where John Shaw's Punch House stood in the eighteenth century. This respectable drinking establishment closed punctually at 8 pm, and if you did not leave when told to, it was possible that your boots would be filled with water. Shaw sold his punch in two sizes, 'P' and 'Q' – possibly pints and quarts, but nobody is absolutely certain what the letters mean.

Close to the Market Place was an area known as Smithy Door. Originally it had been part of the general area surrounding the Market Place, but with the construction of Victoria Street in 1833 it had been left isolated between the new road and Deansgate. The result was that the whole area began to deteriorate. In the early 1870s the City Council decided that the area should be improved and new shops and offices provided. Eventually, in 1875, the Vintner's Arms was demolished together with the remaining buildings of Smithy Door. Although many of the buildings dated from the late eighteenth century, one building, the Vintner's Arms, came from an earlier century. It is not known when this timber-framed building was erected, nor what it was originally used for. The first definite reference to it comes from the late eighteenth century when part of it was used by a butter importer. The Vintner's Arms appears to have sold a type of beer called 'entire', which was brewed by Deakin. According to H.A. Monckton in his book *A History of English Ale and Beer*, entire was a beer that originated in London in the 1720s when the London brewers decided to brew a beer which combined the qualities of brown, old and pale ale. It is claimed that this was later to become porter. The photograph was taken in 1875 as demolition was proceeding.

In 1875 Manchester was presented with a statue of Oliver Cromwell, which was sited close to the junction of Victoria Street, Deansgate and Cateaton Street. The statue was given to Manchester by Mrs Abel Heywood in memory of her first husband, Alderman Goadsby, who had given Manchester the statue of Prince Albert which was the centre-piece of the Albert Memorial. The statue was not universally accepted in Manchester. Some felt there should not have been a statue of Cromwell, while others objected to it being so close to Manchester Cathedral. It was said that Queen Victoria would never come into Manchester through Exchange station as Cromwell had his back to her when she came down the approach. It is also claimed that the reason why Queen Victoria refused to open the new Town Hall in 1877 was because the Mayoress at the time was Mrs Heywood. However, a more likely explanation for this is that her husband, Abel Heywood, had been a supporter of the Chartists in the 1840s, and this movement did not meet with Victoria's approval. Even in recent times the statue has been controversial, in that its location was regarded by road users as a traffic hazard, standing as it did in the centre of the road. In 1969 it was moved to Wythenshawe Park, where it remains today. Behind the statue can be seen the beginning of the approach to the London & North Western Railway's Exchange station, which is in Salford. This station was opened in 1884 when the London & North Western Railway Co. felt their presence at Victoria station was threatened by the continuing expansion of that station by its owners, the Lancashire & Yorkshire Railway. The office block at Exchange station was destroyed in 1940 and the station itself closed in May 1969, the same day as Central station closed.

Victoria Street was constructed in 1833 to improve the link between Central Manchester and the newly completed Bury New Road, which had been built as a turnpike road. In order to make the new road more level, part of it was constructed on a viaduct, which gave rise to the story that there was originally a street under the present road. The photograph, taken in the late 1930s, shows part of a development which took place between 1842 and 1843 when Victoria station was being built. An enterprising developer decided to erect a hotel at the bottom of the approach to the station, the Palatine Hotel. The portion of the building which can be seen on the photograph comprised shops at street level and a riding school on the first floor, access to which was by means of a ramp at the rear of the building. The riding school closed in the early 1850s and the hotel extended. Today the whole building forms part of Chetham's School of Music.

One of the oldest buildings in central Manchester until 1957 was the Rovers Return on Shudehill. It was claimed that the building dated from 1305, although it is unlikely that the building shown here is older than the sixteenth or seventeenth centuries. The pub itself has claimed to be one of the oldest licensed premises in the town, although licensing of public houses did not start until 1552. The building was situated close to the Hen and Poultry Market, hence the caged birds on the left. The Rovers Return was demolished in 1957, not because of demands for redevelopment, but as a result of a fire.

When Humphrey Chetham died in 1651, he left money to establish a school for forty boys of 'poor, painful parents who neither rogues nor vagabonds be'. The boys were to be educated up to the age of fourteen and then apprenticed to a master to learn a useful trade, which in those days would have been the woollen textile trade. Boys were admitted at Easter and were taught subjects which were of a practical nature to equip them for the type of occupation they would follow in later life. As early as 1737 the teaching of Latin and Greek was abolished because there was no practical use for these languages in commerce and industry. Those who were given the responsibility for implementing Chetham's wishes were able to acquire the former home of the Lords of the Manor of Manchester, which had been used by the clergy of the Collegiate Church between 1422 and 1547. When the College of Clergy was dissolved in 1547 the buildings had been acquired by the Earls of Derby, but because of their support for Charles I in the Civil War they had been sequestrated and were owned by the government. Although the buildings were in a state of disrepair they were restored, and the school moved to its new premises in 1655. Chetham's School was housed in the low block of buildings in the centre of the photograph, which had been built by Warden Huntingdon in 1422–3. The taller buildings surrounding the playground are part of Manchester Grammar School, which had been established by Hugh Oldham, Bishop of Exeter, in 1515.

On the north side of central Manchester there are two rivers, the River Irwell and the River Irk. The Irk rises in the foothills of the Pennines near Oldham and flows into the River Irwell at Hunt's Bank, passing through Middleton, Blackley and Collyhurst on the way. In the late eighteenth and nineteenth centuries its banks were lined with factories, in particular ones connected with the bleaching and dyeing industries. Closer to Manchester, in the first half of the nineteenth century, there were tanneries as well as mills using the river water, which by the time it reached the River Irwell was highly polluted. This photograph, taken in about 1859, shows the River Irk near Long Millgate, close to where the Lord of the Manor's mills were once situated. The mills had been given to Manchester Grammar School in 1515 as an endowment and technically had the monopoly of grinding all grain for baking in the township of Manchester. These rights were lost in 1758 after a court case, but the school still retained the right to grind grain for malting purposes. In 1808 Manchester Grammar School sought permission to get rid of this duty as it was becoming difficult to maintain, but this was refused. Consequently they set about trying to improve profitability of the mills, which they did very successfully in about five or six years. Profits continued to improve until the 1830s, after which they began to decline. Eventually the Lancashire & Yorkshire Railway Company offered to purchase the mills as part of their programme to expand Victoria station, and this offer was accepted. The footbridge on the right of the illustration is at approximately the same height above the river as the modern approach to the station, and was probably constructed in the 1850s when Corporation Street was completed to link this road with Victoria station via Todd Street. It was, incidentally, this river from which Jabez Clegg was rescued at the opening of *The Manchester Man* by Mrs Banks and the same river into which he was thrown by boys from the Grammar School when he was at Chetham's School.

During the early nineteenth century some of the worst housing conditions in central Manchester were to be found in the Long Millgate area. The worst places were those which overlooked the River Irk and included, for example, Allen's Court; they were regarded as areas where cholera was likely to visit the town. J.P. Kay, who made this comment in 1831, was proved right the following year when there was a serious outbreak of cholera, not only in Manchester but also in other parts of the country. Although the expansion of the railway resulted in the clearance of many of these very poor houses, it did not account for all of them. In the triangle of land between Long Millgate, Fennel Street and Todd Street was another area of poor housing, centred on Backhouse Court. Here, it is believed, was the Lord of the Manor's oven, which everyone in medieval Manchester was supposed to use to bake their bread, for a fee. The area was partially cleared in the late nineteenth century, revealing these timber-framed buildings, where the wattle and daub had been replaced by brick in-fill panels. One presumes that at the time this photograph was taken, in the 1880s, these properties were still inhabited by a family who could afford to purchase a cycle.

Situated on the edge of central Manchester is Angel Meadow, which is reported to have had a very bad reputation in the nineteenth century, not only because of the behaviour of its residents but also because the housing conditions there left much to be desired. The widest street in the district was Angel Street, which linked St George's Road (now Rochdale Road) with Ashley Street and Collyhurst Road. The population density was very high and there were many back-to-back houses and courts without adequate sanitary facilities. It was one of the areas which the Manchester and Salford Sanitary Association visited regularly in the 1850s, drawing attention to the condition of the houses and streets in their reports. As well as multi-occupation of houses, there were also a number of lodging houses there for those who had come to Manchester to seek work. It was said of the area in the late nineteenth century that the only person who did not live there who was safe was the local midwife. How true this was is hard to tell. This photograph of the 1890s shows what was probably a typical scene on Angel Street as women sit on doorsteps watching the world pass by.

Opposite: Although there were several imposing buildings on Long Millgate, such as those occupied by Manchester Grammar School, the side façade of Victoria station and the Manchester Arms public house, as well as several timber-framed buildings dating back to the sixteenth and seventeenth centuries, there were others which were less imposing but were also an important part of the street scene. This photograph was taken in 1894 and shows the part of Long Millgate beyond the junction of Miller Street, Ducie Bridge and Corporation Street that leads down towards the edge of Angel Meadow and the Irk valley, looking back towards Corporation Street. In the early 1890s these were occupied by people engaged in a wide range of occupations, including a slipper maker, herbalist, earthenware dealer, tobacconist, brushmakers, cork cutter, grocers and butchers. There were also several public houses on this section of road, including the Tin Plate Workers' Arms, the Chetham Arms and the Crown and Cushion, this being behind the photographer. Behind these buildings were several courts such as Berry's Court and Derby Court, where conditions for those who lived there were not very pleasant.

Until the 1850s the main road leading out of Manchester towards Rochdale was rather narrow and caused much congestion, especially when the first tram tracks were laid in the late 1870s. Eventually, when the Lancashire & Yorkshire Railway Co. enlarged their Oldham Road goods depot, the opportunity arose to widen the road and reduce the congestion. The properties at the Manchester end of this important road tended to consist of shops with residential accommodation above. The photograph was taken between 1893 and 1898 near the junction of Angel Street and Rochdale Road, and shows one of several shops in the area which were selling second- and even third-hand clothes and bric-a-brac. Other shops close by included a butcher's, greengrocer's, a fried fish dealer, a clog maker's and a wholesale jeweller's. No doubt with some of the poorer parts of Manchester close by, the second-hand shops would have been very busy with local people looking for bargains.

One street which has changed dramatically in the last half century has been Cannon Street. Today all the buildings shown on this photograph taken in 1920 have been demolished and replaced by the Arndale Centre. During the nineteenth century Cannon Street, which is believed to have got its name because old cannon were used to stop carts crossing the pavements when they turned corners, was a street mainly of warehouses connected with various aspects of the textile trade. One firm which had a warehouse here was that of the Grants Bros of Ramsbottom, whose warehouse was known as Cheeryble House and who were immortalised by Dickens in *Nicholas Nickleby* as the Cheeryble brothers. Their warehouse, which was originally a private house, was demolished in 1907 when part of Cannon Street was widened, but a scheme to convert it to a dual carriageway and close Market Street to traffic was not implemented until 1986. This photograph shows the junction of Corporation Street and Cannon Street and the section which was widened in 1907. Beyond the widened section, the road reverts to its original narrow width.

Until the Manchester blitz of 1940, the Market Place was linked to Manchester Cathedral by Old Millgate, shown here at the turn of the twentieth century. It is believed that the name was derived from the fact that there was a river in the area, the River Dene, and that there was a water-powered corn mill located on it to which the road led. Whether there was a mill there and how long it operated is not known, nor whether it was operational at the same time as the mills on the River Irk or whether they replaced the one on the River Dene. The importance of old Millgate as a route was reduced when Corporation Street was constructed in the nineteenth century.

One of the earliest purpose-built shopping arcades to be constructed in Manchester was Lancaster Arcade, which ran between Fennel Street and Todd Street. It was erected in the early 1850s and built of cast iron, wood and glass. There were small shops on two levels, which in the 1950s and 1960s specialised in numismatics and jewellery. Its appearance gave rise to the story that it had been a former women's prison, but this was not the case. It was from this type of development that other arcades developed, such as Barton Arcade and Exchange Arcade.

Between 1893 and 1903 the area bounded by Hanging Ditch, Fennel Street and Half Street changed dramatically when the new Corn and Produce Exchange was built. The original exchange had been erected in 1837 and was located round the corner in the centre of the photograph. The redevelopment of the site at the end of the nineteenth century resulted in the loss of small streets like Half Street on the left, which was realigned to meet Cateaton Street and renamed Cathedral Street. In the late nineteenth century there were a number of antique shops on Half Street, while in the early years of the century it was where the sweet shop and manufactory of Jane Clowes was located, made famous in *The Manchester Man*. This photograph was taken in about 1890 and shows the buildings which were demolished to make way for the Exchange. Many of those who were affected by the decision to rebuild the Manchester Corn, Grocery and Produce Exchange were themselves members of the Exchange.

Although there were places within the various market buildings at Shudehill where traders could sell their goods, there were others who preferred to stand in the street. Whether the two men on the right were market traders or whether they were using the table as a place on which to rest their belongings while they talk is unclear, but underneath the coat appears to be a suitcase, and to the right of it a hat with a feather in it. Whoever the two men are, they appear to have attracted some attention from the passers-by in this view of the mid-1930s.

One of the buildings which was severely damaged when the IRA bomb exploded in Manchester in June 1996 was the former Corn and Produce Exchange, which was situated on a triangular site between Cathedral Street, Fennel Street and Hanging Ditch. The building shown here was designed by Ball and Elce and erected in three phases between 1893 and 1903 at a cost of £350,000. It replaced an earlier building which had opened in 1837, because the growing importance of Manchester as a centre for the grocery trade and a growth in membership rendered the old building was inadequate. It was, therefore, decided to replace it with this new building, which it was hoped would meet the needs for many years. The main exchange floor, which covers 2,250 square yards, is in the centre of the building and lit by a large dome 85 feet above it. Around the outside of the building are offices for those who traded on the floor, while in the basement there were rooms where produce could be stored.

Between them, Withy Grove and Shudehill constitute one of the old thoroughfares in Manchester. The word 'Withy' implies that the area was rather damp and that willows grew there. It is also believed that originally a small stream, sometimes described as the River Dene, started in this area and flowed roughly along these two roads to Hanging Ditch and the River Irwell. Although it was always a busy road out of Manchester, the removal of most of Manchester's markets to Smithfield in the 1820s and the subsequent development of the wholesale markets in the area resulted in a dramatic increase in traffic. Even before the markets moved, several of the public houses in the area acted as places in Manchester where firms with business premises outside Manchester were able to be contacted on market days. This photograph of 1910 looking towards Corporation Street shows the extent of the traffic. The small gabled building on the left is the Seven Stars public house, while on the right, where the clock is, were the offices of several Manchester-based newspapers such as the *Sunday Chronicle*, *Sporting Chronicle*, *Athletic News*, *Daily Dispatch* and the *Daily Sketch*. The presence of so many newspaper offices in this area meant that there was never a quiet time of day, as even when normal traffic had finished there were vehicles coming and going into the newspaper offices, with newsprint, messages and papers being delivered to either newsagents, wholesalers or the railway stations.

The Seven Stars was one of Manchester's oldest public houses, being one of sixteen on the short Withy Grove and Shudehill in 1851. By 1900 the number had fallen to twelve and was to fall even lower as the twentieth century progressed. The Seven Stars was demolished in 1911 when the site was acquired for redevelopment. In the 1745 rebellion, when Bonnie Prince Charlie passed through Manchester, it is said that some of his troops were billeted here, and there was even a claim that Parliamentary forces stayed here during the Civil War. A literary mention of the building is in *The Manchester Man*, when Tom Hulme, after being told that Bess has been unfaithful to him, retired here before enlisting in the regular army. During the nineteenth century the Seven Stars was a popular meeting place for Manchester's literary community.

In some parts of central Manchester there were a great many second-hand shops selling a wide range of goods. Where this particular shop was located is not recorded on the original lantern slide, but it appeared to be a building which has been whitewashed, possibly to give a black and white half-timbered appearance. The only clue to the building is at the side of the door, where there is the name Springfield.

In December 1905 Alderman M'Cabe, Chairman of the Manchester Markets Committee, gave an address to an unnamed organisation in Ancoats in which he outlined the history of the Manchester markets and how they had developed over the years. According to the newspaper report, which was very detailed and could almost have been a verbatim report of his address, M'Cabe stated that 'The Smithfield Markets . . . said to be the largest covered area of its kind in the country, are, with the exception of London, the greatest centre of distribution for flowers, fruit, vegetables, fish, game and poultry.' He went on to point out that in the 1870s there was only one bank branch in the area; now there were ten and the value of the property had risen over the years with the success of the markets. According to M'Cabe, when the Corporation had taken over the markets in 1846 they covered only a quarter of their present area and they were open to the elements; now parts had been covered over. He also said that the busiest days in 1846 were Tuesday, Thursday and Saturday, but at the end of the nineteenth century every day was busy, with Friday being particularly so, as dealers from outside areas came to collect their supplies that day. He then pointed out that 'there is probably no other centre of trade in the United Kingdom surrounded by an equally large population so devoid of gardens or allotments', with the result that a large fresh vegetable market had developed with produce grown locally being sent direct to Manchester's markets. This photograph, taken in 1894, shows one small section of the markets complex at Shudehill, devoted to fish and game. Fish came to Manchester direct from Grimsby, Hull, Fleetwood, Milford, Lowestoft and Scarborough as well as various parts of Scotland, with only a small amount coming from abroad. Whether this is the wholesale or retail fish market is not clear, but M'Cabe pointed out that both the retail and wholesale fish markets were close together, and that in the 1890s the size of the retail market had been doubled to enable forty stalls to be accommodated. He concludes with the following comments about those who worked in the markets or who were traders there: 'speaking from long personal experience, I can truthfully say that they are among the best I have met with anywhere – brisk, cheery, straightforward, and perfectly natural'. In the photograph are some of these people who may have personally known Alderman M'Cabe.

Although there were many cafés and restaurants in Manchester in the late nineteenth and early twentieth centuries that catered for those who worked in the offices and warehouses, many were not licensed to serve alcohol. Consequently, if someone having a meal in one of these establishments wanted a glass of beer, it was necessary to send one of the waiters or waitresses out to purchase it from a nearby public house or off-licence. This photograph, taken by Samuel Coulthurst in the 1890s, shows two young waitresses carrying what may be jugs of beer back to their customers.

This group of men appears to be about to enter a public house or a beer house on Swan Street in about 1889, but it is not possible to identify which one – as there were five such establishments on the street that year, as well as a coffee tavern.

Opposite: Horses were very important capital assets in the nineteenth century especially if a firm was a carrier, as this was the only means of motive power in the streets of any town. As a result, as much care was taken with the purchase of a new animal as people take today when purchasing a new motor vehicle. The prospective purchaser had to assure himself that the animal was in peak condition and would be able to do the work asked of it. It is not known whether this animal was for sale or whether the rider was seeking advice from the other two men. The photograph was taken in about 1889 on Rochdale Road, and the shop in the background was occupied by James Booth, clog and patten maker, who was also recorded in the directory on one occasion as a clog patten maker and owner of a grindery warehouse. The business was started in the early nineteenth century by W.H. Booth and moved to these premises in about 1879; it continued to occupy them until the 1950s.

Although the area around the markets was busy from early in the morning until late on in the day, there were other parts of central Manchester which saw periods of concentrated activity. One of these was around the Royal Exchange on days of 'High Change', when many firms from outside the city attended. For a short period on two afternoons a week the area was one of frenzied activity with people coming and going. An indication of just how busy the area was can be gained from the figures recorded one day in March 1913: at 1.15 p.m. there were 100 members present, at 2.45 p.m. the number had risen to 5,978; by 3.45 p.m. there were still 1,900 members on the floor, but by 4.45 p.m. only 100 were left. It was claimed that it was quicker to go down the stairs, go round the outside of the building and walk back up the stairs than try to get across the Exchange floor. In fact, many deals were struck not on the floor of the Exchange but in the streets surrounding it. The Portico shown here down which members are streaming fronted Cross Street. It was taken down when the Exchange was enlarged after the First World War so that Manchester could carry out plans to widen and improve Cross Street.

CHAPTER TEN

MANCHESTER AT WAR

There are almost 300 years between the siege of Manchester in September 1642 by Royalist forces under Lord Strange and the bombing of Manchester by the German air force in December 1940. In the intervening centuries Mancunians were involved in wars, but they were wars which did not affect the fabric of the town as did the events of September 1642 and December 1940, when not only lives were lost, but also buildings destroyed.

During the intervening years Manchester men responded to the call to defend the country whenever and wherever the need arose. Men, and later women, from Manchester were involved in events such as the Jacobite rebellion of 1745, the siege of Gibraltar, the French and Napoleonic wars, and the Crimean and Boer wars, as well as the First World War. During the late eighteenth and early nineteenth centuries Manchester men were prominent in establishing volunteer battalions to defend the country from invasion by the French, who they thought might come across the Irish Sea from Ireland. Although these volunteer battalions were stood down in 1802 when the Peace of Amiens was signed, they were reformed when war broke out again and continued to operate until around 1807 when many were disbanded, and those who wanted to enlisted in an enlarged regular army. Mancunians responded to the call for men during both the Crimean and Boer wars, but the numbers involved were small when compared with the numbers who volunteered to serve in the armed forces with the outbreak of war in 1914. So many volunteered or were conscripted that virtually every family and neighbourhood in Manchester was involved directly in the war and the war effort. Even when the war had ended, those who had failed to return were remembered at 11 am on 11 November each year.

Manchester's first memorial to those who had fallen in defending their country or its interests was erected in St Ann's Square in 1908, and was to the 340 men who were killed in the Boer War. After the First World War an official war memorial was erected in central Manchester to all those who had died, but almost every district erected a memorial as well, sometimes inscribed with the names of local people who had died in the conflict. It was these memorials which were the focus of the events each 11 November.

The Second World War brought home to everyone the full horror of war, affected everyone in the city and had the greatest impact on the overall appearance of Manchester. The Christmas blitz of 1940 resulted in the destruction of, or damage to, many familiar buildings in the city centre, such as the Free Trade Hall, Victoria Buildings, the Cathedral and the Royal Exchange, as well as to hospitals, churches, factories and homes. The effect of the bombing was said to have been made worse, according to official reports, by the failure of some businesses to provide effective fire watches, and by a strong wind that blew burning embers into buildings which had escaped destruction and set them alight. However, it should be remembered that not all of Manchester's buildings were destroyed: the Midland Hotel, Town Hall, Watts Warehouse, Central Library and the Art Gallery all escaped serious damage.

Although the bombing destroyed and damaged buildings, it did not destroy the morale of Mancunians, but rather led to a desire to create a better city after the war was over, to not only to reflect the desire for a better life, but also to reflect the historic importance of

Manchester. It was the same spirit that Manchester exhibited in 1940 that was re-awakened after the terrorist bomb ripped the heart out of part of central Manchester in June 1996. The opportunity was taken to look again at the central area and redevelop it for the twenty-first century.

The result of the Manchester blitz was a radical approach to the rebuilding of the city centre. The City's surveyor, Mr R. Nicholas, prepared a grand plan to bring the city into the post-war era. Although never fully implemented, the Nicholas plan served as the basis for the redevelopment of Manchester in the years after the last war.

The photographs in this chapter not only show the damage caused by the Christmas blitz of 1940, but also the men who volunteered for service in the First World War and the remembering of the fallen during the inter-war years. They have come from many sources, and include some that the censors did not allow to be published in 1940.

When war broke out in August 1914, the British army was small compared with those on the continent. However, it soon became apparent that it would have to be enlarged very quickly. There was no shortage of volunteers who were prepared to join the colours and fight to protect English interests. At first, they joined regular battalions, but towards the end of August 1914 the suggestion was made that men who worked together might be more willing to enlist if they were allowed to serve together. The suggestion soon found favour, and within a short period of time four battalions were raised in Manchester which consisted entirely of Manchester men, often men from the same area or company. This photograph show volunteers who have enlisted leaving Platt Fields on their way to the camp at Heaton Park to begin their initial training.

Two of the problems which the authorities had with so many men enlisting were finding suitable places where the men could be trained, and finding material for uniforms and equipment. When it was formed the 16th Manchester City Battalion, the first local volunteer battalion to be formed, was sent to Heaton Park where the men lived under canvas for several weeks until wooden huts could be erected; these were more suitable for the English winter. The volunteers were given a blue uniform similar to that of the tram guards as the government had commandeered all the khaki cloth it could find. The men were not too happy about the uniform as they said that they did not feel they were in the army until they were dressed in khaki. This photograph shows part of the tented camp at Heaton Park, with a crowd of what appear to be high-spirited men tossing a colleague in a blanket.

The men who volunteered to join the 'Pals' battalions had little experience of military life, with the result that officers and NCOs, who had been drafted in from the regular army or recalled from retirement, had to start from the beginning, teaching the men to march in step and to carry out the simplest drill. Gradually the raw recruits were moulded into an efficient fighting force. In some cases, someone who had the basic knowledge of how to march, possibly because he had been in the Scouts, was put in charge of a group, which could result in someone who was a junior employee in a firm giving orders to those who were his superiors at work. As well as carrying out drill and attending lectures on equipment, the men also practised trench digging, as this photograph shows.

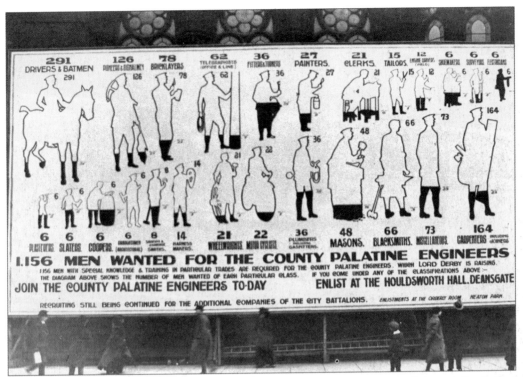

Although the creation of local volunteer battalions increased recruitment into the army, the level of casualties meant that there was always a demand for more men to serve. These two large posters were erected outside Manchester Town Hall to remind people of just how far the recruiting campaign had to go. The top illustration shows the numbers and types of person required by the County Palatine Engineers and just what level recruitment had reached. It also indicates that this battalion was being raised by the Earl of Derby and that the men should enlist at the Houldsworth Hall.

The thermometer approach was taken by the Manchester City battalions and may have been erected in the early days of the war. The thermometer is divided into days and shows how many men volunteered each day towards the target of 1,070. At the very bottom of the thermometer is one of the well-known 'Your Country Needs You' posters, but this is small in comparison with the notices alongside it.

On 21 March 1915 11,000 men drawn from locally raised Manchester volunteer battalions, the Manchester brigade based at Morecambe, detachments of the Lancashire Fusiliers and the Bantam Battalions from Bury and Chadderton were reviewed by Lord Kitchener in front of the Town Hall in Manchester. In his photograph Lord Kitchener is surrounded by other senior army officers and the Lord Mayor of Manchester, Sir Daniel McCabe, and other civic dignitaries. The parade took place a few days before the first of the 'Pals' battalions was posted away from Manchester to finish training.

The First World War saw the advent of aerial warfare. One Manchester firm, AVRO, was involved in the manufacture of aircraft for the Royal Flying Corps. The most successful of their aircraft was the Avro 504, of which over 8,300 were manufactured, almost 4,000 of which were made in Manchester. Whether this aircraft on display in Albert Square is an Avro 504s is not known, but it is possible as they were locally made. The crowds surrounding the planes are an indication of the interest shown in this new form of warfare. Whether the display was part of a recruiting drive or a fund-raising event is not recorded, but it is unlikely that these aircraft would have been displayed unless it was in association with some sort of event. As well as manufacturing aircraft, Manchester also had a small airbase at Princess Road to which newly constructed aircraft were delivered. This field was used after the war for commercial flying, but its location was not really suitable and it was closed down.

Opposite: In April 1915, after seven months of training at Heaton Park, the first of the Manchester Regiment's 'Pals' battalions was moved to Grantham to complete training before being transferred to the front line in France. This photograph shows the men relaxing in Piccadilly, possibly before they boarded the special train to take them to Grantham. From Grantham the 16th Battalion wen to Salisbury, and finally, on 8 November 1915, after some fifteen months' training, the Battalion was moved to France to begin the work for which it had been prepared.

Between 1919 and 1939 those who died in the First World War were remembered at 11 am on 11 November each year. Large crowds would gather by war memorials and the country would stop whatever it was doing for the two minutes silence. This photograph shows the scene in Albert Square on 11 November 1933 at about 11 a.m. Members of the armed forces are lined up in front of the crowd while in front of the Town Hall, on a specially constructed platform, would have been church and civic leaders and senior officers. Behind the representatives of the various armed services can be seen the large number of Mancunians who attended this event each year until 1939. The size of the crowd was so large that the service was relayed by loudspeakers so that all could hear what was being said. From the windows of the surrounding offices members of staff look over the scene, each with his or her own memories of relatives or friends who had been killed or injured during the war.

The original intention of Manchester City Council was to erect the City's Cenotaph or war memorial in Albert Square. However, before this could be done, permission was to be sought from the royal family about moving Prince Albert. Before a final decision could be made about how the issue should be resolved, there was a pressing need to erect the Cenotaph so that Manchester had a focal point for its Armistice Day services. As a result the Cenotaph, designed by Edwin Lutyens, was erected in a temporary position in St Peter's Square on part of the site formerly occupied by St Peter's Church. The intention was that when the question of what to do with the statues in Albert Square was resolved, the Cenotaph would be relocated. The Cenotaph was consecrated in 1924, and although used for wreath laying was not the focal point of Armistice Day until the outbreak of war in 1939. This photograph shows part of the march past on 11 November 1938, the last time it took place before the outbreak of war the following year.

As well as commemorating those from Manchester who had died in the First World War with the Cenotaph in St Peter's Square, there were many other memorials in churches and schools, and in the centre of the various districts that made up Manchester. This photograph shows members of the Manchester Regiment in 1933 marching past the war memorial that had been erected on Ardwick Green to commemorate those from Ardwick and the nearby barracks who had died. The memorial was located in Ardwick Green and bore the battle honours of the regiment, including those for service in France and Egypt.

When war was declared on 3 September 1939 all places of entertainment were closed and members of the public were encouraged not to gather in large numbers. However, it did not stop the people of Manchester remembering those who had died during the First World War at 11 a.m. on 11 November. The tolling of bells and the firing of maroons to signal the beginning and end of the two minutes silence was prohibited so members of the public had to rely on public clocks, one of which can be seen in the top left-hand corner of the photograph. The usual military march past and short service did not take place and those wanting to lay wreaths were given a specific time to do so in an attempt to prevent large crowds gathering. As this photograph shows, these restrictions did not stop a considerable number of Mancunians, including the Lord Mayor, gathering in St Peter's Square at 11 a.m. to pay tribute to those who had died.

During 1939, as the storm clouds gathered over Europe, plans were made to evacuate children and pregnant mothers from cities and towns. Manchester was allocated almost 180,000 places in Lancashire, Cheshire, Shropshire and Derbyshire for its evacuees. In April 1939 a register of children whose parents wanted them to be evacuated was compiled and contingency plans prepared. On 21 August instructions were issued to prepare for the implementation of the evacuation. Although the primary schools had returned from the summer holidays, secondary schools had to be recalled. During the next week the plans were checked, transport arrangements finalised and instructions given. On 26 August a dress rehearsal was organised to ensure that everyone knew what he or she had to do. The date for the start of evacuation was fixed for 1 September, and notices informing parents of the arrangements were posted in playgrounds on blackboards, like this one in Chorlton-cum-Hardy.

When children were evacuated, they were only allowed to take a rucksack or carrier bag with a change of clothes, together with food for the journey and their gas mask. All children were labelled with their name, school and ultimate destination in case they became separated from the group. The ratio of teachers and adults to children was strictly laid down at one adult or teacher to every ten children. When schools were evacuated, they walked to the nearest railway station where this was possible. Here, one of Chorlton-cum-Hardy's schools walks in crocodile along Barlow Moor Road towards Chorlton station ready to catch the train which was to take them to their destination. It is not clear whether the parents walking on the pavement with small children are involved with the evacuation or merely accompanying older children to the station to see them off, although according to the criteria laid down the two women with the small children would have been eligible to be evacuated.

Opposite: This photograph was probably taken a few minutes after the one above and shows the evacuation train leaving Chorlton-cum-Hardy station hauled by an LMS 2–6–0 locomotive. Watching the train depart are friends and relatives of those on board, together with children who had not yet been evacuated or whose parents had decided not to let them go. It is worth noting that if evacuation had taken place a fortnight or so later, the taking of photographs and their publication would have been prohibited, as the Government issued very detailed instructions as to what could and could not be photographed and one of the prohibitions was the recording of evacuations.

All Manchester's railway stations were used in the evacuation. On the first day, 1 September, 109 special trains were run, carrying over 46,000 children, 2,000 teachers and 4,000 helpers. Some children walked to the railway stations, but others were taken by bus and tram. To move such large numbers involved the co-operation of the transport authorities and the police as well as the education department. The police were praised for their work in identifying routes and controlling traffic while the teachers received praise for their work in ensuring that everything went off smoothly. This photograph shows evacuees boarding their train at Chorlton-cum-Hardy station under the watchful eye of railway staff and teachers.

It was not possible to evacuate everyone from the urban areas and so preparations were made to provide those who remained with some form of protection during air-raids. In March 1939 the first distribution of Anderson shelters was made in the Fallowfield and Blackley areas. When the shelters were delivered, it was the householders who were responsible for their erection. An accompanying booklet recommended that the shelter required a site 7 ft 6 in long by 6 ft wide and should be buried to a depth of 4 ft with 15 in of earth on top. Some people even planted gardens over the shelter to complete the camouflage. It was advised that there should be a large box placed inside the door for a step and that the floor should be created by either using a duckboard or laying clinker. This photograph shows an Anderson shelter being delivered to a council house, possibly in the Fallowfield area, in the spring of 1939.

Opposite: Although all schools were evacuated from Manchester, including those in Wythenshawe, as the phoney war continued and no air-raids materialised children started to drift back to Manchester. Although provision had been made for those children who had remained behind, with schools opening for limited periods each day, as the number of children returning home increased so more schools were re-opened. As a result, it was necessary to provide some form of protection in case of an air-raid when the children were at school. Shelters and trenches protected by sand-bags were constructed on playing fields and in playgrounds. This photograph shows the girls of Sharston Senior School entering the shelter which had been built in their playground. Notice that each girl is carrying her gas-mask, which everyone was supposed to carry with him or her at all times.

As well as shelters for people in their own homes, the authorities realised that it was necessary to construct public shelters in areas where people shopped and worked and in residential areas where gardens were not large enough for an Anderson shelter. One area in central Manchester where public air-raid shelters were constructed was Piccadilly Gardens, shown here in this photograph of June 1940. Wardens were appointed to look after the shelters, which were open from 8 am to 7 pm each day, and to take control when they were in use. There were complaints that many of these public shelters were damp, badly ventilated and poorly lighted.

On the fears of the authorities when war became imminent was that the Germans would try to use gas to subdue the civilian population, and so everyone was issued with a gas-mask, even babies. Everyone was supposed to carry it wherever he or she went. In fact, to gain entry to some places of entertainment, such as Belle Vue when it re-opened after an initial closure when war was declared, you had to show that you had your gas-mask with you. Schoolchildren were given regular practice in putting on their masks even before war broke out so they were familiar with what to do if the need arose. It was also to encourage them to carry their gas-masks at all times. So successful was the Education Department that it was able to claim in February 1941 that 99 per cent of all elementary school pupils carried their gas-masks with them everywhere they went, and suggested that adults should copy the behaviour of the children in this respect.

Damage caused by the blast from exploding bombs came to be as devastating as a direct hit itself. Consequently many buildings were protected by sandbags. This photograph shows men erecting sandbag protection at Manchester Grammar School's buildings in Rusholme. The school had originally been evacuated to Blackpool, but had returned because the staff felt that the boys were not getting adequate education. Whether these sandbags were filled by the boys themselves or by others is not known, but there is at least one photograph which shows the boys filling sandbags, possibly as a welcome break from the daily round of lessons.

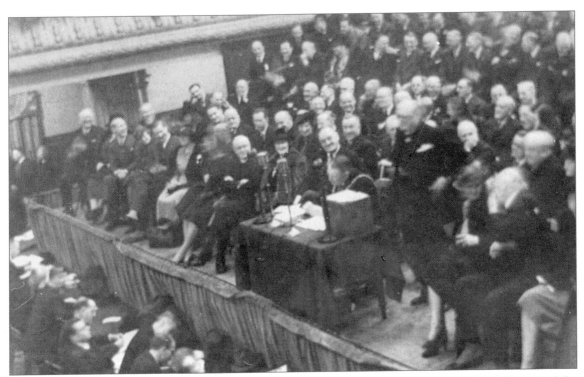

On 27 January 1940 the Free Trade Hall was the setting for a major speech by Winston Churchill in which he encouraged the British people to stand firm against the Germans. It has been variously reported as the 'Let us to the task, to the battle, to the toil' speech and the 'A time to dare and to endure' speech. Whichever interpretation is correct, this was the last major public meeting to be held in the Free Trade Hall before its destruction in December 1940. This rare photograph shows Churchill delivering his speech to a packed building with a line of reporters sitting at tables in front of the stage. Later in the war, after the Blitz, Churchill was to visit Manchester as Prime Minister to inspect the damage caused by the German bombs. His visit in 1941 was intended to be secret, but word soon spread that he was in the city and large crowds gathered to meet him on his tour of inspection of the bomb damage. Later, on 26 July 1945, he paid Manchester a compliment by beginning his General Election campaign in the city, when he was welcomed by crowds of about 80,000 people. Despite Churchill's popularity as a prime minister, the Conservatives lost five Manchester seats to Labour.

Although a few German bombs had been dropped on Manchester and the surrounding area in 1940, including an incident when a Salford policeman was injured when he was hit by a bundle of propaganda leaflets dropped from the air, it was not until the evening of 22 December 1940 that Manchester was subjected to its first sustained air-raid. The Manchester blitz took place over two nights, 22–23 and 23–24 December 1940, and when it was over parts of central Manchester were a smoking ruin. The day after the first raid, newspapers merely reported that a North West town had been raided the previous evening, and it was not until after Christmas that the *Manchester Guardian* disclosed that the mysterious town was in fact Manchester, a fact which Mancunians and those in the surrounding areas knew only too well.

On 22 December 1940 the sirens sounded at 6.38 p.m. and the raid continued for over five hours, during which time countless incendiaries and 233 high explosive bombs were dropped on central Manchester, Salford and Trafford Park. The following night the raid started at 7.15 p.m. and continued until 1.29 a.m. the following morning. As with the previous night, a mixture of incendiary and high explosive bombs were dropped, but the damage was made worse by the wind, which strengthened during the evening and blew burning embers and sparks into buildings which, although damaged, had not been destroyed or set on fire. The result was that many more buildings were affected than might have been the case. This photograph shows the remains of the Market Place after the blitz. Although the surrounding buildings have been damaged, the Wellington Inn and the adjoining Sinclair's Oyster Bar remained virtually undamaged. Among the buildings which were destroyed in the area around the Market Place were Victoria Buildings, the Falstaff Hotel, the Bull's Head and the Coal Exchange. The nearby Royal Exchange was also damaged, but within a few months its members were back on the floor carrying on their usual business. The tower in the centre of the photograph is that of the Corn Exchange on Hanging Ditch, while in the background is Manchester Cathedral, which suffered damage from a landmine that exploded nearby.

When Mancunians returned to work after the blitz, they found buildings destroyed and streets blocked by rubble or not accessible because of the danger of buildings collapsing. This photograph shows Miller Street, looking from Rochdale Road towards Corporation Street. Before the war one of the most important firms with premises on Miller Street was Baxendales, a long-established and well-respected firm of ironmongers, who could supply anything from a drain cover to agricultural machinery. As the photograph shows, people are beginning to pick their way through the rubble to discover what was left of their places of employment. Immediately after Christmas, the *Manchester Guardian* reported that 'Manchester men and women have used the Christmas holiday to put right, as far as possible, what has been torn down and burnt out by German bombs. . . . Today life is a little more normal and there is an increasing semblance of order. . . .'

The task of trying to prevent the centre of Manchester being completely engulfed in flames fell to the Manchester Fire Brigade, supported by members of the Auxiliary Fire Service. At the height of the blitz there were some 400 extra fire appliances and 3,400 extra men involved in fighting the fires in central Manchester. Not only had they to contend with the raging fires, but also unexploded bombs and collapsing buildings. The remains of one such can be seen in this picture as firemen direct their hoses into the remains. According to official reports, during the two nights the fire service had to deal with six conflagrations, twenty major fires and about six hundred less serious ones. Their efforts were hampered by damage to the water mains bringing water into the city centre, although it was still possible to draw water from the canals. After the blitz it was decided to turn the basements of destroyed warehouses into static water supplies in case of a further raid. Despite the heroic efforts of the firemen 9¼ acres of central Manchester were destroyed, or, putting it another way, some 31 acres within a mile of the Town Hall were affected to some degree by the Christmas blitz.

Not even the equipment used by the fire service was immune from damage. This photograph shows the remains of a fire engine in St Mary's Gate; it appears to have been crushed by debris falling from a nearby building.

Local railways were severely affected by the blitz. Although London Road and Central stations escaped serious damage, the office block at the front of Exchange station was destroyed and a landmine fell on platform 16 of Victoria station, putting a large part of it out of action for a time. Severe damage was caused at Oldham Road Goods Depot, shown here, and to the viaduct carrying the important commuter line between Manchester and Altrincham near Hulme Locks. Fortunately, the rail network was brought back into full service relatively speedily.

Among the buildings that were destroyed during the Manchester Christmas blitz was the Free Trade Hall, regarded as a symbol of Manchester's nineteenth-century greatness and influence on economic thought during the mid-nineteenth century. The Free Trade Hall had been opened in 1856 and is said to have been the only public hall in the country to commemorate an economic concept and not a local worthy or a saint. Not only did the destruction of the hall deprive Manchester of the city's main hall for public meetings, but it also deprived the world-famous Hallé Orchestra of the home it had occupied since its foundation in 1858. Inspecting the damage the morning after the bombing, the Lord Mayor vowed that one of the first tasks of the City Council at the end of the war was to secure the rebuilding of this symbol of Manchester's greatness, which it achieved, despite many difficulties, in 1951.

Opposite: Damage was not limited to places of employment and public buildings. Residential property was also damaged or destroyed during the Christmas blitz, and other raids as well. However, it was during the Christmas blitz that the most serious damage was inflicted on Manchester's housing stock. This photograph shows houses on Chester Road which were damaged as a result of the two nights' air raids. Between September 1939 and May 1945 it was estimated that 389 houses had been destroyed by enemy bombs, 1,562 so badly damaged that they had to be demolished, 4,537 'badly damaged, but repairable' and 24,085 'slightly damaged'. The Christmas raids resulted in 369 civilians being killed, 453 seriously injured and 728 slightly injured. During the whole war 559 Mancunians were killed by air-raids and a further 572 seriously injured.

Public buildings, factories, churches and theatres as well as private houses and even hospitals were damaged during the Christmas blitz and a second concentrated raid at the end of May 1941. This photograph shows nurses carrying babies from the bomb-damaged building. Although not identified, it is possible that this is St Mary's Hospital at Hathersage Road, which was hit in the Christmas blitz. Other hospitals which suffered from bomb damage included the Royal Infirmary, the Eye Hospital and the Royal Manchester Children's Hospital at Gartside Street. In all cases, casualties appear to have been limited to staff rather than patients in the hospitals.

After the bombing the city had several distinguished visitors who came to see the damage for themselves and to offer moral support to the residents. Among them were Winston Churchill and the Duke of Kent, but the most popular visit was by George VI and Queen Elizabeth, accompanied by the Home Secretary, on 13 February 1941. Their visit was meant to have been a secret, but news of their arrival soon spread throughout Manchester and large crowds gathered to greet them. During their visit, they saw some of the results of the Christmas raids – including the damage to the floor of the Royal Exchange, where they were photographed. The Queen appears to be asking a question about either the building or the damage, while in the background a group of men, possibly members of the Royal Exchange, stand watching the visitors. The members of the Exchange continued to meet after the blitz in the Houldsworth Hall, but finding this was not suitable they moved back to the undamaged part of the Exchange building.

During the early months of 1941 the ruins of burned-out buildings were gradually demolished and a semblance of normality began to return to the city centre. Buses replaced trams where the damage to the overhead wires was too great to be repaired. Some of the material from the demolished buildings was salvaged and re-used. For example, over 5,000 tons of metal was recovered from damaged buildings in Piccadilly alone. In order to help the fire services in the event of another raid, the suggestion was made in April 1941 that the basements of warehouses which had been destroyed and demolished should be turned into static water tanks, so that if water supplies were cut during a raid there were supplies available to fight fires. This photograph was taken looking across Piccadilly towards Mosley Street early in 1941. The site, which was occupied by several large warehouses before the blitz, is being cleared and made safe. Later, several large static water tanks were created in the basements of these buildings. The white building in the background is Colwyn Chambers on the corner of York Street and Mosley Street, while looming on the skyline is the Midland Bank on King Street.

Opposite: After the blitz the Lord Mayor launched an appeal to raise money for those families who had lost everything as a result of the air-raids. On 17 April 1941 he was presented with a cheque for £6,250 by Bertram de N. Cruger of the British War Relief Society of America, which had raised substantial amounts of money to help air-raid victims in England. The presentation of the cheque to the Lord Mayor (Alderman R.G. Edwards), shown here, took place in the ruins of the Free Trade Hall. Other aid from America came in the form of donations to purchase equipment and food for immediate use by those made homeless. For instance, some money was spent in purchasing mobile canteens to feed those whose homes had been destroyed or were too badly damaged to be made habitable again.

Early in the war the authorities in Manchester appreciated the fact that should the city be bombed, there would be problems with feeding people, especially if gas, water and electricity supplies were out. In order to overcome this, the council decided to establish a number of centres where people could get hot meals. The first of these feeding stations to be opened was the Bank Meadow Communal Feeding Centre at Pin Mill Brow, which opened on 2 December 1940 with a three course meal costing just 9*d*.

The feeding centres that the council had established late in 1940 became the nucleus of the emergency feeding arrangements which had to be adopted as a result of the blitz and the damage to residential property. It was claimed that these five feeding centres, later to become known as British Restaurants, were able to serve 70,000 hot meals a day by the time the city faced further air-raids during the Whitsun period of 1941.

Although 8 May 1945 marked the end of the war in Europe, it was another three months before the war against Japan ended. When the end of the conflict was announced at midnight on 14–15 August, there was dancing in the streets, with the *Manchester Guardian* reporting that at least one girl was dancing in her pyjamas. The official celebrations began at 10 a.m. on 15 August with an announcement from the steps of the Town Hall, which was followed by a civic service in the Cathedral. Throughout the day people sang and danced in the streets (residents of Rosamond Grove are shown here), bands played in the parks and services were held in churches. At night illuminated trams and buses toured the streets, while at 9 p.m. the King's message to the nation was relayed through loudspeakers to crowds assembled in Albert Square.

CHAPTER ELEVEN

WEATHER

People have always made fun of Manchester's weather, claiming that it is always raining in the town. Some historians have said that this story was invented by Londoners who were jealous of Manchester's commercial success in the nineteenth century. In fact, Manchester does not have a very wet climate, and there are many more places which have higher annual amounts of rain. However, in Manchester's case it appears to be more in the form of drizzle rather than downpours. In 1814 Johann Escher, from Switzerland, commented that people lit fires in Manchester in the morning not because it was cold, but because it was 'damp and foggy'. It is also likely that Manchester's reputation for being wet was enhanced by the fact that in 1880 the test match was washed out completely, the first time this had happened. Manchester was also the place where waterproof cloth was developed by Charles Macintosh, giving rise to the 'mac'.

On the other hand, Manchester does have some very sunny days when people can sit outside in the parks and squares and enjoy the sun. However, in the nineteenth century the sun was obscured by the atmospheric pollution caused by thousands of 'smoke pouring shafts' which, according to A.B. Reach of the *Morning Chronicle* in 1849, turned the sky 'smoky brown'. Perhaps the most graphic description of the atmosphere comes from Alexis de Tocqueville in 1835, when he commented that 'a thick, black smoke covers the city. The sun appears like a disc without rays. . . .'

Collecting of weather statistics has been carried on in Manchester by individuals since the late eighteenth century when the first figures were collected by John Dalton and reported to the Manchester Literary and Philosophical Society. In 1851 another member of the Lit. & Phil., Robert Angus-Smith, started to collect data on pollution and discovered and reported on 'acid rain'. Twenty years later he drew attention to the effect of acid rain and pollution on buildings, coming to the conclusion that all were affected in some way. A good example of this was the Albert Memorial, erected in 1867, which by 1890 was suffering from the effect of acid rain and pollution and had to be restored for Queen Victoria's visit to open the Manchester Ship Canal in 1894.

Manchester also has its fair share of snow, which at one time was said to have turned black as a result of the air pollution. Central Manchester, although getting some heavy falls, does not get as much as the suburban areas or the surrounding Pennines. When it does snow, it rapidly turns to slush with the wheels of vehicles and feet of pedestrians. During the nineteenth century, when it did snow heavily, men from the council were employed in clearing it as quickly as possible and, presumably, tipping it into the rivers or canals.

These photographs record some of the weather conditions experienced in Manchester over the years. Not only have there been heat waves and floods, but also thick fogs and blizzards which have disrupted traffic and the everyday lives of Mancunians.

The increasing use of coal as a fuel from the sixteenth century onwards resulted in an increase in the amount of fog. This increased as the steam engine took over as the main provider of power for factories and transport in the nineteenth century. One prominent geographer once said that going to school one morning he saw the Pennines for the first time, and realised that this was possible because industry had ground to a halt because of a miners' strike. Local authorities tried to limit the amount of smoke pollution. For instance, Levenshulme Local Board of Health took action against factories and even railway companies who produced too much black smoke. However, controls were limited and it was not until the advent of clear air legislation that things started to improve. Fog was not only bad for people's health, but also delayed public transport. Trains took much longer to reach their destinations, and when the motor bus was introduced special provision was made to guide them: a tricycle, similar to the one shown here, would travel in front of the bus so the driver could find his way. So the bus driver could see the tricycle, there was a battery of red lights attached to the rear.

On some occasions the fog was so dense that it turned day into night. Much of the problem was caused by the smoke produced by factories and also railway engines and domestic fires burning coal. In the early 1920s Manchester attempted to reduce the amount of smoke pollution and clean up the atmosphere by proposing the introduction of a smokeless zone, where the burning of coal was prohibited, but it took several decades before the whole city was covered by orders prohibiting the use of smoke-producing fuels. The photograph opposite was taken during a November day in 1962 when Manchester experienced a very serious fog; it caused many problems not only for public transport and the drivers of private cars, but also for members of the public with respiratory difficulties.

Manchester has often been described as a rainy city and this picture of St Peter's Square does nothing to alter that impression. In the foreground is the cross erected to commemorate St Peter's Church which stood here from 1794 until 1907, when it was demolished. In the background is the Midland Hotel, completed in 1903, which rapidly established itself as Manchester's leading hotel. It was said that if you arrived in Manchester and wanted to stay at the Midland, but did not have a reservation, it was unlikely that you could be accommodated. It was at this hotel where Henry Royce met Charles Rolls, a meeting which resulted in the creation of the Rolls-Royce car. Later, in the inter-war years, Henry Hall, the renowned dance band leader, also started his career at the Midland Hotel.

The gleaming wet pavement of Piccadilly Esplanade in the 1920s reflects the street and shop lights as people make their way home. In the background are Lewis's and Royal Buildings while the statue is that of Sir Robert Peel, unveiled in 1856.

There are four main rivers which flow through Manchester, the Irwell, Irk, Medlock and Mersey; they are fed by numerous streams and watercourses, which were culveted as Manchester expanded. All the main rivers rise in the Pennines and are subject to repid rises in level and consequent flooding. Manchester's best known novel, *The Manchester Man* opens with a flood on the River Irk while within living memory both the Irwell and Mersey have broken their banks and caused widespread flooding and damage. This photograph shows a horse being led to safety in February 1946 when, after a period of exceptionally heavy rain, the River Mersey broke its banks and flooded a wide area around Didsbury, Northendon and Chorlton-cum-Hardy.

Manchester is not all rain and fog as these citizens show as they sit on the wall surrounding Piccadilly Gardens, which appears to be the wall that originally surrounded the Manchester Royal Infirmary, and was left in place when the Infirmary was demolished. This wall **was** always a favourite place for people to congregate and watch the world pass by. There are other places equally as pleasant, such as the gardens created from the former churchyards that surrounded St Mary's Church behind Kendall's shop and St John's Churchyard at the end of St John's Street. In addition, when St Peter's Church was demolished, the site was paved but later landscaped, while across the road a stone seat was provided at the side of Central Library, both of which locations, despite the traffic, are popular with those working in the city centre on summer days.

When snow fell on central Manchester in the nineteenth century it could cause many problems, especially disrupting the trams. On occasions the falls were so great that the unemployed were used to help council workmen remove the snow from the streets. For instance, over Christmas 1878 between 300 and 400 unemployed labourers were employed by the council at 4*d* a day to clear snow from the streets of central Manchester. In total, over six days, over 35,000 loads of snow were removed. Although the pay was low, it would have been welcome, as it was a time of high **unemployment** and would have provided little Christmas cheer. This picture, taken from a glass lantern slide, shows men clearing snow from the city centre's pavements to enable pedestrians to get to and from work and the shops. Whether the cart on the right is being used to take the snow away and tip it into the River Irwell is uncertain.

It has been said that central Manchester does not get heavy snowfalls, but this is not necessarily the case. If the snow falls during the day, it tends to get churned up and it is possible to keep the roads open. This photograph shows a snow storm in central Manchester in March 1930. The pavements are already covered while the roads have been kept partially clear by traffic.

Few people seem to have ventured out into Whitworth Park, Chorlton-on-Medlock, after this fall of snow. In the background, rising above the trees, is the Union Chapel on the corner of High Street (now Hathersage Road) and Wilmslow Road. The chapel had been built in 1869 for the Baptist Church, which had been established in 1842 on Park Place, a short distance away. The chapel was designed by Medland Taylor at a cost of £22,000. The chapel closed in 1951 when the site was acquired by St Mary's Maternity Hospital, and it was demolished.

CHAPTER TWELVE

WHEN NOT AT WORK

During the last fifty years the way people have used their leisure time has changed dramatically with the advent of radio and television. Until their arrival, the only way to hear music or a particular artist was to go to a concert, and the only way to see the news was to go to the cinema, and that news was not 'instant'; it was always a few days or even weeks old. Today concerts are broadcast over the radio, there are twenty-four hour news programmes and sporting fixtures are beamed directly into the home. There is no need to go out of doors to see or listen to events if the weather is bad. This is very different from the nineteenth and early twentieth centuries when there was no radio or television.

To many people the nineteenth century was a period when it is generally believed there was little spare time for anything other than working, sleeping and eating. Lives were ruled by the factory bell or hooter, and for the average working man or woman wages were only just sufficient to provide for food, heating and the rent. This is a picture which is far from accurate, however. To start with, working hours were gradually reduced throughout the nineteenth century. The Factory Acts of 1850 and 1853 introduced the 10½ hour day, that is 6 a.m. to 6 p.m. with 1½ hours for meals. At the same time the Saturday half-holiday was introduced, with the lead being taken by William Marsden and George Wilson in Manchester. The aim was for firms to close at 1 pm on Saturdays, giving their employees a Saturday half-day holiday, which was further increased by another hour in the early twentieth century when S. & J. Watts announced they were going to close at 12 noon rather than 1 p.m. Other warehouses soon followed.

During the nineteenth century the average working person appears to have had an increasing amount of disposable income. Between 1840 and 1875 it is said that real wages rose by 40 per cent and by another 33 per cent in the last quarter of the century. This was brought about by falling prices. For instance, bus fares fell from 6d per journey in 1840 to 1d by 1900, and although railway fares rose, the increase was very slow. It was claimed that during the last half of the nineteenth century, many people opened friendly society and Post Office savings accounts. Saving was no longer the preserve of the wealthy or middle classes.

The nineteenth century also saw the beginnings of the rise of the annual holiday, or Wakes Weeks as they were referred to in the north-west. Employers began to appreciate that maintenance work on machinery could be carried out more efficiently if their employees were absent, and so they began to give their employees a week's unpaid holiday. There were also those unofficial holidays when workers took an extra day off without permission, usually Monday and sometimes referred to as 'Saint Monday'. There was also the appreciation of the fact that those who worked in warehouses, offices, banks and shops did not get the same time off as those in mills and factories, and so the Bank Holiday Act was introduced in 1870 to force these organisations to close down for several days each year. It is worth noting that in the eighteenth century the Bank of England closed for forty-seven days each year, which was reduced to forty-four in 1808, to forty in 1825, eighteen in 1830 and just four in 1834 (Christmas Day, Good Friday, 1 May and 1 November).

Perhaps one of the biggest influences on leisure time in the nineteenth century was not the reduction in working hours or the rising wages but the railway, as it reduced the time taken to travel between places considerably and increased the mobility of people generally. Initially, people could go away for the day and return to take part in local events in the evening, but these day trips gradually extended into a week's unpaid holiday at the seaside.

Railway excursions from Manchester were particularly popular around Whit Week in 1848: it was said that 116,000 passengers left Manchester Victoria for the coast during Whit Week, and two years later the number exceeded 202,000. Gradually the number of excursions and trips organised by railway companies increased – to local and national events as well as to race meetings, football and cricket matches, and even half-day trips to places like the Peak district on Saturday afternoons.

The nineteenth century also saw the growth of organised activities by churches, clubs and other bodies. For example, in the late nineteenth century Levenshulme Conservative Club travelled out to Disley one Saturday afternoon in July for a picnic, while the YMCA Hiking Club travelled to Middlewood and walked via Disley, Strines, Cobden Edge and New Mills before returning to Disley to catch the train back to Manchester. Cycling clubs, athletic clubs and sporting events all gained support in the late nineteenth century.

There was also a growth in the number of organisations that provided what could be described as 'do-it-yourself' entertainment. Sometimes it was centred on a business and encouraged by the owners, as at J. & S. Watts where there was a dramatic society, or developed at a church, often to raise funds for a specific purpose.

Although there were organised activities, there were still events and activities that people could either do on their own or attend, sometimes for free. Those who could not afford to visit places, go on trips or visit the music halls or theatres could make their own entertainment – for example, children using pieces of rope to create swings.

The illustrations in this section show people enjoying themselves in many ways or the provision that was made for people to spend their leisure time if they wanted to get away from home. Sometimes these events involved the whole community; sometimes only a few people or even people on their own. The important thing to remember is that there were many ways for people to use their free time in the era before radio and television. What might not satisfy twenty-first century people would certainly have pleased our forebears.

When Manchester's first public parks were first opened in 1845, there were few facilities for children provided. However, by the end of the nineteenth century it was realised that children required not only swings and other playground facilities, but also areas where they could run around and even sail model boats. In 1895 Manchester City Council took a lease on a plot of land at the corner of Moss Lane East and Wilmslow Road from the trustees of Sir Joseph Whitworth's estate with the specific intention to create a park that was aimed at children. The central feature was a large ornamental lake where children could sail model boats and also use small rowing boats. Another concession to the children was that there were no 'Keep off the Grass' notices and few flower beds, so that the children were able to run freely throughout the park. The new park had no facilities for adults except a bandstand, where those accompanying the children could listen to music on Saturdays and Sundays. This Edwardian photograph shows the lake with boys sailing their boats. To prevent children from running into the lake as they raced around, a low railing was erected.

Opposite: Although open space was at a premium in the densely populated parts of Manchester surrounding the city centre, the local authority did try to find small plots of land which could be converted into playgrounds for the local children. This particular playground, which was described as a 'recreation ground', may have been the one marked on the 1893 map as lying between Cheltenham Street, Church Street, Harrowby Street and Willert Street Police Station in Collyhurst. Whether the boys, who appear to be playing an organised game of some description, possibly football, have been brought here from a local school is not certain, but there are certainly children looking on as the game is played. The presence of an adult gives the impression that the game is more than just a group of children spontaneously kicking a ball around an open space. In the background can be seen the swings, a feature of many children's playgrounds and recreation grounds.

These children appear to be having a good time on the swings at the Manchester University Settlement on Every Street in Ancoats, away from the dangers of busy roads and the nearby Ashton and Rochdale Canals. The Settlement was established in 1895 after a meeting at Owens College (now Manchester University) attended by students, academics and professional people. At the first annual general meeting in 1896 it was explained that the Settlement had been founded in the 'hope that it may become common ground on which men and women of various classes may meet in goodwill, sympathy and friendship, that the residents may learn something of the conditions of an industrial neighbourhood and share its interests, and endeavour to live among their neighbours a simple and religious life'. The movement made Ancoats Hall its centre. After refurbishment work the first Settlement workers moved in during 1898. The Settlement also acquired the use of the house that stood in front of the Roundhouse, which had been the home of Dr Scholes, who had founded the Roundhouse Chapel in 1820 as a non-conformist place of worship. Although the Settlement did not take over the Roundhouse until 1929, it acquired the surrounding graveyard (which had been closed in 1854) in 1900, and created a children's playground there with swings and other play equipment. Although the University Settlement still exists, both the Roundhouse and Ancoats Hall have been demolished and the area has changed dramatically since 1900.

Opposite: Many churches had football teams drawn from those who attended both the church and the Sunday school. This photograph shows the team which played for St Wilfrid's, Newton Heath, during the 1911/12 season. When the team was formed is not recorded, although the booklet from which this picture was taken includes a photograph of the team in 1909.

In the nineteenth century many of Manchester's districts and surrounding communities had sports clubs which played in local leagues. This undated photograph shows some of those who played for Levenshulme Cricket Club, possibly at the beginning of the twentieth century. Their ground was bounded by Slade Lane and Park Grove and was visible from the railway line between Manchester and Stockport, and later from the Styal line. The plot of land which was originally their ground is now owned by Manchester City Council.

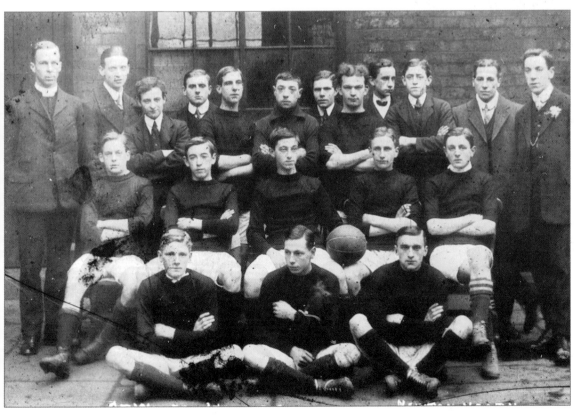

The team that was to become Manchester United had its origins in a football team which played for Lancashire and Yorkshire works at Newton Heath in 1878. In 1885 the team changed its name to Newton Heath and finally, in 1902, it became Manchester United. Since 1910 the team has been based not in Manchester but in Stretford, at Old Trafford, but when this photograph of the team was taken in 1905/6 the club was playing at Bank Street in Clayton, where they had moved in 1893 from North Road at Monsall, which was close to the works. While the club was at Bank Street they won the First Division Championship for the 1907/8 season, and in the following season they defeated Bristol City 1–0 at Crystal Palace to win the FA Cup. According to a note on the reverse of the photograph this team cost less than £1,000, and was built around Charlie Roberts (second from the left on the front row), who cost the club £400 from Grimsby Town in 1904.

Founded two years after Manchester United, Manchester City owes its origins to a team known as West Gorton St Marks, which amalgamated with Gorton Athletic, formed in 1884, to become Ardwick FC in 1887. Finally, in 1894, the club changed its name to Manchester City. Unlike Manchester United, Manchester City had several grounds in east Manchester before moving to Maine Road. These included Clowes Street in Gorton (1880–1), Kirkmanshulme Cricket Club (1881–2), Queens Road (1882–4), Pink Bank Lane (1884–7) and Hyde Road until 1923. When the Football League Second Division was formed in 1892, Ardwick was one of the original members. This photograph shows the team that won the First Division Championship for the 1936/7 season, the first time Manchester City had achieved this although they had been runners-up twice before, 1903/4 and 1920/1. Among the players in this team photograph are Frank Swift (back row, third from right), Eric Toseland (second row, first on left), Alex Herd (next to Toseland) (Herd's son, David, later played for Manchester United), and Fred Tilson (next to Herd).

In the middle of the nineteenth century Manchester looked outside the boundaries of the town for supplies of fresh, clean water. The location of the new water source was the Longdendale valley, east of Manchester. However, by the mid-1870s the demand for water was such that the existing supplies were proving to be inadequate and Manchester was forced to look elsewhere for additional supplies. In 1878 it was decided to pipe water from the Lake District to augment that from the Pennines. Having obtained Parliamentary approval for the work, the residents of the village of Mardale were relocated and the Thirlmere scheme was started. Work on constructing the lake and the pipeline to Manchester was completed in 1894 and officially opened in October that year with two ceremonies. The first was at the pumping station at Thirlmere and the second in Manchester, when a fountain in Albert Square was switched on in the presence of between 20,000 and 30,000 people. The original fountain was replaced in 1897 by one designed by Thomas Worthington, executed by J. and H. Patterson and donated anonymously to Manchester. The new fountain bore the inscription 'Erected in the Sixtieth Year of the Reign of Her Most Gracious Majesty Queen Victoria. Eighteen Hundred and Ninety Seven.' This photograph shows the original fountain in Albert Square as it was commissioned in 1894.

The River Mersey, like all of Manchester's rivers was badly polluted, but this did not stop people wanting to use the rivers for pleasure, especially where they flowed through open countryside. This photograph was taken in the 1930s at Northendon, which at the time was still a pleasant village in a rural setting, but it was not to remain so for long as the authorities began to develop Wythenshawe by building housing for those displaced by slum clearance programmes. The river at this point is relatively shallow, there being several fords in the area as well as a weir for a former corn mill.

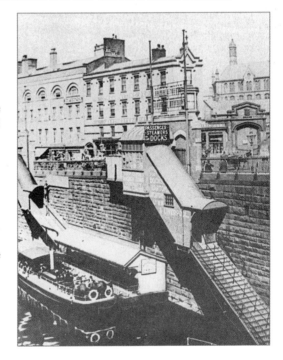

The opening of the Manchester Ship Canal attracted a great deal of attention among Mancunians with people wanting to see ships from all parts of the world so close to the centre of Manchester. A landing-stage was constructed on the River Irwell, close to Manchester Cathedral, access to which was down the flight of steps shown in this photograph. The first trips were made in 1895 and soon proved very popular with over 200,000 passengers being carried in the first half of 1897. The tall building to the left is the Palatine Hotel, opened in 1843 to cater for people arriving at Victoria Station. The gateway on the right leads into the playground of Chetham's School and was part of the unauthorised pathway which boys from the Grammar School took to get from Long Millgate to Victoria Street. It was this path and gateway which the boys from Chetham's are described as defending in *The Manchester Man*.

One of the best-known places of entertainment in Manchester, which attracted thousands of visitors each year, not only from Manchester but also from a wide area of the north of England and north Midlands, was Belle Vue. Belle Vue was started in 1836 by John Jennison when he moved his collection of birds from his property in Adswood, Stockport, to a new site on Hyde Road. The following year he added some small animals and laid out pleasure grounds where members of the public could promenade. In spite of difficulties in the 1840s Jennison's venture flourished, and gradually an extensive zoological collection was built up. Among the earliest animals he acquired were ones from the Broughton Zoological Gardens, which closed in 1842. These included 'carnivorous animals, gallinaceous birds, monkeys, foreign birds, elephants, bears, eagles, polar bears and pelicans'. However, Jennison's financial position was far from secure and he was not in a financial position to purchase the animals at auction. Nicholls, in his books on Belle Vue, suggests that Jennison was probably given the smaller and less exotic animals which did not sell. Gradually the collection of animals grew, new cages were added and old ones were improved, to provide better conditions for the animals and to enable the public to have better views. In 1870, for instance, a new lion house, a polar bears' den and a monkey house were built, the last being regarded as the finest in Europe at the time. It was a policy which continued for many years. For example, in the 1930s a 'monkey mountain' was constructed as well as a new outdoor area for reptiles. This was intended to recreate something of their natural surroundings and enable the public to have a better view of them. This photograph shows Gerald Iles, who had come to the zoo in 1929, had taken a degree in zoology at Manchester University in 1930 and become the youngest superintendent of the animals in 1933, showing some of the snakes, which had been moved to their new quarters, to a group of interested boys.

Water was a feature of Belle Vue from its early days, with the first lake being created from a pond in the mid-1840s. This lake, later known as the Firework Lake, was enlarged on several occasions and had a building which was used as a natural history museum erected on an island in the centre; access was by boat. Later, in about 1858, Jennison constructed a large lake, known as the Great or New Lake, which was enlarged and turned into a pear-shaped feature in 1876. The lake boasted two small paddle steamers, *Little Briton* and *Little Eastern*, one of which is shown in this photograph.

On 21 March 1898 the last concert of the 1897–8 season at the Gentlemen's Concert Hall took place, a concert which marked the end of an era, for this was the last concert to be held in the building before its closure and demolition to make way for a new hotel. The Gentlemen's Concert Hall had been opened in 1831 by the Gentlemen's Concert Society as a replacement for an earlier building off Mosley Street. The Society had been founded in the early 1770s by a group of twenty-four gentlemen flautists who wanted to play together. Gradually a society evolved, which began to put on regular concerts for its members and on occasions for members of the public. As membership grew, the original building became too small and so a new one was built on the corner of Peter Street and Lower Mosley Street. Such was the popularity of the Society that attendance at concerts was restricted to members only, and at one time there was a lengthy waiting list to join. It was the Gentlemen's Concert Society that invited Charles Hallé to come to Manchester in 1848 to assume the role of conductor of the orchestra. When he arrived he was not at all impressed with the orchestra and threatened to return to London. However, he was persuaded to stay and began to raise standards. Hallé left the Gentlemen's Concert Society in 1857 to establish an orchestra to play at the Art Treasures Exhibition, and then his own orchestra. During the latter half of the nineteenth century the Gentlemen's Concert Society faced a series of financial crises as the effect of Hallé's concerts began to be felt. Chamber concerts were held, ladies were admitted to membership and the hall leased for bazaars and for the staging of plays. When the closure of the building was announced, the *Manchester Guardian* commented that it was 'not without regret that the removal of so conspicuous a public building – a hall consecrated by so many musical and social memories – can be contemplated'. The final concert had a varied programme with works by Gluck, Chopin, Massenet, Brahms, Franz, Blow, Rosenthall and Beethoven being performed. The conductor at this last concert was F.H. Cowen and the soloists were Rosenthall and Mrs Hutchinson, who sang three songs and an aria. The building was demolished shortly afterwards and, as part of the deal to sell the site, the Midland Railway agreed to incorporate a theatre in the new hotel which could be used by the Society.

In 1858 Charles Hallé decided to establish a professional orchestra in Manchester which would give concerts at reasonable prices to all who wanted to attend. At the end of his first season Hallé made a profit of 2s 6d, which he regarded as satisfactory. As a venue for his concerts Hallé used the recently completed Free Trade Hall, although he called for a purpose-built concert hall and opera house to be built in the city. Over four decades Hallé and his orchestra began to introduce to Manchester audiences concerts in which complete works were played rather than just a series of single movements. At the same time many pieces new to Manchester audiences were introduced as well as several United Kingdom performances and world premières as well. Hallé's death in 1895 put the concerts under threat, but with the support of some of his friends, who guaranteed the orchestra's financial security for the next three years, the concerts survived and were eventually taken over by the Hallé Concerts Society. Eventually Hans Richter was appointed conductor and he was succeeded by Michael Balling. As well as permanent conductors there were a succession of guest conductors, including Henry Wood. The First World War was a difficult time for the orchestra, but not as severe as the 1920s when there were several financial crises. In 1924 it appeared as if England's oldest professional orchestra would have to close and be disbanded, but salvation came in the form of financial aid from Manchester City Council who also sponsored some concerts. The conductor at this time was Hamilton Harty, pictured here on the podium at the Free Trade Hall in the early 1930s. Under Harty the Hallé began to broadcast on the wireless so that its music began to reach a wider audience. When Harty departed in 1933 he was succeeded by Thomas Beecham, whose reign not only saw world-famous soloists performing with the orchestra but also the development of more varied programmes. When Beecham left in 1939 he was succeeded by Malcolm Sargent, who left in 1944 and was succeeded by John Barbirolli, whose name will always be associated with the Hallé Orchestra. During the Second World War the destruction of the Free Trade Hall made it homeless, but after playing in a series of cinemas the orchestra found a temporary home in the King's Hall at Belle Vue, until the Free Trade Hall had been rebuilt.

In June 1882 Daniel Adamson called a meeting at his home, The Towers in Didsbury, to which he invited political and business leaders of the Manchester area to discuss a proposal to construct a canal between the Mersey estuary and Manchester, capable of bringing ocean-going vessels almost into the heart of the city. The result of this meeting was the formation of a provisional committee to investigate two rival schemes and make recommendations regarding which was the more practicable, and to raise funds to secure Parliamentary approval. By autumn of 1882 a decision had been made and plans were made to present a bill to Parliament. The proposal received support, not only from the business community in Manchester and surrounding area but also from trade unions and the public generally. The first bill was presented to Parliament at the end of 1882, but there was a lot of opposition and the bill failed to reach the statute book because when it was sent to the House of Lords it was the end of the session, and the bill lapsed. A second bill was presented in 1883: this time it started its life in the House of Lords, but again failed as when it reached the Commons the session was almost over and the bill once more ran out of time. In the autumn of 1884 a modified third bill was presented, which eventually reached the statute book at the beginning of August 1885. Adamson was greeted by large crowds on his return to Manchester. This photograph was taken in Didsbury and is dated 1884. It has been suggested that the banner might have been strung across the road to show support for the bill, but it is also possible that the date on the photograph is incorrect, and that it was taken in August 1885 when Adamson returned triumphantly when the Manchester Ship Canal Act had reached the statute book.

Work on the construction of the Manchester Ship Canal started in November 1887, with Thomas Walker as contractor; it was optimistically stated that the work should be completed by 1892. However, owing to problems such as bad weather, the death of Walker and financial problems, it was not until November 1893 that the Ship Canal was completed and everything found to be in working order. The Ship Canal Company had hoped that Queen Victoria would officially open the canal, but as it was midwinter it was decided to open the canal to traffic and have an official opening later in the year. For the Queen's visit on 21 May 1894 Manchester's main streets were decorated with bunting and triumphal arches. The Manchester Fire Brigade used a pair of extension ladders to form an arch across Deansgate. This photograph shows the arch in place, prior to being manned by firemen when the Queen passed under it.

This is the same arch as in the previous illustration, but this time the photograph was taken just before the arrival of the Queen. Firemen manned the ladders and the structure was partially hidden by flags. On one side there was the motto 'Success to the Ship Canal' and on the other 'Welcome to our Queen'. The Queen's route from London Road station was via Market Street, Cross Street, Albert Square, Oxford Street and Oxford Road to Stretford Road and the docks. Her return from the docks was via Salford and then into Deansgate and to Exchange station, where she boarded the royal train to go to Scotland. On the evening of the opening only essential traffic was allowed in central Manchester so visitors could look at the street decorations, but all they would have seen here was the ladders – the firemen having departed either to go on duty or to go home.

Among the highlights of the year for many children living in central Manchester were the annual Whit Walks. Started in 1801, by the end of the nineteenth century there were two separate walks for children from the various Sunday schools in central Manchester: the Church of England on Whit Monday and the Roman Catholics on Whit Friday. The children taking part in the walks, irrespective of denomination, had new clothes for the walks, which meant that some parents had to save very hard. This photograph shows some of the children from St James the Less in Ancoats marching either to or from the main procession. St James's Church was located on Little Newton Street, just off Great Ancoats Street. In 1850 the site was covered by poor-quality housing including Willoughby's Court, which contained a block of back-to-back houses. The acquisition of the land and the erection of a church on the site was an improvement, but where did the residents go after they were displaced – it is not known. The church was opened in 1870 and was one of a number of churches which the Church of England had in the area. Within a few minutes' walk of St James's Church there was St Peter's on Blossom Street, St Paul's at New Cross and St Jude's on Mill Street. St James's Church was surrounded by rows of terraced houses, while close by there were still back-to-back houses on John Street and Pott Street. St James's Church was closed in 1937 and the building demolished as part of a rationalisation programme by Manchester diocese, as the population of the area was falling and there was no need for so many churches so close together. Today the site is covered by several large stores: Comet, Toys R Us and others.

Although Wood Street Mission was not attached to any particular religious denomination there was a Sunday school, and this took part in the Whit Walks as this photograph of the 1920s shows. Whether Wood Street took part in the Whit Monday walk is not clear, but it is possible that they staged their own walk around the Deansgate area where they were most active.

In the days before radio and television one way in which people could hear music was from street musicians. The person in the centre of this small crowd of children appears to be playing an accordion and has attracted some interest among the children, while the adults stand at the doors listening or watching the children. The fact that there are men present and children around suggests that the photograph might have been taken on a Sunday morning. Another clue which supports this is the presence of two small birdcages which can be seen to the left of the doorways. The absence of any women suggests that they were either preparing a meal or doing the weekly cleaning, and that the birds had been put outside for some fresh air while the housework was being completed. The size of the cages would be criticised today as not allowing the birds enough room to move around, but the birds themselves would have livened up a drab house.

Children living in the over-crowded areas of Manchester had few facilities for playing, especially if they lived in back-to-back or court-type housing where there were no back yards or gardens. Consequently they had no option but to play in the street, improvising with whatever was available. These children were probably living in back-to-back houses somewhere in inner-city Manchester, if the juxtaposition of the doors, windows and expanses of blank wall at the end of the building are a guide. If they are back-to-back houses, they would have been built prior to 1844, when the Police Act stipulated that all new property should have adequate sanitary facilities. Although one small group of children is playing in the gutter, the two little girls by the house have put a piece of rope over a hook or some other projection from the wall and created a crude but effective swing. Children living in these areas would adapt even simple things to provide themselves with play equipment. It is probable that the hook was used on washing days as the anchor point for the clothes lines which would stretch across the street to a similar hook on the opposite side.

In 1909 Edward VII made his second visit to Manchester, to open the new Manchester Royal Infirmary of which he was patron. Although it was July the day began with heavy rain, which gradually became a fine drizzle, but this did not deter the crowds who came out to greet the royal visitors. The route appears to have been from London Road station, through the city centre to Oxford Road and so to the Infirmary. This photograph shows some of the crowds lining the route along Oxford Road on that rather damp July morning.

The coronation of George V was the last one to be held before the advent of radio enabled the events in London to be heard by large numbers of people as they happened. It was, therefore, left to local authorities to organise events to mark the day. In Manchester a civic service was held at the Cathedral and services were held in other churches. Bands played in parks, teas were organised and children were given mementoes of the occasion. At night the streets were toured by a decorated tram and bus, the latter shown in this photograph.

George VI's coronation in 1937 was the first to be broadcast live, but this did not stop Manchester organising a full programme of events to entertain its citizens. As in 1911, a special service was held in the Cathedral, while open-air services were held in the larger parks and concerts were held in central Manchester. Streets were decorated and some of the more imposing buildings were floodlit for the occasion. Events were organised for ex-servicemen, pensioners and children, the latter receiving a fountain pen or a souvenir booklet. At night there were firework displays in Heaton Park and at Platt Fields, while decorated buses and trams toured the streets. This photograph shows the bus that was decorated for the occasion. Its streamlined appearance reflected the spirit of the age.

The junction of Ardwick Green South, Hyde Road, Higher Ardwick and Stockport Road was an important place of entertainment between the wars. Les Sutton, in his three-volume work on Ardwick, paints a picture of the area being alive with activity especially on Friday and Saturday evenings, as busy as Oxford Street in his opinion. By 1938 there were three large places of entertainment within a short distance of each other: the Apollo (opened in 1938), the Empire (opened in 1904 and renamed New Manchester Hippodrome in 1935) and the Ardwick Victoria (opened in 1912 as the Victoria Picture Theatre, then the Victoria Picture Palace and finally the Ardwick Picture Theatre), shown here in this 1930s photograph. The Victoria was licensed as a cinema in 1912, the same time as the nearby Ardwick Empire and the Coliseum. The Ardwick Picture Theatre continued to attract patrons until March 1941 when the front was severely damaged in an air-raid, with the result that the building had to be demolished.

The Palace Theatre was opened in 1891 as the Palace of Varieties, providing, according to the *Manchester Examiner and Times*, 'high class variety'. The new theatre attracted some of the leading music hall stars of the age including Harry Lauder, Vesta Tilly, Charlie Chaplin, Dan Leno and Harry Champion. Between 1912 and 1913 the Palace was closed for refurbishment, in order to meet the expected competition from the New Theatre, now the Opera House, on Quay Street. The Palace continued to stage variety shows until 1921, when it was decided to start staging more conventional dramatic productions and musicals, but from time to time revues were staged, and in the late 1930s big bands and radio stars began to make their appearance. During the Second World War the Palace continued to entertain its audiences with a mixture of variety acts, radio stars and musicals. One of the major events of the 1940s occurred in 1949, when Danny Kaye appeared at the Palace for a week from 13 to 18 June. It is said that his one-man show attracted over 25,000 people and had them rolling in the aisles with laughter. Here, the queue waiting for tickets to see him is blocking the pavement on Oxford Street.

One of the hazards of early cinemas was that film was inflammable and there was always the risk of it catching fire and destroying the building. Several cinemas suffered this fate, including the Tivoli on Peter Street in 1927 and the recently opened Capitol Cinema in East Didsbury in 1932. When the Capitol had opened in 1931 it could seat 1,400 on the ground floor, where there was also a café, and a further 500 in the balcony. The photograph not only shows the devastation caused by the fire but also one of the older buildings in the neighbourhood, which was originally a farmhouse. Although development was taking place in the area, it had not yet spread along this part of Parrs Wood Road. However, it was not long before this occurred, encouraged by the building of Kingsway and the existence of a commuter line into Manchester. According to France in his history of Didsbury, those attending Capitol Cinema by car did not need to park their cars as there were attendants to do it for them who were all 'skilled mechanics' who could carry out 'running repairs' while 'the patrons are enjoying the entertainment'. The Capitol also claimed to have one of the most advanced theatre organs in the country and was also equipped so that the stage could be used for live theatre as well, and as such was used from time to time by the Didsbury Amateur Operatic and Dramatic Society. The building closed as a cinema in 1956 and converted into a television studio, before being turned back into a theatre in 1971 by Manchester Polytechnic.

Opposite: Cycling became a popular hobby during the latter half of the nineteenth century and continued to be so through the first half of the twentieth, with clubs being formed by many organisations so that members could venture into the surrounding countryside. Manchester was fortunate that in the early years of the twentieth century the Manchester Athletic Club in Fallowfield added a banked cycle track to its stadium, which could be used for races. In 1955 it was purchased by Reg Harris who renamed it the Harris Stadium, and it continued to be used for cycling events. This photograph, however, was taken not in Fallowfield but at Heaton Park in about 1950, when a 50-mile cycle race was organised there. The photograph shows some of the competitors before the start of what must have been a difficult race, as the land to the north of Manchester is not exactly level.

In 1912 Manchester Corporation Waterworks Department handed over to the Parks Department surplus land around Debdale Reservoirs. Although there were formal walks and flower beds in the new park, much of it was devoted to sport. The new park had tennis courts, bowling greens, football, cricket and hockey pitches, although no water sports were allowed on the reservoirs. This photograph shows girls playing hockey on one of the pitches in about 1914. Notice the long skirts they are playing in: they must have got rather dirty as well as making it difficult for the girls to play, but it has to be remembered that this was the dress of the period, and there were few sports girls and women could engage in competitively.

The sound of people making music in the street is not always welcome to pedestrians today and certainly was not to the author of an article which was published at the end of the nineteenth century in the series 'Bye-ways of Manchester life: XII Street Musickers'. To the author, the sounds which the various types of street musician made had little to do with performing music, but with persuading people to part with their money in the hope that the musician might stop either singing or playing. He briefly mentions the players of street pianos or organs, including the comment: 'Of the Italian organ-girls, mostly hailing from county Cork: of their young men; of their regular "pitches", their gains, and so-forth, we cannot stay to speak. They seem commonly prosperous, well-fed, well-clothed, and in generally good condition.' Was he, perchance, referring to girls like those in this 1889 photograph taken in the Swan Street area? Who they were and whether they owned the instrument or merely hired it by the day is not certain, but they do have a certain air of determination to make as much as they can from the instrument.

CHAPTER THIRTEEN

CHILDREN & CHILDHOOD

It is often said that 'Childhood is the happiest time of one's life'. Theoretically this should be the case, as it is generally assumed that children should not have worries about whether their employment will continue, where money is coming from to pay the bills and for food, heating and lighting. It is assumed that it is a time for learning and playing. However, for many children their childhood was far from easy and worry-free, especially if they lived in the poorer quarters of the town where there was the ever-present threat of unemployment for parents, disease was endemic and bad housing conditions abounded. For children living in the poorer parts of Manchester, their childhood years were ones which they must have regarded with mixed emotions.

Although the nineteenth century is often regarded as a period of *laissez-faire* and a reduction in government intervention in everyday life, this is far from the truth. Throughout the nineteenth century government interference in all areas of life increased. Regulations and laws relating to children were among the earliest attempts to introduce regulations to control what they did and how they could be treated. Many of the early Factory Acts included provisions which gradually reduced the hours that children worked and the age at which they could start work. Later compulsory education was introduced while specialist hospitals dealing specifically with children and their illnesses also developed. There was also a growth in the number of toys, games and children's books available during the late nineteenth century.

However, there were many children in areas like Ancoats, Angel Meadow and behind Deansgate where the effect of such changes was limited. Many of the children living here were still expected to try to make a contribution to the family economy as soon as they were old enough to find even a part-time job. It was for these children, in the poorer parts of central Manchester, that organisations came into existence to try to provide some help and assistance. There were several such bodies in Manchester who worked exclusively with children such as Wood Street Mission, the Boys' and Girls' Refuges in Strangeways and the various ragged schools, while others, like the Manchester and Salford Methodist Mission and the Manchester City Mission, although helping adults, were also helping children as well. Such organisations worked in the poorer parts of Manchester, helping those who lived there, but there were also children whose parents either abandoned them as babies or infants or whose parents were the inmates of the various workhouses that served the city. These children were brought up in an institutionalised atmosphere, often with a strict regime. Looking at the lives of children brought up in the workhouse, it could be said that they were given three meals a day, had a bed to sleep in and a roof over their heads and were educated and trained in a manner which was intended to give them the opportunity to earn a living in the world outside.

This selection of photographs of children, together with those to be found elsewhere in the book, taken in the closing years of the nineteenth century and early years of the twentieth century, has a theme; it is children not at work or at school, but doing things which children prefer to do if the opportunity arises – doing very little or playing, even if there are dark clouds on the horizon. As well as photographs from individual children and groups, there are a number that depict the work of Wood Street Mission, who recorded their work for posterity.

These children were photographed in Rusholme at the beginning of the twentieth century. Who they were and why the photograph was taken is not recorded. The photograph clearly shows the dress of the children and the fact that film speeds were still relatively slow, as several of the children have moved their heads, creating an indistinct effect. On the extreme right an older boy is trying to persuade a smaller child to either sit down or face the camera.

Dancing round the maypole was just one of the events of May Day. Another custom that took place during the nineteenth and early twentieth centuries was the adorning of carriers' horses with polished horse brasses and harnesses before parading them through the streets. These children in Rusholme appear to have been celebrating May Day by dancing round the maypole.

What these four boys have been doing is anyone's guess. Although three of the boys have shoes, the one second from the right lacks footwear, his trousers appear to have been torn and even his shirt appears to have lost some buttons.

Who this little boy is and why he was photographed is not recorded, although it does show the clothes that some of the smaller children must have worn in the poorest part of Manchester. The fact that he does not appear to be camera-shy leaves one wondering whether the photograph was 'set-up' for a particular purpose, with the lad being deliberately dressed like this to enable the photograph to be taken.

These three boys appear to be engrossed in a comic or some sort of newspaper. Whether the boys could read it or whether they were just looking at the illustrations will never be known. Since 1871, however, all children were supposed to have had some education, but whether all the boys and girls who lived in the slums of central Manchester received this or were able to benefit from it is not recorded. Prior to compulsory education being introduced, one of the most important educational bodies was the Sunday schools movement, which taught reading and writing. Although the intention was that the children should be able to read the Bible and prayer book, they could also go on to read books and newspapers as well. One Sunday school, that of St Matthew's on Liverpool Road, actually commented in an annual report on the number of children who could read and write and on the progress they were making.

In the mid-1840s Manchester Borough Council realised that to improve the health of its citizens something had to be done to provide them with a regular supply of clean water. The previous sources of water, the rivers and streams of the area together with wells and water supplied by the Manchester and Salford Waterworks Co., were not sufficient and did not meet the higher standards that were required if cholera and other waterborne diseases were to be eliminated. During the late 1840s and 1850s several of the Longdendale valleys were dammed and reservoirs created to provide Manchester with regular supplies of clean water. One side effect of this was the gradual introduction of drinking fountains at different places throughout the town, where people could obtain a drink of fresh, clean water. One such fountain was at Bank Top, near London Road station, and it is shown here. The cup was chained to the fountain so that no one could walk away with it. Although it might have left something to be desired in terms of hygiene, the water that was drunk was certainly better than that which was previously available.

It is not known who these children were, or why they were sitting in deck-chairs and what appears to be a pushchair or pram. What is known is that the photograph was taken by or for William Royle, an important figure and local historian in Rusholme in the early twentieth century. It is possible that the building in the background may be part of Platt Hall, which was offered for sale together with the surrounding estate in 1901 as a potential development site. It was offered for sale again in 1906, but failed to reach the reserve price. In 1907 a Town Meeting recommended that Manchester purchase the hall and estate as a public facility. This they did, and Platt Fields was opened to the public in 1910.

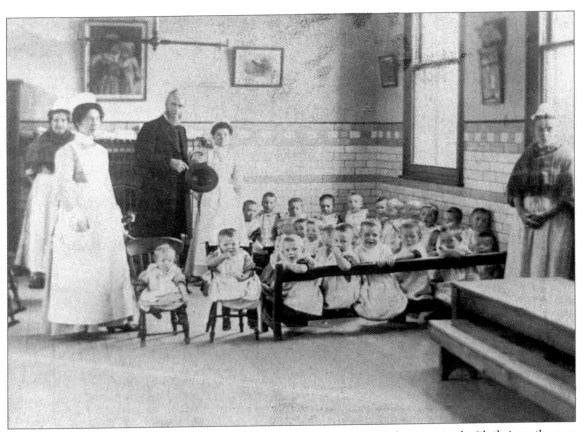

When children were born at the Chorlton Union Workhouse at Withington, they remained with their mothers up to the age of about two, when they were moved to a separate building and joined those older children who had been admitted as orphans, had been abandoned, or whose parents had been admitted to the workhouse. The buildings where the children were housed were on the opposite side of Nell Lane to the main workhouse. They had their own staff, including teachers who taught the older children useful trades so that when they were old enough they could find a job and would no longer be a charge on the rate-payers. Although the regime was hard, the children were given three meals a day, which was possibly more than they would have got in the outside world. According to the Handbook issued by the Chorlton Board of Guardians in the early twentieth century, children under the age of seven had 5 oz of bread and half a pint of milk for breakfast; for dinner, bread, potatoes and 2 ounces of boiled bacon or beef, except on Thursday when they received meat pie and bread pudding and Fridays when it was Irish stew; for supper, it was back to bread and milk with a little margarine and, as a special treat, an ounce of jam on Sundays. Although milk was the usual drink, cocoa and coffee were supplied occasionally. This photograph shows a group of small children with the Workhouse's chaplain and the staff responsible for looking after them. It is possible that the two women wearing shawls are inmates from the adult workhouse who have been recruited to help look after the smaller children in return for a small payment and, according to official records, increased rations.

A scene that must have been repeated many times over, as children pass a sweet shop and stop to look in the window. However, when this particular photograph was taken, these children were on their way to Varna Street School before being evacuated; they have taken the opportunity to have one last look in the window of what might have been their favourite shop. It was not long after the outbreak of war that sweets were rationed, not to be freely available for over a decade.

One of the best-known organisations in Manchester that helped children who lived in the poorer parts of central Manchester, especially at the western end of Deansgate, was Wood Street Mission, which had been founded by Alfred Alsop in 1869. Alsop began in a modest way by holding an open-air service in the area, which had a very bad reputation for crime. The first building he occupied was on Lombard Street, but in 1873 it was acquired by the Cheshire Lines Committee for their Central station and so Alsop moved to new premises on Wood Street. Alsop's aim was not to convert the residents of the area, but to provide them, and in particular their children, with help to improve their condition. Food was provided through soup kitchens, which must have been welcome to some of the street children some of whom, according to reports, spent the day begging and trying to collect money so their parents could spend it on drink. As well as providing food, Wood Street Mission, as it became known, also provided clothing and clogs for those who were in need. The cost of running the mission was met by donations from members of the public. In the 1880s Wood Street started organising day trips to the seaside for the children of the area; these later developed into week-long holidays. This photograph shows the boys queuing to get places on one of the camps that Wood Street organised at St Anne's. On page 162 there is the companion photograph to this one, showing the girls queuing for their places.)

Opposite: There were many children who lived rough on the streets of Manchester during the late nineteenth and early twentieth centuries. Wood Street Mission was one organisation that tried to help them, as did the Boys' and Girls' Refuge in Strangeways. Although some were found positions in England, others were given the opportunity to start a new life in Canada, often being employed on farms. Not all those who went were happy with their new surroundings, and there were reports of boys absconding and ill treatment. Before they left Manchester they were received by the Lord Mayor and wished *bon voyage*. This photograph shows a group of boys with the Lord Mayor prior to their departure in about 1910.

The railway made it possible to move large numbers of children to the seaside. In the 1880s day trips to the seaside at Southport were organised by Wood Street Mission and were well supported and appreciated by the children who went on them. According to some reports, they started queuing at about midnight although the trains did not leave until 6 a.m. When they reached Southport the children were taken to the beach, where they could play and paddle, and they were then entertained and fed before being taken back to Manchester. The trips were paid for by public donations and this policy continued when the summer camps were organised at St Anne's. The parents were expected to make a small contribution to the cost of the trip. In this photograph, taken between 1923 and 1939, children from Wood Street are seen leaving Manchester, possibly from Victoria station, for the seaside in two coaches attached to the front of the train.

When the children got to St Anne's they were originally housed in purpose-built huts among the dunes. Most of the huts were used as dormitories, each child having his or her own bed. Other huts were used as a dining room, kitchens, washrooms and recreational rooms. The camps were designed to take 120 children at any one time. The emphasis was on supervised outdoor activities. These boys are enjoying playing in the sea, which would have been much cleaner than the rivers and canals which some of them may have swum in back in Manchester.

These girls are playing in the sand at St Anne's while taking part in the Wood Street Mission's summer camp there. Several of the girls have buckets and spades, which may have been donated. All the girls are wearing smocks and, like the boys in the earlier photograph, are wearing hats, which may have been made from a thick, stocking type of material.

Another important event in the lives of the children connected with Wood Street Mission was Christmas. In the late nineteenth century children were given breakfast on Christmas Day, there were Christmas dinners and even suppers for the adults and, of course, small presents. All this was paid for by donations. In common with many charitable organisations, notices appeared in the local papers about a fortnight before Christmas asking for donations from the public to help meet the cost of the celebrations. This photograph shows the arrival of Father Christmas at Wood Street at some time in the years between the wars. The faces of the children appear to be full of expectation.

Every picture tells a story. This boy appears either to be suffering from toothache or to have had his ears boxed for misbehaviour. If he is suffering from toothache, he would have had to 'grin and bear it' unless his parents could afford to pay to have it treated by a dentist, or the boy was prepared to go through the agony of having it pulled out by a travelling dentist. There were few dentists who were prepared to treat the less well off, such as McDonald's 'Free Dentorium' situated in Piccadilly in about 1888, who treated those who could not afford a dentist, provided that they had a letter of support from a prominent local person who knew them. Such people were, however, few and far between.

As the number of motorised vehicles increased, it became increasingly important that children were taught to cross a busy road safely. Alternatively, they could cross roads at specially created crossings or with the help of an adult. Here two little girls are taken across what would have been a very busy Upper Brook Street by a policeman. In the background are the motor car showrooms of William Arnold. This firm had been started in the early twentieth century by William Arnold, who made carriages and then moved into motor cars. It is probable that in the early days of motoring Arnold was one of a number of carriage builders who would construct customised car bodies on chassis that the owners had purchased. Later, when mass production of cars came in and cars were supplied complete with their bodies, he moved into selling cars for several different manufacturers. The advert in the picture shows that he sold both MG and Bentley cars, and he appears to have been awaiting the arrival of a new American model, the Hudson.

ACKNOWLEDGEMENTS

In the first volume of *Manchester in Old Photographs* I expressed my grateful appreciation and thanks to a large number of people who had photographed Manchester over the years and had made their photographs available to the general public through libraries or, more recently, in books. Those sentiments, which were expressed in 1996, hold true today for the collection of illustrations in this volume. The number of photographs appears to be endless, with so many still coming to light in private and family collections. I hope that some of the captions in this book will help readers look more closely at the old photographs they own to see that there is often more to be discovered than just the subject in the foreground.

My thanks are also due to Manchester Public Libraries, and in particular the Local History Library, now the Local Studies Department, for their work in collecting and preserving so many photographs. My thanks are due to the staff there, in particular David Taylor, for their help over the years when researching for this and other books. I should also like to express my support for proposals to put them on to CD-Rom to make them more generally available to the public.

I wish to thank Ted Gray, Salford Archives Department, Manchester, and Salford Methodist Mission, Wood Street Mission and Manchester Public Libraries for permission to reproduce some of the illustrations used in this book. I apologise in advance if I have overlooked anyone who should have been acknowledged and has not been included.

I wish to thank Simon Fletcher and Sarah Moore of Sutton Publishing for their help, and also Sutton Publishing for giving me the opportunity to compile this collection of illustrations on Manchester. Without the work of publishers like Sutton, photographs of towns and villages would not be so readily available, and many people would not have come to appreciate the historical importance of their own community.

My thanks are due to David Brearly, who has copied some of the lantern slides used in this book. It is his work that has made it possible to include material which might otherwise have been difficult to use.

On a more general front, I would also like to thank everyone who purchased the first volume and for the comments you have made, which have been very much appreciated. I hope you will enjoy this volume as well.

Finally, I would like to thank my wife Hilary and my children Peter and Anna for their interest in the pictures, and for making helpful comments when looking at them with fresh eyes.

PART THREE

MANCHESTER
A THIRD SELECTION

Piccadilly in the 1890s.

Pigeons and starlings are among the most common birds in the centre of towns and cities. They congregate in such large numbers partly because waste food is thrown out by restaurants, cafés and snack bars, but also members of the public feed them. This photograph shows a man feeding the pigeons in Albert Square, possibly in the 1930s. In the background is the Town Hall while to the left are the ornamental railings around the base of the Albert Memorial – they were designed to prevent members of the public climbing on the monument. Pigeons have presented a serious problem in Manchester and other cities for many years as they roost on ledges and window sills, coating everything with a layer of droppings which does little to enhance the appearance of buildings and can cause serious damage to the stone work. Various methods have been tried to keep the birds away, including the use of a very fine mesh netting which does not detract from the appearance of the building.

INTRODUCTION

T he end of the twentieth century, irrespective of whether 2000 or 2001 is the start of the new one, provides an opportunity to look back at the history of Manchester and recall some of the events that have influenced its development over the 150 years since the advent of photography. After all, it is the photograph that has made this book possible.

It might be said that photography was a kind of watershed in that it enabled things to be preserved accurately in pictorial form for the first time. Before the invention of the camera, artists recorded what they saw, but only included in paintings and drawings what they felt was most attractive and tended to ignore the more unpleasant side of their subject. With the invention of the camera, it became possible to record exactly what was there, although sometimes the stage was carefully set to get the best results. Today, with digital cameras, there are ways of altering how a photographic image turns out, thus weakening the statement that 'the camera never lies'.

The importance of the camera as a means of recording the present for the future was recognised early in its development. In about 1874, an article in the *Builder* suggested that photography ought to be used to record all the historical buildings of a town before they were demolished in the name of redevelopment and suggested that such records were kept in libraries or museums. Twenty years later, Manchester Amateur Photographic Society made just such a survey of Manchester and Salford, although it should be pointed out that photographers such as James Mudd, Fischer and Brothers had already been recording the town since the mid-1850s. Some of the photographs in this book, and the previous two volumes in the series, were taken by these very able photographers. It is also fortunate that at the end of the nineteenth century, the City Engineer's Department started using photography to record the town and that organisations, like the Manchester and Salford Methodist Mission, began to use photographs to illustrate their annual reports. In the twentieth century, newspapers started to use photographs to accompany stories – another important step forward.

Manchester, like all towns, has been affected by events, both local and national. For example, at the end of the Napoleonic Wars in 1815 many of those who were discharged from the forces headed for the growing industrial towns rather than their former homes in the countryside. Central Manchester's population rose from around 42,000 in 1788 to almost 187,000 in 1851. The effect of major twentieth-century wars was different, however: they involved the whole population in some way or other. For instance, the air raids of the Second World War destroyed not only military targets, but also the homes and workplaces of those who were not directly involved in the fighting.

Looking back over the 150 years since the first photographs of Manchester were taken, what have been the watersheds or events that have influenced the growth and development of 'this capital of the spinners and weavers of the world', as Reach put it in 1849?

It appears that the approach of 1900 did not generate the same level of discussion about when the new century would begin as there has been in recent times. According to one article there was no argument – the twentieth century began on 1 January 1901. In some respects, the death of Queen Victoria early in 1901 seemed to reinforce the idea that a new century had begun, but in reality the 'Naughty Nineties' merged into Edwardian England. A different head gradually began to appear on coins and stamps, but there was no announcement 'All change. It is now the twentieth century' or 'It is now the Edwardian period'. Life went on very much as it always had done for the vast majority. The outbreak of war in 1914 was to have a far more dramatic effect on people's lives.

Although the pace of change was probably more rapid in the twentieth century, the nineteenth century saw many important and dramatic developments which affected everyone's lives. For example, the fastest means of travel in 1815 was the canal or the horse. Railways carrying passengers hauled by steam engines were still fifteen years in the future when the Liverpool and Manchester Railway opened and introduced a gradual reduction in what might be called 'time distance' – by this I mean journeys that would have taken several hours or days could now be completed in a few hours. For example, the trip from Manchester to Liverpool took virtually all day by canal and several hours by stage coach, but by 1900 it was only 43 minutes on a non-stop train from Manchester Central station.

Railways were intended to carry goods as well as passengers, but Manchester's greatest desire in freight transportation was a direct link to the sea. This was achieved in 1894 with the opening of the Manchester Ship Canal, which enabled ocean-going vessels to dock within a couple of miles of the Town Hall. More recently, the airport has been the centre of expansion both in passenger traffic and freight sent overseas. However, the growth of freight traffic has to a large extent been the result of the changing nature of the goods made in Manchester. Until well into the twentieth century items for export tended to be heavy and bulky, ideal for transport by sea but not by air. Today exports tend to be small, high-value items which are ideal for air freight.

In 1815, the majority of people lived in the countryside, but the 1851 census revealed that over half the country's population lived in towns of more than 10,000. At the same time there was a movement of the middle classes into the countryside, encouraged by the growth of more efficient transport – the railways and, in urban areas, the horse-drawn bus and later the horse-drawn tram. The first horse-drawn buses were operating in Manchester in 1824 and the first horse-drawn trams in 1877. By 1901, electricity was beginning to be used for public transport and for the wealthy, private cars were beginning to replace carriages. Changes in transport prompted the outward expansion of Manchester and the growth of residential suburbs.

This was further encouraged by the fact that industry and commerce took over old residential areas in the centre of the city, forcing the residents to move away. This trend continued in the twentieth century with slum clearance programmes which involved not only the remaining poor quality houses in the centre of the city, but also in the surrounding inner suburbs such as Ardwick, Hulme and Chorlton-on-Medlock. People from these areas were decanted into districts like Withington, Fallowfield, Wythenshawe and, since 1945, outside the boundaries of the city to places like Hattersley, Handforth and Middleton where overspill estates were constructed by the City Council's housing department.

The nineteenth century was a period of new ideas. In the 1830s and 1840s, the concept of free trade took hold and then gathered momentum as the century progressed. The principle behind it was a move to get rid of as much red tape relating to exports as possible. However, by the end of the nineteenth century protectionism had reared its head and there was a growing demand for Britain to impose tariffs to protect its own industry from foreign competition. In some respects one can see a parallel today with the European Union and the same splits between and within political parties – protectionism *v* free trade – as there were in the late nineteenth century. It is interesting to note that among the strongest supporters of free trade in the nineteenth century were the textile manufacturers of Lancashire, but in the twentieth century the same industry was seeking quotas and tariffs to protect it from foreign competition.

But what of other changes in the nineteenth century? Gas began to be used for lighting and by the 1890s many houses were lit using it; gas was also used for heating, cooking and providing hot water.

By 1900, the supremacy of gas was being threatened by the arrival of a new industry – electricity.

The supply of clean water is taken for granted today, but this was not the case in 1815 when people relied on wells, water tanks, rivers and streams for their supply. In the middle of the nineteenth century, Manchester became the first town to look outside its boundaries for clean water. In the late 1840s and early 1850s, major engineering works were completed in the Longdendale valley which resulted in the construction of the Longdendale Reservoirs to supply the city and its neighbours. By the 1870s, Manchester discovered that it again needed to increase the supply to meet the growing demand and began to draw water from the Lake District via the Thirlmere Aqueduct. At the same time, the existence of adequate supplies ensured that an effective sewage disposal system could be introduced. The result was the construction of the Davyhulme Sewage Works on the edge of the Manchester Ship Canal. Not only was Manchester involved in trying to clean up its act, its neighbours, like Withington Local Board of Health, did the same. Withington built its own sewage works on the banks of the River Mersey at Chorlton and this also handled sewage from Levenshulme.

Other areas of life where change was also very noticeable in the nineteenth century included education. By the end of the century, elementary education was compulsory and secondary and further education were beginning to grow with the appearance of new universities and colleges. School boards of the 1870s and 1880s gave way in the 1900s to local authority education committees.

In the field of social care, there were also changes. The old Elizabethan Poor Law had been replaced in the 1830s by the New Poor Law, characterised by the dreaded 'bastilles', as some called the new, more efficient and cost-effective workhouses, but these were changing by the end of the nineteenth century. Voluntary organisations began to make their mark in helping those who had fallen on hard times.

Attempts were made to remove the slums. The 1844 Police Act in Manchester banned the construction of houses without adequate sanitary facilities while the Artisans Dwellings Act of the 1880s, and its subsequent amendments, resulted in local authorities being able to encourage the building of new houses to established standards. It was not, however, until after 1919 that housing and the clearance of the slums became an important priority for both central and local government.

New hospitals, particularly specialist ones, also made an appearance in the nineteenth century while medicine made important advances. And developments came even faster during the twentieth century. Old hospitals were replaced by new ones, but it was not until 1948 that medical treatment became available to all through the National Health Service. During the early twentieth century, those who could not afford a doctor still had to rely on charity to get treatment. Some diseases appeared in the nineteenth century, but improvements in social conditions resulted in their being brought under control. Epidemics of cholera and typhoid were countered by improvements in water supply while smallpox was brought under control by vaccination and the realisation that isolation could stop illnesses spreading. The appointment of medical officers of health was an important step forward in the area of prevention, as even the smallest local boards of health had their own part-time medical officer of health, often a local doctor.

Local government was also shaken up in the nineteenth century. The Municipal Corporations Act of 1835 reformed local government and provided a means by which growing industrial towns, like Manchester, were able to apply for charters of incorporation as boroughs. This meant they could adopt a more efficient method of administration and dispense with other forms of government, some manorial in origin. Other changes, such as the creation of new local government structures including local boards of health, resulted from the fear that slums were developing in the areas around towns that were not under any form of municipal control. In 1888 county councils were introduced and in the 1890s urban district councils, with wider powers than their predecessors, took over from local boards of health. In 1885, Manchester began to enlarge its area of jurisdiction by taking over neighbouring local boards and urban district councils such as Bradford and Rusholme in 1885 and Moston, Blackley, Crumpsall, Openshaw, Newton Heath and part of Gorton in 1890. This was two years after a proposal to create a Manchester County Council, similar to the London County Council, was put forward and rejected. The twentieth century opened with Manchester continuing its expansionist policy by taking in Heaton Park in 1903, Moss Side, Withington, Didsbury and Chorlton-cum-Hardy in 1904, Levenshulme and West Gorton in 1909, Wythenshawe in 1931 and Ringway in 1974.

The nineteenth century was also an important period culturally. Theatres flourished, libraries and museums came into existence, art galleries were opened and books became more common place as prices began to fall. Even newspaper circulation rose, especially after the abolition of the newspaper tax in 1851. Manchester was the first place to have a public library under the terms of the 1850 Public Libraries Act – Manchester Free Library opened in September 1852 in a converted building. The purpose-built Central Library in St Peter's Square did not open until 1934. Manchester City Art Gallery was acquired by the City Council in the 1880s when its owners, the Royal Manchester Institution, found that they could not afford to maintain it and continue to add to collections. By the twentieth century, space for the collections was limited but recently a much-needed extension has been begun. Musically, the group formed by Sir Charles Hallé for the Art Treasures Exhibition of 1857 was to lead to the foundation of the Hallé Orchestra in the following year. It provided regular concerts for the general public at affordable prices. However, Hallé's dream of a purpose-built concert hall was not realised until the 1990s. The twentieth century saw many changes in Manchester's cultural life, with live theatre being replaced by cinema, although with the opening of the Royal Exchange Theatre in the 1970s there was a revival of that art form.

The nineteenth and twentieth centuries witnessed many changes in Manchester's appearance. Old, familiar buildings disappeared and were replaced by new ones. For example, the Infirmary moved from Piccadilly to a new site in Chorlton-on-Medlock and the old building was demolished, leaving an open space which today is prompting great controversy. The former Town Hall on King Street was declared unsafe and the Free Reference Library which was housed there was forced to find temporary accommodation. The Gentlemen's Concert Hall, the People's Concert Hall and Lower Mosley Street

Opposite: St Mary's Gate is one of central Manchester's oldest streets. It linked Market Street with Deansgate. The name may have arisen because it led to a pre-Conquest church that originally stood close to the corner of Exchange Street and St Ann's Square. The street is mentioned in the earliest surviving Court Leet records of 1552 as having its own scavengers and by-lawmen. According to the 1690 Manchester Poll Book, twenty-one households with a total of forty-five people were recorded for St Mary's Gate. When the first directory for Manchester was published in 1772, thirteen people were listed as living here, although it should be remembered that the directory was not comprehensive. A similar number are listed for 1800, including Edward Holme, a doctor, and John Ollivant, a silversmith, who founded the well-known Manchester firm of Ollivant and Botsford. This postcard view of St Mary's Gate was taken in about 1904, looking towards Market Street. On the left is Victoria Buildings, which was destroyed in the Christmas blitz of 1940. The tower in the centre is that of the Royal Exchange while to its right can be seen buildings which had shops at street level and offices on the upper floors, and the entrance to the Exchange Arcade (extreme right). When the photograph was taken, among the firms that had retail premises here were the Maypole Dairy Company (nos 2–4), Lockhart's Café (no. 8) and Burgons, who were grocers (no. 12).

Schools were demolished to make way for the Midland Hotel, and the former Natural History Museum in Peter Street was replaced by a new YMCA building. This was the period when the north side of Deansgate was cleared and Deansgate itself was partially widened. The Great Northern Warehouse was also built, completing the clearance of an area of poor quality housing between Watson Street, Deansgate, Great Bridgewater Street and Peter Street.

Over the 150 years since the first photographs were taken in Manchester, much has changed. Buildings have been erected, torn down and replaced. The way people travel, live, work, spend their leisure time and are governed has also altered dramatically. Many of these changes have been recorded by the camera to the benefit of the present generation of local historians. It is the current generation's task to ensure that the present day is recorded photographically so that in another 150 years it will be possible to look back to see how we lived and worked at the end of the twentieth and the beginning of the twenty-first centuries. There will be other watersheds in the history of Manchester, but will they be as significant as those in the past? It is not possible to say at present. Only time will tell.

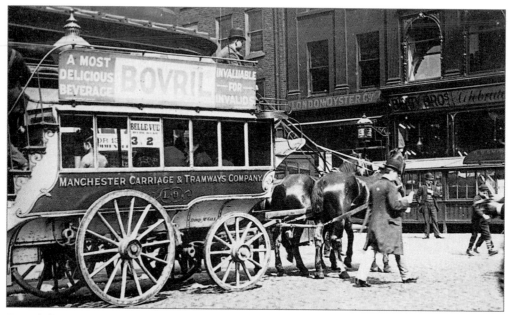

One of the many horse buses that operated in Manchester before the introduction of the horse trams waits near Victoria Buildings, St Mary's Gate, before setting off on its journey to Belle Vue sometime after 1880. This route was converted to horse tram operation in the late 1870s, but horse buses continued to be used to provide additional services at certain times of the day and to serve the outlying districts where the construction of a tramway was not economic. This bus, L9, was based in Longsight, possibly at the Grey Street Depot, and was built to the designs of John Eades. It is not clear from the photograph whether the bus is in its original condition with the top deck seating facing outwards or whether it has been rebuilt with the seating facing towards the front. Note that if you travelled outside, you paid less for your journey. Just above the front wheel is the name of the secretary of the Manchester Carriage and Tramways Company, David McGill.

CHAPTER FOURTEEN

CENTRAL MANCHESTER

To many people, Manchester appears on a map as a long, sausage-shaped area, but this is only the present-day city. The origins of Manchester proper lay in a relatively small area bounded on the south by the River Medlock and on the north and north-east by the rivers Irwell and Irk. This is the township of Manchester and was the only area referred to by that name until the creation of the borough in 1838.

Until the last half of the eighteenth century, Manchester was a small, compact area which could be crossed in about half an hour. Even in the 1780s it was said that it was possible to stand in Piccadilly and watch the hunt in Ardwick. In fact, until the construction of the Infirmary in Piccadilly in 1754–5, the only building in this area was Alkrington Hall, the town house of the Lever family, which was sold in 1786 and converted into the White Bear Inn. In 1757, the population of the township was only about 17,000 people, but within a short period, it exceeded 22,000, almost doubling by 1788 to around 42,000. When the first census was taken, it had risen to over 70,000 and continued to rise until the 1850s when it reached 180,000. By 1850, almost all the open space in Manchester had been built on, either for commercial buildings or houses, with as much as possible squeezed on to the available space. Back-to-back houses, course dwellings and other sub-standard housing were constructed as quickly as possible. Little thought was given to the need for sanitary facilities or running water. It is little wonder that diseases such as typhus and typhoid were endemic and that cholera spread rapidly in 1832.

It was not until after 1851 that the population of what was to become central Manchester began to decline, albeit rather slowly at first. This trend gradually gathered momentum as the nineteenth century progressed, fuelled not by the desire to escape the poor conditions, but by the pressures of commerce and the retail trade for space to erect new warehouses, shops and offices. This movement had already been noted in the 1840s when Mosley Street was transformed from a thoroughfare lined with gentlemen's and merchants' houses to one of warehouses, offices and public buildings. This was the time when churches like Mosley Street Unitarian Chapel, Mosley Street Independent Chapel and St Chad's Roman Catholic Church on Rook Street moved to what are often described today as the 'inner city suburbs'.

Possibly one of the most dramatic effects of commercial development on the population and on the nature of the buildings in central Manchester took place in the 1870s when Central station was built. Twenty years later, the Great Northern Railway's warehouse was erected. In the area covered by these two buildings, there were some 6,500 people in 1865. When the area was redeveloped, the people had to find new homes. Some moved into the adjacent districts of Hulme and Chorlton-on-Medlock while others moved to the New Cross area. The effect on central Manchester was dramatic. Churches like St Matthew's on Liverpool Road and St Peter's in St Peter's Square felt the effect quickly as their congregations declined. On the other side of the township, St Paul's Church on Turner Street was closed and replaced by St Paul's New Cross in the 1870s. St Clement's on Lever Street was also closed in the 1870s and the money from the sale of the site was used to build and endow churches in areas including Openshaw and Chorlton-on-Medlock. St Mary's in Parsonage Gardens was also closed as a result of the declining population of the area. The local magazine *Sphinx* visited several of these inner city churches in the 1860s and referred to them as 'Manchester's deserted churches', most having a congregation of only a few people. The article on St James's Church in George Street referred to its congregation as having changed from those of a 'better sort' to one where the main worshippers were 'of a lesser sort'.

During the twentieth century, the decline in the population of central Manchester accelerated, but more recently, this has been reversed with warehouses being converted into desirable residential accommodation and even purpose-built housing has begun to make an appearance. In some respects, history is repeating itself in that the centre of Manchester, or rather the former township of Manchester, is now regaining some of its lost inhabitants. Even trams reappeared in the last decade, providing an efficient alternative to the motor car as a means of commuting into the central area from places like Bury, Altrincham and, more recently, from Salford Quays and Eccles. In some respects, Manchester is rediscovering itself and emphasising its status as a regional centre.

With the clearance of the remaining market stalls from the Market Place in 1891, the public was able to gain a proper impression of the size of the Market Place and how small it was compared with other towns. The changes also allowed the buildings that surrounded the Market Place to be seen without obstructions for the first time. Also clearly visible is Old Millgate with the east end of the Cathedral closing the view. This road is believed to have been named because of the presence many centuries before of a water mill on the River Dene, which flowed down Withy Grove; its role was later taken over by the mills on the River Irk. When the area was redeveloped in the 1960s and 1970s, Old Millgate was restricted to a simple pedestrian footpath alongside a modern building, but in the post-1996 redevelopment all traces of Old Millgate have been completely obliterated. Among the buildings that can be seen in this photograph are the Wellington Inn, the Cotton Waste Exchange, which also housed the Coal Exchange, Yates, who were suppliers of plants and seeds, and the Falstaff Hotel.

Opposite: There are two other photographs of St Mary's Gate in this volume, both taken in the early twentieth century (see pages 297 and 303). This particular image was taken shortly after the IRA bomb blast on 16 June 1996 and shows the full effect of the blast on the Market Place development and the bridge over Market Street. Today, all this has changed yet again: the City Council took the opportunity afforded by the damage to reconsider how the centre of Manchester should look.

Another of central Manchester's old streets which still follows its original line and retains many of its twists and turns is Long Millgate. Until about 1850, Long Millgate extended from Fennel Street to Red Bank, but with the construction of Corporation Street it was divided into two sections. This photograph shows the section between Corporation Street and Red Bank, which drops down to the River Irk, flowing by this time underneath the railway viaduct leading to Victoria station. Most of the houses in this section appear to date from the mid-eighteenth century, as Manchester's population began to rise, although the building with three gables in the centre may be earlier as it appears to have timber framing. When this photograph was taken in the late nineteenth or early twentieth centuries, this part of Long Millgate was still largely residential in character.

St. Mary's Gate, Manchester.

Many photographs of St Mary's Gate were taken looking towards Market Street, but this particular one shows the view in the opposite direction towards Blackfriars Street and Bridge. The prominent structure on the right is Victoria Buildings, designed by William Dawes and completed in 1878 on the site of an area known as Smithy Door. Its construction was encouraged by the City Council because it felt that there was a serious shortage of good quality shops in the St Mary's Gate/Victoria Street and Deansgate area. Victoria Buildings incorporated shops at street level, offices on the upper floor and, as the site was triangular, a hotel overlooking the junction of Deansgate and Victoria Street. Running through the building was a shopping arcade. The site was an awkward one as it sloped downhill towards the river. Consequently, the shops which fronted Deansgate had very high ceilings and several of them were able to install a mezzanine floor to provide additional space. Victoria Buildings was destroyed in 1940 and the site was landscaped until the late 1960s when it was incorporated in the Market Place redevelopment. Today, as a result of the IRA bomb in 1996, the area has been redeveloped yet again. In the background are the buildings lining Blackfriars Street, which were mainly warehouses and offices.

Opposite: For many years part of Withy Grove and Shudehill was the home of a street market. Originally, it was the hen and poultry market, but latterly it was the location for open-air secondhand book stalls. This photograph, taken towards the end of the nineteenth century, shows the area when it was the hen and poultry market on what was a relatively quiet day with only a few stalls around. In the background several warehouses can be seen as well as the Rovers Return, the black and white building, which was demolished in 1957. Today, the whole of this area is covered by the Arndale Centre while the stalls, which now appear to concentrate on records rather than books, have been moved to the corner of High Street and Church Street. The market is but a shadow of its former self.

Deansgate is the main east–west thoroughfare through central Manchester and is always busy, although this particular postcard from *c.* 1904 seems to give a somewhat different impression. The photograph was taken looking along Deansgate towards central Manchester. The building on the right was originally the Manchester School Board premises and was on the corner of Jackson's Row. Most of it was taken up with offices and what would today be called interview rooms for the staff of the board and for inspectors, but on the first floor was the boardroom. When the Manchester School Board ceased to exist in 1903, the building was taken over by Manchester's Education Department, which continued to use it until its offices in Crown Square were completed in the 1960s. After a period as Manchester's main register office, the building has now been converted into a restaurant. On the left is the building which was formerly used by the Inland Revenue, but is now part of the Crown Court. Beyond are premises which housed several offices as well as the Manchester premises of the *Daily Mail*. This building was demolished and replaced in about 1932 by Northcliffe House, which included facilities for the *Daily Mail* to be printed in Manchester. In about 1968 the *Manchester Evening News* and the *Guardian* moved from Cross Street to share these premises with the *Daily Mail*, but now all three papers have moved out of central Manchester and the site has been redeveloped as a hotel. These buildings, erected in the last two decades of the nineteenth century, gave Deansgate an impressive appearance and make it a kind of grand entry into the city centre proper.

According to the note on this photograph from the early 1920s, it is intended to show a traffic jam at the junction of Deansgate, Peter Street and Quay Street, although by the standards of the twenty-first century traffic is flowing smoothly and only waiting for the policeman on point duty to allow it to start moving again. The junction of Quay Street, Peter Street and Deansgate was created in the 1740s when Quay Street was constructed to link the main road with the newly completed warehouse and quay on the River Irwell. At that time, there was a short row of cottages across the road from Quay Street on a road known as Yates Street, which was extended to meet Oxford Street at St Peter's Church in about 1793 and was renamed Peter Street. The photograph also shows two of the houses which were built on Deansgate as the road developed in the nineteenth century – these are the two low buildings next to the one with the cross. Eventually, they were demolished and replaced by new buildings after the Second World War.

Throughout the latter half of the nineteenth century there were complaints about traffic congestion on Market Street and how dangerous it was to cross. In the early twentieth century there were proposals to pedestrianise Market Street and turn Cannon Street into a dual carriageway. However, nothing was done and Market Street continued to be a source of problems until 1986 when it was closed to traffic. During the first half of the twentieth century traffic congestion was made worse by the trams which ran in the centre of the road, meaning that other road-users had to pass between the trams and the pavement as can be seen in this photograph of the junction of Cross Street, Market Street and Corporation Street in the 1930s. It was suggested on several occasions that trams should not be allowed to go down Market Street but should terminate in Piccadilly on the grounds that this would reduce traffic congestion and that it was quicker to walk along Market Street than travel in a tram. The line of trams stretching along Market Street certainly reinforces that impression because once one tram had stopped to pick up passengers, others had to wait, causing delays and further congestion. The building on the corner of Corporation Street and Market Street, occupied by Burton's, was originally the premises of J. & S. Moss, gentlemen's outfitters, who opened on this site in the early 1930s.

St Ann's Square came into existence in the early eighteenth century when part of Acres Fields was used for the construction of St Ann's Church, which was consecrated in 1712. The Act of Parliament which authorised its construction also laid down that there had to be space left between any buildings that might be erected so that the annual fair could continue to be held there. This fair started in 1222 and was eventually moved in 1821 as it was considered not to be a suitable event to be held in what was becoming a fashionable shopping area. During the nineteenth century, the original residential properties that once lined the square were replaced by buildings which had shops at street level and offices on the upper floors. By the middle of the nineteenth century, St Ann's Square had taken on the appearance which it has in this postcard with the statue of Richard Cobden, one of the leaders of the Anti-Corn Law League, and the memorial to those who had fallen in the Boer War. According to the directory for 1912, the year this postcard was sent, the occupiers of the buildings on the right included Verey's Limited (ladies outfitters), Mappin & Webb (silversmiths), Stephenson & Sons (glass and earthenware dealers), Emma Wilson (milliner), J.E. Cornish (bookseller) and Thomas Parker & Sons (cooks and confectioners). Among the professions to be found in the offices above the shops were solicitors, cotton merchants, estate agents, accountants, an architect and a consulting engineer. The building on the extreme left of the photograph was demolished shortly after the end of the First World War to make way for the extension to the Royal Exchange.

The corner of St Ann's Street and St Ann's Square has always been very busy with people passing to and from Deansgate to Cross Street and into St Ann's Square. This photograph was taken in the early 1890s as part of the first photographic survey of Manchester and Salford and shows Baynes & Co., hatters, at 23 St Ann's Street. This firm appears to have been in existence for only a short time because by 1901 no. 23 was not recorded in the directory although next door at no. 21 there was a café. By the 1920s, the building shown in this picture had been replaced by a new one which was occupied by Weatherall's, outfitters. St Ann's Street, which links Deansgate with Cross Street, was originally known as Toll Lane; it was the only means of access into Acres Field where the annual Michaelmas fair was held. As late as the 1820s, it was still the only way to get into Cross Street because there was no proper entrance to the latter from Market Street.

Opposite: One of the busiest junctions in central Manchester was at the point where Cross Street and Corporation Street met Market Street. The area around the Royal Exchange was always very busy with pedestrians because of the number of offices in the Royal Exchange building itself and the fact that Corporation Street was the main access to Victoria station, one of Manchester's busiest. To these people were added those who arrived at Exchange station and made their way to the Exchange and the various financial institutions in and around the King Street area. In April 1914, a survey of both road and pedestrian traffic within a 1-mile radius of the Exchange showed that in a 24-hour period, over 1.13 million people entered the area, of whom over 440,000 were on foot, over 425,000 used the trams and 206,000 came by train. The survey also found that there were almost 100,000 vehicle movements past the 76 observation points that had been set up, of which almost 19,000 were tram car movements. The survey concluded that there had been a 5 per cent increase in traffic since 1911, when the first such survey had been held, and that there was also a 16.7 per cent increase in motor cars and 7.8 per cent increase in heavy motors, presumably meaning goods vehicles. This photograph accompanied the report and shows what purports to be ordinary traffic controlled by a policeman. Another illustration, on the back cover, shows the junction without a policeman on point duty. The newspaper headline is worthy of note: it reads 'Buckingham Palace Intruder. Court appeal for . . .' The rest is not easily legible, but could the missing word be 'clemency'?

One of the clues in dating postcards is a postmark, but sometimes postmarks can be very misleading. The postmark on this card is 25 April 1925, but the evidence in the picture indicates that the original photograph was taken during the Edwardian period as the trams are open top. There is a further clue to the fact that the photograph may date from either 1902 or 1903 because just to the right of the electric tram is what appears to be either a horse-drawn tram or bus and these were phased out in the first two or three years of the twentieth century. The main building in the photograph is the Cross Street façade of the Royal Exchange which was taken down when the Exchange was enlarged after the First World War. The demolition of this impressive portico was carried out at the request of Manchester City Council which wanted to widen Cross Street and agreed not to oppose the plans for the extension if the portico was removed. Although the scene at the corner of Cross Street and Market Street looked relatively peaceful when the photograph was taken, it was a hive of activity on Tuesdays and Thursdays, which were days of 'High 'Change' at the Royal Exchange.

An evening tram waits for the traffic lights at the junction of Cross Street, Market Street and Corporation Street on a wet night in the 1930s. Behind the line of cars, also waiting at the lights, is the ground floor of the Royal Exchange which was occupied by retail premises. The use of the ground floor for shops was a feature of many buildings erected in the latter half of the nineteenth century because of the high cost of land. The shop with all the lights on is Boots the Chemist, which first appeared in the 1923 directory as occupying the Market Street/Cross Street corner of the Exchange. The problem of servicing the shops in the Royal Exchange was solved in a novel way when it was enlarged. A special lift was constructed at the end of Bank Street which allowed a vehicle to be lowered into the basement. At the end of the underground service road there was a turntable so that the vehicle could be turned round and leave the building facing the correct way to drive out. Today, all new major shopping developments have an area for service vehicles, but the one at the Royal Exchange was among the earliest to be constructed and helped to reduce traffic congestion in the area.

For almost a century, Cross Street was associated with the *Manchester Guardian*, founded in 1821 as the voice of liberalism in Manchester. Originally, it was a weekly, but as the nineteenth century progressed it was published first twice a week and eventually became a daily. In 1868, the *Manchester Guardian* acquired the *Manchester Evening News*, founded to support the election campaign of Mitchell Henry who was dissatisfied with the coverage of his campaign to elected a Liberal MP for Manchester. The move was not unexpected as both papers shared the same liberal outlook on events. In 1886, both papers moved into purpose-built premises on Cross Street, which included editorial offices, newsrooms and presses. In 1959, the *Manchester Guardian* changed its name, dropping the word *Manchester* from its mast-head, a move which recognised its national readership. Both newspapers remained at Cross Street until about 1968 when the site was required for part of the Arndale development. Coincidentally, the move came at a time when new technology was beginning to appear, the buildings needed modernising and access to them for lorries carrying newsprint was not easy. A decision was taken to move from Cross Street and share the same building and presses as the *Daily Mail* on Deansgate, although there were no connections between the two papers. This photograph shows the beginning of the demolition work on the old *Manchester Guardian* and *Evening News* buildings, severing the link this part of Cross Street had had with the newspaper industry since the first half of the nineteenth century.

Manchester's original post office was in the Market Place, but when the Exchange opened in 1809, provision was made for it to be located there. However, with the introduction of the Penny Post, the post office was moved to its own building on Brown Street. It was argued that everyone had a right of access to the post office and that it should not be located in a building whose owners could exclude people without a good reason. The Brown Street building was enlarged in 1861, but the growing pressure on services and the increase in the number of letters and parcels handled resulted in the need for new accommodation. This was opened in 1884 and cost £120,000. The new post office not only included counter facilities, but also sorting offices. In 1890, the postmaster claimed that the sorting office handled 2 million letters, parcels and newspapers each week and this had risen to 4 million by 1900. It was claimed in 1895 that Manchester was responsible for about one-twelfth of all correspondence that emanated from the United Kingdom and was second only to London in the amount of post it generated. This photograph shows the building as it appeared in 1866 after its enlargement.

During the latter half of the eighteenth century, several new streets were created on the south side of the built-up area as landowners, like the Mosley family, began to sell the property they held there. One of the earliest of the new roads was Mosley Street. It was not entirely residential in character as several public buildings were to be found there. The earliest of these was Mosley Street Unitarian Chapel, which stood at the corner of Mosley Street and Marble Street (on a site now occupied by the Bradford & Bingley Building Society) between 1788 and 1834 when it moved to Upper Brook Street. In the same year, Mosley Street Independent Chapel was opened at the corner of Mosley Street and Charlotte Street, where it remained until 1848 when it moved to All Saints, becoming known as the Cavendish Street Chapel. In 1792, on the opposite corner to the Independent Chapel, the Manchester Assembly Rooms were opened. The Assembly Rooms were regarded as one of the most fashionable places in early nineteenth-century Manchester, but with changing tastes and the outward movement of the membership to the suburbs, they were closed in 1850 and the building was demolished. At the end of the eighteenth century the Manchester Academy fronted Mosley Street between Princess Street and St Peter's Square. John Dalton, the scientist who discovered colour blindness and the atomic theory, taught there from 1793 until the academy moved to York in 1803. An important building erected in the early nineteenth century was the Portico Library and Newsroom, designed by Thomas Harrison and opened in 1806; here members could read the current papers and borrow books. In this photograph of Mosley Street in the 1890s the building on the right is the Manchester City Art Gallery, designed by Sir Charles Barry for the Royal Manchester Institution and completed in 1829, while behind it is the Union Club, opened in 1825.

In July 1880, the Cheshire Lines Committee opened its new terminal station in Manchester. Central station replaced a temporary one on Watson Street that had opened in 1877. The main feature of the new station was a 210ft single-span arch, the third largest in the country, which is clearly seen in this photograph taken in about 1930. Unfortunately, the office block and hotel planned for the front of the station were never constructed which gave it the appearance of only being partially completed. Central was used by trains from three different companies: Manchester, Sheffield & Lincolnshire Railway; the Midland Railway; and the Great Northern Railway. Trains, or through coaches, from Central station ran to Chester and Liverpool as well as to London (St Pancras) via the Peak District, to Sheffield and to many other parts of the country. It was the Cheshire Lines Committee that introduced the policy of rounding fares down so that passengers and staff did not have to deal with small change – if the fare was 2s 7½d, it was rounded down to 2s 6d. The company also developed a reputation for efficiency, especially on its services to Liverpool, which were completed in 43 minutes non-stop or 45 minutes if a stop was made at Warrington. Central was one of the busiest of Manchester's commuter stations with passengers arriving from expanding residential areas like Flixton and Urmston to the west, and Withington, Didsbury and Chorlton-cum-Hardy to the south. Not all of the platforms were to be found under the arched roof. There were a couple on the Lower Mosley Street side of the station which handled local services; access to them was by the sign indicating the way to platforms 8 and 9. Today, the station has been converted into the GMEX exhibition centre.

During the first decade of the twentieth century, the section of Whitworth Street between Princess Street and Oxford Street underwent a dramatic transformation. The canal wharves in the area were sold for development. Several large and impressive warehouses were erected which gave the street the appearance of a canyon, clearly visible in this 1940 photograph. Some of the new warehouses were owned by Lloyd's Packing Company which leased the space at a low rent on condition that Lloyd's despatched all the goods that left the buildings. On the left is the Palace Theatre while on the right are the offices of the Refuge Assurance Company, which extended its frontage onto Whitworth Street in the 1930s. Today, several of these large warehouses have been converted into apartments while the former Refuge building is now a hotel.

In the late nineteenth and early twentieth centuries the southern end of Oxford Street underwent a dramatic transformation. The four corner sites at the junction of Oxford Street with Whitworth Street and Gloucester Street (later to become Whitworth Street West) became available for development and four new buildings were erected. Two of these, the Palace Theatre, completed in 1892 on the northern corner of Whitworth Street and Oxford Street, and St Mary's Hospital, completed in 1893 on the corner of Whitworth Street West and Oxford Street, are shown in this photograph. The other new buildings were the Refuge Insurance Offices, built between Whitworth Street and the railway line to Oxford Road station, the first part of which was completed in the 1890s, and a furniture shop, Shaws, at the junction of Oxford Street, Whitworth Street West and the approach to Oxford Road station, which was built in around 1905. In this picture, the site of the furniture shop is surrounded by hoardings. The tower in the middle distance is that of the St James's theatre, opened in the 1880s and closed in 1910, which described itself as the home of 'heavy drama'. Next to it was the St James's Hall, which was used for exhibitions of all kinds as well as for early cinematograph shows. These were eventually replaced by St James's Buildings. Just beyond the horse-drawn cart on the left is another vacant site which was to be developed as the Hippodrome, completed in 1904. In order to advertise what was being built, the developers have put a large notice around the top of the hoarding which prevents unauthorised access to a dangerous construction site. The tower which appears to be in the centre of Oxford Street is that of St Peter's Church, which was closed in 1906 and demolished in 1907, the outward movement of population from the area reducing the size of the congregation attending the church to virtually nothing.

Although the junction of Market Street, Cross Street and Corporation Street was regarded as one of the busiest in central Manchester, another hectic spot was the junction of Market Street, Piccadilly, Mosley Street and George Street by the Royal Hotel. In this photograph of the junction, taken in about 1903 or 1904, pedestrians, horse-drawn wagons and electric trams all vie for space. On the left of the picture is the Royal Hotel and Lewis's store while the large block of buildings on the right was the hub of the Rylands empire. The firm of John Rylands & Sons was established in 1823 by John Rylands when he came to Manchester from Wigan and set up a textile warehouse. Gradually, he expanded his interests to include spinning cotton, weaving and bleaching cloth and making cloth into clothing and other household items. His mills and works were scattered throughout the Manchester area from Wigan to Gorton, as well as being at Crewe. It is claimed that his firm was a good example of an integrated business, controlling everything from manufacturing the raw materials through to selling the finished product. John Rylands gradually extended the size of his warehouse in Manchester until it covered the area between High Street and Tib Lane and fronted on to Market Street. As well as clothing and household fabric, the firm also moved into making and selling furniture, some of it being manufactured at the former cotton mills on Oxford Road which were eventually demolished to make way for the Regal Twins, a cinema complex built in the early 1930s. John Rylands died a wealthy man, leaving over £1 million. His third wife used some of her fortune to establish the John Rylands Library on Deansgate. John Rylands lived his last thirty years at Longford Hall in Stretford, where he pursued his interest in gardening. He is said to have worked from 8 a.m. to 6 p.m., even when he was an old man.

Until the middle of the eighteenth century, the only building in what is now known as Piccadilly was Alkrington Hall, the town house of the Lever family. It was said to have been a black-and-white, half-timbered building with a small garden in the front. The Levers last used the building in 1771 when it was advertised for sale, the suggested uses being an inn or a school. By this time Piccadilly, or Lever's Row as it was known, was becoming more important because the Infirmary was located nearby. The building was sold in 1772 to John Travis, who converted it into an inn. Whether Travis gave it the name of the White Bear is uncertain but by 1801 it had become a coaching inn. A contemporary advertisement claimed that 'the only coach from Manchester to London without changing, the London and Manchester commercial post coach sets off from the above inn every Sunday, Tuesday and Thursday, to the Golden Cross, Charing Cross, in thirty-six hours, being quicker than any except the mail coaches'. However, the White Bear, seen here in 1904, was never a leading inn for long-distance coaches, although it was the starting and arrival point for the services that covered the local communities. During the nineteenth century, it was said to have been a popular place of entertainment for 'Manchester's tradesfolk' – this meant the men rather than their masters. The building was sold in the early twentieth century and demolished to be replaced by a restaurant.

This is the view you might have had if you were sitting on the upper deck of a horse-drawn tram entering Piccadilly in the 1890s. On the left is the Bridgewater Arms and Royal Hotel, built as a private residence around 1772 and converted into a hotel in 1828 when the Bridgewater Arms was displaced from High Street by warehouse developments. Beyond the hotel is the famous tower of Lewis's department store, which opened its doors in Manchester in 1877 and rapidly established itself as an important force in the city's retail trade. Not only did the store open on Saturdays, but it was also proud to deliver to the suburban area three times a day. Its market was the growing number of office and warehouse workers who poured into Manchester each day from residential suburbs like Rusholme, Fallowfield and Levenshulme. On the right is a building used by Black and Green, tea merchants, and next to it is the Mosley Hotel and beyond that, the White Bear. The Mosley Hotel moved to Piccadilly in the 1820s when its original premises on Market Street were required for road widening. In 1891 the Mosley Hotel was again demolished and a new hotel erected on an enlarged site; it was described as the 'largest and most commodious hotel' in Manchester with a clientele from all parts of the world.

During the first forty years of the twentieth century, Piccadilly underwent a series of changes. The demolition of the Manchester Royal Infirmary in 1910 resulted in the creation of a large open space and the council spent a considerable amount of time discussing what to do with it. However, in 1912, when the former Town Hall at the corner of Cross Street and King Street was declared to be structurally dangerous, temporary huts were erected on part of the former Infirmary site to house the reference library. These huts can be seen on the right of the photograph, just beyond the landscaped area. The building on the left-hand side of the picture is the Albion Hotel which was closed and demolished in 1926, the site being used for a new Woolworth's store. Next door to the Albion Hotel is a building which was demolished in about 1926 or 1927 to make way for a new bank at street level and offices on the upper floors. In 1928, the latter were taken over by the BBC as its Manchester studios.

This image of Piccadilly and the gardens is considerably less cluttered than the previous one. A large part of central Manchester had been damaged in the Christmas blitz of 1940 and the work of reconstruction and redesigning part of central Manchester was just beginning to get under way when this photograph was taken in 1957. Parker Street bus station in the foreground was created in the 1930s to reduce the congestion so apparent in the previous photograph – it looks very bleak in this picture. Although some bus shelters have been erected close to Piccadilly Gardens, passengers waiting for buses which departed from the central part of the station had to brave the elements. Eventually, shelters were erected to protect them. Today, Metrolink has its Piccadilly station where the buses are waiting, close to the gardens, and the whole area is being refurbished and improved. The photograph also shows how the landscaping of the gardens themselves had become well established, providing a pleasant, green, open area in the centre of the city. In the background are the buildings housing three of Manchester's largest shops – Lewis's, Rylands and Littlewoods.

London Road station, now known as Piccadilly station, was the terminus on the south side of Manchester for the London & North Western Railway (LNWR) and also the Manchester terminus for the Manchester, Sheffield & Lincolnshire Railway (MS & L). The original station, built by the Manchester & Birmingham Railway, later part of the LNWR, was opened in 1842 and consisted of two platforms, one for arrivals and the other for departures. The station was rebuilt between 1860 and 1866 to cater for the rapidly growing number of people travelling by train. The office building in the centre of the picture was jointly shared by the two companies, whose relationship in the 1840s and 1850s was far from cordial. When the station was rebuilt, not only was there a fence erected between the platforms used by the different companies, but they were even designated differently: the MS & L lettered its platforms while the LNWR used numbers. By the right-hand edge of the office block is the arched roof covering platforms 8 to 12 which were constructed by the LNWR in the 1880s to cater for the increased commuter traffic and the milk traffic from north Cheshire. On the left is a signal arm which controlled access to the MS & L's goods yard and warehouse which was located at the side of the approach to the station where Gateway House and the station car parks are now located. The office building in front of the station was replaced in 1958 when British Railways began a programme of modernisation and electrified the line to London. (*J. Ryan*)

London Road station was built at the end of a viaduct which carried the railway over the River Medlock and gave a level approach to the station. Initially, access was via steps from Store Street, but in the 1850s, an approach road was constructed which allowed vehicles to take passengers and goods right up to the front of the station. This photograph from the early twentieth century shows the approach road, which was used by taxis and hansom cabs, together with the warehouse belonging to the Manchester, Sheffield & Lincolnshire Railway (left). To the right of the station approach is the beginning of London Road, which drops down to cross the River Medlock near where Mancunian Way now crosses the main road. The chimney on the right is part of a cotton mill, of which there were several on London Road in the nineteenth and early twentieth centuries. One mill has been preserved and converted into a hotel, a reminder of the days when this part of central Manchester was industrial. The two cupolas in the background are on the London Road façade of the fire station, completed in 1904. This must have been a very dangerous junction for pedestrians to deal with in the days before lights and crossings. From the photograph, it appears that the island occupied by the street light and the column for the overhead tram wires was used as a refuge by those waiting for a gap in the traffic. (*J. Ryan*)

Opposite, top: The approach to Piccadilly station (the modern name for London Road station), *c.* 1970. Central to the photograph is the 'lazy S' of Gateway House, which is said to have been developed from a doodle on a menu. The building replaced the railway warehouses which formerly stood on the site. When this photograph was taken, the shop units had still to be let. To the right of Gateway House are the offices and booking hall of the station, which replaced the 1860s building when British Railways decided a new development was more in keeping with its modern image. Behind the booking hall are the arches of what is often referred to as the 'train shed' but is the place where trains arrive and depart. The 'train shed', the basic structure of which dates from the mid-nineteenth century, has recently been refurbished and the details on its columns have been picked out.

In 1820, a new Roman Catholic church was opened on the edge of Manchester – St Augustine's, Granby Row. This church rapidly attracted a large congregation as well as a reputation for fine singing. It is said that when there were visiting Italian opera companies in Manchester, they would augment the church choir and give performances which attracted a large number of non-Catholics to hear mass being sung. The church closed in 1906 and the congregation moved to York Street in Chorlton-on-Medlock. The reason for the closure was not the declining population of the area, but because the noise and vibration caused by machinery and equipment at the nearby College of Technology (now UMIST) affected the building and disturbed worshippers. This postcard, dating from about 1905, shows the interior of St Augustine's church with its high vaulted roof, which must have produced very good acoustics for the singers. The replacement church was destroyed in 1940 during the Christmas blitz and worshippers eventually merged with another Catholic congregation to form a new church at All Saints.

This photograph and the ones that follow were taken in 1979 from the very top of Piccadilly Plaza, looking south towards Piccadilly station. The view is dominated by the Minshull Street police courts, now a crown court, which were designed by Thomas Worthington and opened in 1868. During the 1990s, the building was refurbished and extended after the building to the left of the original courts was demolished. In the top left-hand corner is Gateway House, often described as being in the shape of a 'lazy S', which was built on the site of the former Manchester, Sheffield & Lincolnshire Railway goods warehouses. In the background is Piccadilly station with the arches which cover the platforms clearly visible, together with the modern tower block which was erected when the station was modernised in the early 1960s. The view also shows the triangular shape of London Road fire station, opened in 1904, while in front of it are the remains of two cotton mills, which have since been converted into a hotel.

Looking westwards from the roof of Piccadilly Plaza, along Mosley Street, it is possible to see the Midland Hotel (centre), the former Central station (behind) and the Town Hall extension (right) together with the roof of the Art Gallery and a small part of Central Library and the Town Hall. The former Central station was opened in 1880 and the Midland Hotel in 1904. Adjacent to the former Central station is the Great Northern Railway company's warehouse, opened in 1898, which was one of the earliest steel-framed structures in the country. When this photograph was taken, the railway no longer used the warehouse or the adjacent railway sidings. The place which they once occupied had been turned into car parks to cater for the growing number of people who travelled into Manchester by car. The tall white building on the left is Peter House. It partially covers the site of the former Prince's Theatre, which closed in 1940.

Manchester's Town Hall is one of the most impressive in the country and dominates Albert Square. The Town Hall dominates the left-hand side of this photograph with its Princess Street elevation clearly visible. On the opposite side of the Albert Square, facing the Town Hall, there is a large vacant site visible. Originally there were a number of warehouses here, including the offices of Blacklock's, who published Bradshaw's railway timetables. The warehouses were demolished to make way for modern office buildings in a scheme which also incorporated the pedestrianisation of Brazennose Street and the creation of Lincoln Square. It is also possible to see the 'Hidden Gem', otherwise known as St Mary's, Mulberry Street. This Catholic church was opened in 1794 and rebuilt in 1844. It was the second Catholic church to be opened in Manchester.

This particular view from the roof of Piccadilly Plaza concentrates on King Street and looks towards Salford. In the foreground, surrounded by scaffolding, is Lutyens' Midland Bank, a steel frame encased in white Portland stone, completed in 1929. Partially hidden behind the bank is Harry Fairhurst's 1926 building for the Manchester Ship Canal Co. On the opposite side of King Street, across the road from the Midland Bank, the upper part of the Reform Club is visible, completed in 1871 to designs by Edward Salomons. The structure dominating the right-hand side of this photograph is the black stone-clad NatWest Building completed in the 1960s on the site of the District Bank, which had been erected over the site of the York Hotel, where the Anti-Corn Law League held its earliest meeting. Peeping out from behind the NatWest building is the Edwardian baroque of Lloyds Bank, completed in 1912 on the site of Manchester's original Town Hall. Looking into the background, it is possible to see where the railway line from Liverpool to Manchester Exchange and Victoria stations joins with the line from Bolton and Preston, both built on viaducts to provide the trains with easy gradients in and out of Manchester.

Looking down from the top of Piccadilly Plaza across Piccadilly, the Woolworth's store, which was opened in 1926 on the site of the Albion Hotel, can be seen. According to a French visitor to Manchester in the mid-nineteenth century, this hotel had a plain brick exterior, but its cuisine was among the best in Europe. Like other hotels in central Manchester in the nineteenth century, its manager was from continental Europe while guests came from many parts of the world. In the nineteenth century, many of the city's leading hotels were to be found in the vicinity of Piccadilly. Next door to Woolworth's was the home of the BBC for around forty years. The building, erected in the mid-1920s, had a bank at ground-floor level while the upper floors housed radio and television offices and studios. By the time the BBC moved from here to new premises in Chorlton-on-Medlock, its offices had expanded into the adjoining building to the right, which had been erected by Kitson's who were tailors. On the right-hand side of the photograph, there is a small building which appears to have been 'squashed' in between other buildings. In fact, the others were built around it. This small building is the last of the type which would have once graced Piccadilly. Many were occupied at the beginning of the nineteenth century by members of the medical profession because they were close to the Infirmary, which was located on the site of Piccadilly Gardens.

CHAPTER FIFTEEN

POSTERS

Until the middle of the twentieth century, advertising was mainly found in newspapers, magazines, on hoardings or on gable-end walls of houses and factories. Advertisers tried to catch the eye of the passer-by rather than his ears. Many posters were very striking, their image being more important than their words. Today, things are somewhat different. Commercial television and radio now bring advertisements more into the home and there is greater emphasis on the moving image, the spoken word, music and jingles. This chapter is not concerned with advertisements which appear in magazines, newspapers, on television or radio, but with the posters that were pasted on walls, gable ends and hoardings, adding colour to the streets of many towns and villages. Today, painted adverts on gable walls are no longer permitted but it is still possible to see the faded remains of some of them, especially where the gable wall has had a later building erected against it.

Although many posters and advertisements had relatively long lives, some were only short lived. Their importance lies in the immediacy of their message. Examples include notices or advertisements chalked on boards or walls or the newspaper billboard. Advertisements in this category can be changed quickly, but their objective is to encourage the public to enter the premises and purchase the product. Longer-lived advertisements and posters were those that were specially printed, stuck to walls and hoardings and could only be changed by sticking a new poster over them or being worn away by the weather.

Hand-bills and official notices can be traced back to the sixteenth and seventeenth centuries, but it was developments in printing in the nineteenth century that enabled the advertising industry to take advantage of the hoardings around building sites, gable-end walls and even special sites purchased on railway stations or on the sides of trams and buses. These advertisements show the gradual development of commercial pressure on people to buy goods which they might not otherwise have considered purchasing and also to make them aware of the existence of a particular shop or product.

Not all posters were used to advertise products or shops. The entertainment industry made extensive use of the medium, often outside theatres and music halls. In some cases, posters provided the only information available about what a particular place of entertainment was putting on. They were aimed at getting the general public inside the building and this was also true of posters outside churches, which have recently adopted a higher profile.

Although posters are generally associated with selling, some gave official information, such as details of election candidates or the compulsory purchase of buildings to enable redevelopment to take place. Sometimes posters and advertisements like the ones shown in this section are the only sources of information on a particular product or firm.

It is interesting to note that old advertisements, or rather the characters or images of these advertisements, occasionally reappear today. When this happens, one wonders whether the creator has been looking through old photographs for ideas.

As many posters were stuck on walls and hoardings, the photograph has enabled details of what they looked like and their message to be preserved for posterity. Many more posters have survived on photographs than in material collected by libraries and archive departments or in copies retained by printers for their own records. This chapter reveals some of the many posters on the walls, hoardings and gable ends of buildings in central Manchester which have survived through the medium of photography. Many of the photographs which are reproduced in other parts of the book also include advertisements and posters as part of the background.

When the block of buildings bounded by Lloyd Street, Cooper Street and Mount Street were demolished in the early 1930s to make way for the Town Hall extension, one enterprising firm, Poster Advertising, took advantage of the hoardings around the site. Unfortunately, it is only possible to read some of the advertisements. The first, for the company responsible for the advertisements, proclaims 'Posters bring definite results'. Others are for Rozalex soap, Worthington's beers, Palethorpe's sausages, Symington's coffee and Imperial bricks. There is also a bill for a show or a film, but it is not possible to identify where this is being staged or shown. The building being demolished looks like a former warehouse with the large entrance gateway on the left, although there is no evidence of a yard. Perhaps the goods were lifted by hoist directly into the building.

Although the Gentlemen's Concert Hall had an imposing front elevation, the side on Lower Mosley Street appears to have been a very plain brick wall with only three windows and possibly two doors. It was an ideal site for posters: not only could a large number be displayed, but it was near a major road junction and would be seen each day by hundreds of people passing along Oxford Street to Peter Street or entering central Manchester by way of Lower Mosley Street and from Central station. It is not known when the Gentlemen's Concert Society first allowed the wall to be used for posters, but it is possible that it was not until the 1880s or 1890s when the society was having difficulty in attracting audiences and raising money to maintain the building. This photograph was taken on 5 March 1897, just over twelve months before the building was closed and demolished to make way for the Midland Hotel. The wall includes advertisements for Nestlé's milk, Symington's coffee essence, Chiver's jellies, Zebra grate polish, Compo for colds, Seymour Mead's tea (which cost 1s 10d a pound!), Smith's pianos and Lewis's 'Sovereign' suites, as well as two posters for theatres' productions – *Babes in the Wood* at the Prince's Theatre on Oxford Road and *Antony and Cleopatra* at the Queen's Theatre on Bridge Street.

Between the wars, there was a proposal to build a new hotel at the bottom of the approach to London Road (now Piccadilly) station on the site now occupied by the Rodwell Tower. The notice on the warehouse in this picture from the 1930s warns of the development. It looks as though only the ground floor of the warehouse was still occupied with Themans, who were tobacconists, while on the first and second floors there appear to be lights in the windows, suggesting that this part of the building was still in use. The advertising hoarding conceals the Rochdale Canal as it passes under Piccadilly, where there was a small wharf which serviced the warehouse and buildings behind. However, the most striking thing about the photograph, other than the lack of traffic on what was, and still is, a very busy road, is the posters. Among them are several for places of entertainment including Belle Vue Circus, George Formby at the Apollo in Ardwick, *Dick Whittington* at the Palace Theatre, *The Lady Vanishes* at the Deansgate cinema, Vivien Leigh and Charles Laughton starring in *St Martin's Lane*, *The Saint* at the Paramount (now the Odeon) on Oxford Street and *This Way Please* at the Hulme Hippodrome. The adverts include several for alcoholic drinks such as Guinness, Johnny Walker, Bass No. 1 Barley Wine, Threlfalls Mild Ale and Mackeson's stout, while others encourage the observant reader to consider purchasing Atora suet, Bovril and Mazda light bulbs.

Sometimes notices or advertisements are very ephemeral – merely chalked on a board, with the result that they are easily removed either by individuals or by the weather. This photograph was taken late in 1922 or early in 1923 and shows the former Sun Inn at Poet's Corner on Long Millgate where the photographer has captured two different types of poster. The most obvious one, and the easiest to read, is chalked on a former shop sign for the company which was located there. It is for 'wireless supplies' and dates from the days of the 'cat's whisker', when broadcasting was still in its infancy. It is possible that at this time Manchester was still known by its call-sign '2ZY' and was still broadcasting from Trafford Park. The other poster is of the more traditional type and relates to the sale of antiques; a close examination reveals that the antiques are furniture and that the sale includes seventeen eight-day grandfather clocks, six Chippendale mahogany chairs and Lancashire oak settles. However, more interesting is the wording which appears just below 'Capes, Dunn & Co.', which indicates that the building itself was being sold at the same time 'without reserve', on Wednesday 13 December 1922. The Sun Inn was demolished shortly after it was sold and central Manchester lost one of its oldest surviving buildings. A link with the city's literary past was severed for it was here in 1842 that a group of local poets used to meet and read their works. As a result, the bend on Long Millgate where the building was located had become known as Poet's Corner.

Long Millgate is one of the oldest streets in Manchester and still retains its medieval twists and turns. This photograph was taken looking towards Poet's Corner on 17 December 1921 and shows the building adjoining the former Sun Inn. The building seems to have been a bookshop but its gable wall had become a regular site for one of Manchester's bill posting companies. As well as advertisements for Ideal Milk (the poster at the top of the display), Palethorpe's sausages, Harris's Wiltshire sausages, Toblerone and Seymour Mead's tea, there is also a poster promoting Veno's cough mixture, which is partly obscured by a sign prohibiting motors from entering the back yard. Behind the gate is an advertisement for the Midland Picture Theatre. This was located in the former concert hall inside the Midland Hotel which had been converted into a cinema earlier in 1921.

Although this photograph was taken in a residential part of Manchester, possibly the Hulme area, the advertisers have still made full use of all the available space to get their message across. There are adverts not only for bicycles such as Centaur and Golden Sunbeam, but also for Lewis's hats, for Blackpool as a holiday resort and for OK Sauce. On the right can be seen some of the many newsprint billboard posters which were published each week. These have been pasted to the walls and doors of a small newsagent's kiosk, presumably to attract customers. At the very top of the left-hand hoarding is a notice advertising the fact that the site was for sale and that the auctioneers were W.H. Robinson's. The latter was established in the mid-nineteenth century and was one of Manchester's leading property auctioneers. Although the illustration is not dated, there is a clue on one of the newspaper billboards which refers to 'Daily Mail Pension experiment'; this suggests that the photograph might have been taken in about 1907. Mention is also made of suffragettes taking over a Liberal Party meeting. The photograph shows the way in which posters were stuck one on top of another; when they began to peel off, the old ones were exposed again.

Opposite: This collection of posters and shop adverts from about 1921 or 1922 was to be found on Charles Street. The photograph clearly shows how every available site was used for advertising in the days when posters were one of the main ways of getting a message across. According to local trade directories, the shop selling furs was occupied by an H.A. Blaiwais and was only there for a short time before the building was demolished to make way for a new development. Previously, the premises had been occupied for many years by a firm of clothiers trading as the Oxford Clothing Company. According to the directory of 1922, E. Hood of the Cosy Café in the picture was Evelyn Hood, who was a fried fish dealer: the café is first recorded in 1921. In 1923 there are no entries for the Cosy Café, which had been open for almost twelve hours a day to serve those who lived and worked in the area. Earlier directories list the previous occupier as a Sarah Ann Whalley, who was a shopkeeper. The adverts to the left of Cosy Café are mainly for entertainment, including *Tom Tom the Piper's Son* which was on at the Opera House. It appears that this was the Christmas pantomime, but the fact that the Palace Theatre was advertising *Mona Vivian* suggests that the pantomime season was over and that the opera house's poster had not been replaced. The very dark poster is for the Majestic, but it is not possible to make out who was appearing there at this time.

Newspapers were often distributed by sellers walking the
streets. In the early twentieth century, there were a great
many of these, but now the numbers are declining and they
tend to have fixed pitches or sites. This particular seller is
carrying a poster encouraging people to purchase the paper
with news of the relief of Ladysmith in 1900 during the
Boer War.

During the interwar years, the number of motor vehicles on the roads increased dramatically, as did their speed. In order to make the general public aware of the dangers of motor traffic and encourage them to be more road safety conscious, Manchester City Council came up with the idea of a mobile advert. It decided to use one of its trams and covered it with road safety adverts. Whether the tram remained parked in one place or moved throughout the city is not clear as it was photographed in the depot. The tram itself was built in the early 1920s and was capable of carrying seventy-eight passengers in normal service.

Opposite: One of the perennial problems facing businesses which occupy only part of a building or are located in a court is ensuring that customers know where to find them. Some businesses overcame this difficulty by placing their name on a board at the entrance to the court or building so that customers knew who was where. This collection of nameboards was located at the Corporation Street end of Bull's Head Court and represented an interesting array of businesses. The first shop on the left of the illustration does not really need any written text to tell the passer-by what it offered – it was a locksmith's as the key clearly shows. Further along the court another three-dimensional advert can be seen – a large pair of spectacles which were used by an optician to advertise his presence. At the far end of the court, just beyond the figure, is the corner of the Wellington Inn, located in the Market Place.

This photograph clearly shows how poster companies used every available space to advertise their clients' products. Apart from two well-known firms – Quaker Oats and Greenhalgh's Preserves – there are posters for the *Manchester Weekly Times*, which ceased publication in 1922, and for two places of entertainment, the Alexandra on Hamilton Road in Longsight and the Hippodrome, which was on Oxford Street in central Manchester. The Alexandra's poster gives a date, 13 October, but no year. Assuming that the film opened on Monday evening, the year the photograph was taken would have been 1913 or 1919.

Posters were not only to be found in the centre of towns. Vacant sites or gable walls in the suburban areas were also very much favoured. This collection of posters was to be found on Factory Lane in Blackley in 1907 and brightened up a rather dreary corner. The products advertised included well-known brands such as Oxo, McDougall's flour, Seymour Mead's tea, Bass beer and the products of one of Manchester's local brewery's, Walker & Homfray's. However, others are equally interesting such as John Hill & Sons' cream crackers, Remy's starch and a powder which killed all types of insects. As well as the advertisements for products, there are also two for places of entertainment: Belle Vue and Queen's Park Hippodrome. (*Victorian Society*)

CHAPTER SIXTEEN

SUBURBAN MANCHESTER

Until 1838, the name 'Manchester' was applied only to the centre of the present-day city. The surrounding areas were independent townships within the parish of Manchester and as such were responsible for their own administration, if any proper administration existed. However, as conditions in the central area deteriorated, those who could afford it began to move to more pleasant surroundings on the edge of the town. Each of the new townships was centred on a village or hamlet which gave it its name and these have been preserved today as the titles of districts. Although most people regard suburbs as residential areas, it should be remembered that suburban areas can be divided into three general groups: residential, industrial and those where there is a mixture of both industrial and residential premises.

The earliest suburban development in Manchester appears to have taken place in the St John's Street/Byrom Street area in the 1770s, but by the beginning of the nineteenth century, the trend was starting to move into surrounding townships like Ardwick and Cheetham. These areas were within easy reach of central Manchester where the factories, warehouses and other business premises were located, yet far enough away to provide a rural setting for the new homes.

However, to the east, still within the township of Manchester, the industrial suburb of Ancoats, dominated by multi-storey mills on the banks of the Rochdale and Ashton Canals, developed in the late eighteenth and early nineteenth centuries. At the same time, the part of Chorlton-on-Medlock closest to Manchester also began to become an industrial area with the erection of Chorlton Mills on the banks of the River Medlock. Industrial suburbs were characterised by factories, mills and often poor quality housing.

Improvements in transport gave further impetus to the outward expansion of Manchester and the development of residential suburbs. In 1824, the first horse-drawn omnibus was introduced from Pendleton into Manchester. Shortly afterwards, other routes were developed to areas including Greenheys to the south. Throughout the nineteenth century horse bus, and later horse-drawn tram, routes expanded and fares fell making it easier for people to move away from the overcrowded central area. After 1851, the population of central Manchester began to fall, slowly at first, but at an accelerating rate. At the same time, the popularity of places like Rusholme, Levenshulme, Withington and Crumpsall as residential areas increased. Often it was the redevelopment of residential parts of the city centre that forced people to move. The poorest, who were often those most affected, moved only short distances into adjacent areas. Those already living just out of the city centre either stayed or moved a little further out. Often those who had moved into a new area from an adjacent one were often regarded as being of a lower social status and were therefore considered to be lowering the character of the area. Existing residents often moved on to a new area, creating a sort of ripple effect of movement outwards.

The industrial suburbs tended to be concentrated on the eastern side of Manchester. Richard Peacock of Beyer Peacock summed it up when he said that the reason why he chose Gorton for the Manchester, Sheffield & Lincolnshire Railway's works in the 1840s was that this was the first place where the land and the railway were at the same level,

The area often referred to as Ancoats sweeps round the eastern end of the township of Manchester, linking the Rivers Irk and Medlock. It was never an independent township like Ardwick or Cheetham although technically it is not one of Manchester's suburbs either. For many centuries, one of the area's most important buildings was Ancoats Hall, was one of the homes of the Mosley family in the seventeenth century. The original half-timbered building was demolished in the early nineteenth century and replaced by the Georgian one shown in this late nineteenth-century photograph. The Mosleys ceased to use it in the late eighteenth century and sold it. During the nineteenth century the building was not only used for residential purposes. In the 1880s, it was converted into an art museum by Thomas Horsfall, who aimed to bring some culture and appreciation of the fine arts and countryside to the residents of this overcrowded edge of central Manchester. Eventually, after being used as a railwaymen's social centre for several years, the building was demolished because the land was required for a road improvement scheme.

but also that the rates were lower, the land cheaper and that there was access to the skilled labour in nearby Manchester.

It was not until 1838 that the borough of Manchester was created, comprising the townships of Manchester, Hulme, Chorlton-on-Medlock, Ardwick and Cheetham. These latter areas provided Manchester with its first residential suburbs, but as the town grew, they became increasingly built up and the wealthier residents began to move away. Almost fifty years later, in 1885, the boundaries of the city were extended to include Rusholme, Harpurhey and Bradford, whose populations had been swelled by those who moved away from Manchester to live in more pleasant surroundings.

The next phase of Manchester's expansion took place in 1890 when Clayton, Crumpsall, Moston, Blackley, Openshaw and part of Gorton joined the city. The beginning of the twentieth century saw further expansion. In 1904, Withington, Didsbury, Chorlton-cum-Hardy and Moss Side became part of Manchester, although in the case of Moss Side, there was a strenuous rear-guard campaign to try to prevent the inevitable. Expansion into the south-east part of Lancashire was completed in 1909 when Levenshulme and West Gorton became part of the city. However, Manchester still needed more space, especially with the advent of slum clearance programmes between the wars. In 1931, a portion of north Cheshire was taken over to form Wythenshawe, which was to be a new town for those displaced by slum clearance in areas like Hulme, Ancoats and Ardwick.

This selection of photographs does not cover all the suburbs of Manchester – space does not permit. It should also be remembered that there are photographs of some of the suburbs in other sections of the book. For example, there are images of firms like Clayton Aniline, which is in Clayton, and Beyer Peacock, located in Gorton, in the section on industry, while others appear in the section covering recreation.

The railway line linking London Road station with Oxford Road station forms a sort of dividing line between central Manchester and the surrounding inner-city suburbs. Until the construction of the Mancunian Way in the late 1960s and early 1970s, this was very noticeable on London Road. To the north of the railway were large, impressive buildings while to the south the road was lined with small shops, some of which had living accommodation on the upper floors. This photograph of London Road, taken in the early 1950s, shows the spot where London Road, central Manchester, becomes London Road, Ardwick, the boundary being the River Medlock, the bridge over which the van in the photograph is crossing. In 1939, the shops on this section of London Road were selling everything from dog food to wireless parts, from confectionery to baby clothes. There was even a tattoo artist recorded in the directory for that year. After the war, the shops were less varied, but in 1951, there were still stores selling baby clothes, surgical rubber goods, radios, tyres, bar fittings, confectionery and newspapers. Other businesses found in this area included a butcher, a wood carver and a hairdresser. In the background is the roof of London Road station. All this area has since been demolished and is now covered by the Mancunian Way and its associated roads.

The boundary between central Manchester and Ancoats is difficult to define. However, it is often assumed that Great Ancoats Street/Swan Street is a kind of dividing line between the two. This photograph, taken between 1893 and 1898, reveals the view along Rochdale Road towards Collyhurst and Harpurhey, and shows the junction with Angel Street which led down to Angel Meadow where living conditions left much to be desired. The shop on the corner of Angel Street and Rochdale Road is Steel & Cleaver, butcher, which occupied 31 Rochdale Road between 1893 and 1898. Previously the premises had been used for a chemist's or druggist's shop. After Steel & Cleaver left, the building continued to be used as a butcher's for a number of years before the area was demolished as part of Manchester's slum clearance programme. The family are passing in front of a wholesale jewellers while the secondhand shop which the man is passing also housed an insurance company.

Opposite: About 4 miles east of central Manchester lies Charlestown, which was described in 1890 as a 'picturesque and quaint little village' close to the Rochdale Road at Blackley. Despite its proximity to Manchester and the industrialised valley of the River Medlock, Charlestown retained its rural appearance and atmosphere into the twentieth century. One of the area's most prominent residents in the nineteenth century was the radical author Samuel Bamford, who is said to have written many of his most important works here, including *Passages in the life of a radical*, *Walks in South Lancashire* and a glossary of Lancashire words and phrases. When Bamford moved to Charlestown, the area was still relatively free from pollution and considerably quieter than his former home in Middleton, which was a rapidly growing mill town. At Charlestown, Bamford ran the local post office. His garden was reported to be 'neat . . . laid out with daisies, wallflowers, sweet pink, white rock, polyanthus, and rose trees, and a beautiful woodbine . . . entwined over the door'. This photograph, taken in the 1890s, shows the rural nature of the community.

In the nineteenth and early twentieth centuries, the temperance movement was very strong in Manchester, especially in the Methodist Church and its various branches. This photograph shows Chancery Lane Wesleyan School and Mission in Ardwick. According to Les Sutton in his unpublished work on Ardwick, this chapel could trace its origins back to the late eighteenth century when a Sunday school was established in the area. The chapel prospered in the nineteenth century attracting a large congregation of local people. In 1879, it was decided to replace the original chapel with a larger one, which opened in 1880. Chancery Lane Sunday School had a sick club for teachers and scholars as early as 1821 while Bank Meadow School, which eventually merged with Chancery Lane's school, had its own sick and burial society. The latter's work was taken over by the temperance movement. This photograph, believed to have been taken in the early twentieth century, shows what must be a Sunday school procession, possibly during Whit Week when the scholars and teachers paraded around the district in their best clothes with Sunday school and temperance banners. The clean white clothes of those taking part in the procession contrast with the dress of the bystanders on the pavement, some of whom may have been members of the church. The building was demolished in the mid-1950s as the area was gradually redeveloped.

In the Middle Ages, Blackley was part of a deer park which belonged to the lords of the manor of Manchester. Whether it included the large open space acquired by Manchester City Council in 1894 and known as Boggart Hole Clough is not known, but it is more than likely that it did as records refer to deer leaps in the area. The land on which Boggart Hole Clough was created included a stream with steep sides which was of little use for development purposes. The land acquired in 1894 provided the parks department with an ideal spot for growing plants which could not be cultivated elsewhere in the city because of atmospheric pollution. As well as pleasant walks, the department also created a boating lake, which was said to provide views across the Irk valley towards the Pennines and to be above the pollution which often blanketed the area. This photograph, which may have started life as a family snapshot, shows 'Reg and Meg' in a rowing boat, possibly during the interwar years.

As Manchester expanded in the late eighteenth century, the number of people living in the surrounding townships also increased, although more slowly than in the centre of the city. For those living at the northern end of the township of Cheetham, it was a long walk into Manchester to attend the nearest Church of England place of worship, which was the Collegiate Church. Consequently, the church authorities were prepared to look favourably on proposals to erect new churches in outlying areas. Technically, new churches were chapels and not parish churches in their own right although they performed the functions of a parish church. In 1790, Charles Ethelson proposed that a new church be built at the northern end of Cheetham, close to its boundary with Crumpsall. The new church, shown here in about 1918, was consecrated in July 1794 and dedicated to St Mark. The Ethelson family continued to provide the clergy for St Mark's Church until 1872 when Revd Hart Ethelson died. When the church was built, it was a simple brick building: the tower was not added until 1894. It was surrounded by what were described as 'merchants' or gentlemen's villas'. Some of these properties still remain although they have been converted into offices and shops. The church itself is hidden from the main road and today its future is in doubt as a viable place of worship.

In 1890, St Luke's Church on Cheetham Hill Road was described in *Manchester Faces and Places* as being 'surrounded by a forest of gravestones' and that 'with its fine crocketted spire and pinnacles', it was a 'noteworthy object in the Cheetham Hill district'. This photograph, taken in the early twentieth century, shows how impressive the church appeared from the main road. Built at a cost of £23,000, it was designed by V.W. Atkinson and is said to have been modelled on Louth parish church, Lincolnshire. It was consecrated in 1839. The organ, built by Hill's of London, was said to have been one of the finest in Manchester. When it was inaugurated in 1840, St Luke's choir was augmented by members from the choirs of Westminster Abbey, St Paul's Cathedral and the Chapel Royal. When Felix Mendelsohn visited Manchester to conduct 'Elijah' at the Gentlemen's Concert Hall Society in April 1847, he stayed with Charles Souchay and visited St Luke's Church where he spent 1½ hours playing the organ. At the time of its construction St Luke's was a fashionable church in a select residential area, but as the nineteenth century progressed, the merchants and businessmen moved further away and the open fields which surrounded St Luke's were built on. Today, only the lower part of the tower remains – the church developed dry-rot in the 1970s and had to be demolished. The organ was removed and taken to St John's in Radcliffe.

In 1838, the township of Cheetham was incorporated in the new borough of Manchester. At that time it was becoming a residential area for merchants and businessmen as it lay only a short distance away from both Manchester and Salford and had pleasant views across the Irk valley to the Pennines. This early twentieth-century photograph shows Cheetham Hill Road (originally known as York Street). In the mid-nineteenth century several imposing buildings were built along the road; these included the Assembly Rooms, offices for the Prestwich Board of Guardians, Cheetham Public Hall and Baths, erected in the 1850s (the tower of which can be seen in the photograph), and several synagogues, for Cheetham Hill was the centre for Manchester jewry. This photograph shows the junction of Cheetham Hill Road and Heath Street, looking towards Manchester. In 1876, *City Lantern* pointed out that the residents of Cheetham Hill had no need to go into Manchester to shop as everything they might require was available there – except banks and pawnbrokers!

The River Mersey formed part of the southern boundary of the city of Manchester between 1904 and 1931 and, with its wide flood plain and tendency to burst its banks, formed a natural barrier against development – it still does today. Attempts to reduce the effect of flooding and make the land economically viable were made in the Middle Ages when the first embankments were constructed to contain the river. However, flooding continued and even today, with the original embankments raised and reinforced, floods still happen along the Mersey in Manchester, especially in the Northendon and Didsbury areas. As a result, development on the Mersey flood plain has been restricted to a few farms, an inn and, in the late nineteenth century, Withington Local Board of Health's sewage facilities in Chorlton. The farms and cottages built close to the Mersey tended to be on the river terrace, above the usual flood level. One of these was Hardy Lane Farm, shown here in 1931 when Hardy Lane was a pleasant rural road. Hardy Lane itself led to Jackson's Bridge and the Bridge Inn, which was the only place to cross the river in this area.

Opposite: Between 1596 and 1845 the Mosley family were Lords of the Manor of Manchester. The first Mosley to hold the position was Sir Nicholas, who purchased it for £3,500 from John Lacy of London. Nicholas was a member of the City of London and became Lord Mayor of London in 1599. The family, however, was not new to the Manchester area as Jenkyn Mosley, one of Nicholas's ancestors, is recorded as having lived at Hough End Hall in about 1465. At that time it was probably a black-and-white, half-timbered house, but when Nicholas took up residence, he had the hall rebuilt in brick. It is said that he used brick because he did not like living in timber-framed buildings, having lived in brick ones in London. The new building, shown here in about 1906, was described in the early twentieth century as 'a charming, well-proportioned example of one of the most interesting phases of English architecture', although by the time this was written, the building had been altered from its original state and portions of it had been rebuilt. The brick walls, constructed on a thick stone plinth, were said to be 2ft 1in thick at ground-floor level. The Mosleys continued to live at Hough End until 1720 when it appears to have become a farmhouse, which it remained to the end of the nineteenth century. At various times, its existence has been threatened by road schemes, but nothing has ever come of them. In 1927, it was suggested that the building, which was gradually deteriorating, should be restored and converted into a hall of residence, leased to a society or turned into an art gallery. Ten years later, the cost of restoring the building was put at between £2,000 and £6,000, but little was done until the 1970s when it was converted into a restaurant. Today, the hall is hidden from view by a modern office block.

During the last seventy-five years the part of Barlow Moor Road which is in the centre of Chorlton village has changed little. This picture was taken in the early 1950s and shows the portion of the road between Wallworth Avenue (later renamed Needham Avenue) and Wilbraham Road, which was formerly known as Pemberton Arcade. (By the 1930s, this name had been dropped from the directories.) Over the years, the type of shops here changed. In 1906, they included a chemist, a photographer, a fruiterer, a draper, a confectioner, butcher, provision merchant and a hairdresser. Thirty years later, there was a wine merchant, paint merchant, a milliner, a grocer, a bootmaker, a hairdresser and an outfitters occupying the range of shops shown in the picture. By the beginning of the 1950s, many of the stores established before the war were still trading there, although they had been joined by other firms such as Singer Sewing Machines and Shropshire Farm Produce, which was a grocer. (*J. Ryan*)

The first station after leaving Manchester Central for Stockport and the Peak District was Chorlton, located close to Wilbraham Road and now the site of a supermarket. The station was opened in 1880 when the line between Marple, Stockport Tiviot Dale, Heaton Mersey and Manchester Central was completed by the Midland Railway company. The arrival of the railway in the area resulted in new development, encouraging a growing number of office workers to consider moving to suburbs like Chorlton-cum-Hardy. The train service provided a quiet and efficient means of commuting to work each day and enabled people to enjoy the benefits of living in a leafy area, away from the pollution of central Manchester. Like other stations on the line, Chorlton had its own bookstall, which can just be seen beyond the footbridge, enabling passengers to purchase their morning paper while waiting for their train. As well as trains to Manchester and Stockport, Chorlton station also had a few services that went via Alexandra Park, Fallowfield and Levenshulme to Fairfield junction on the Manchester, Sheffield & Lincolnshire Railway's line between Manchester and Sheffield. This line was never a success as it was a much slower route for those from Levenshulme and Fairfield who wanted to get into Manchester. However, it was a useful line for freight traffic and passenger services using the Cheshire Lines routes to the west of Manchester to gain access to services that ran eastwards out of Manchester and vice versa. Possibly the best known of these was the one that ran from Liverpool via Manchester to Harwich to connect with the night sailing to the Hook of Holland. (*J. Ryan*)

This view shows the beginning of Oxford Road in Chorton-on-Medlock, looking towards Oxford Street and St Peter's Square in about 1930. Originally, the whole length of the road from St Peter's Square to Hathersage Road (formerly High Street) was known as Oxford Street, but in about 1886, it was decided to rename the section through Chorlton-on-Medlock as Oxford Road, the change taking effect from the railway bridge in the picture. The bridge was opened in 1849 and carried the Manchester, South Junction & Altrincham railway line from London Road station to Oxford Road station and then on to either Altrincham or Ordsall Junction. Just in front of the bridge, the road crosses the River Medlock, which was the boundary between the townships of Manchester and Chorlton-on-Medlock and could be said to mark the southern edge of what is called central Manchester today. The road on the left of the picture leads into an area which was notorious in the mid-nineteenth century for its poor housing conditions – Little Ireland. It was built on low-lying land on the banks of the river and the cholera epidemic of 1832 caused many deaths in the area. The white building on the right was known as Shell-Mex House and was built in the late 1920s, replacing a row of shops. The BSA shops are now the BBC's regional headquarters and studios. The trams in the photograph were on cross-town routes. In 1930, service no. 13 ran between Hightown and either Brook's Bar, Victoria Park or Chorlton (Chorlton-cum-Hardy), while the no. 27 ran from Old Trafford to Piccadilly, Clayton, Edge Lane or Droylsden. Tram no. 450 had been introduced during 1901/2 and was originally open topped, but in 1905, a cover was fitted and later, during 1922/3, it was rebuilt and improved.

In 1838, the Manchester School of Art was established by the Royal Manchester Institution in the art gallery which it had built on Mosley Street (now the Manchester City Art Gallery). The Art Gallery remained the School of Art's home until 1881 when it was decided that because of rising student numbers and the fact that the Royal Manchester Institution was considering donating the art gallery to the City Council, the School of Art should move to separate premises. A site was acquired at All Saints, adjacent to Chorlton Town Hall, and G.T. Redmayne was commissioned to design the new building, which was opened by the Earl of Derby. In 1898, the school was extended to provide a gallery where students' work could be displayed. Today, the buildings form part of Manchester Metropolitan University. This photograph was taken in about 1895 and shows the original building fronting Stretford Road. To the left of the School of Art was Chorlton Town Hall and a small portion of its front portico can be seen above the tram. Chorlton Town Hall was designed by Richard Lane and completed in about 1830/1 for the Chorlton police commissioners. The 5th Pan-Africa Congress took place in the Town Hall in 1945 and was attended by future leaders of African states including Jomo Kenyatta and Kwane Nkrumah. The former Town Hall was demolished in the mid-1970s although the façade was incorporated into a new building on the site. On the left of the photograph by the lamppost the offices of the Chorlton Poor Law Union can be seen. Its workhouse was originally located in Hulme, but moved to Withington in the 1850s.

When John Owens died in 1845, he left over £168,000 of which £98,000 was given to establish a place of higher education where no account was taken of the religion of either students or staff, in contrast to some other institutions where membership of the Church of England was a criterion for admission. The only criterion that Owens did impose was that priority should be given to those who came from Manchester or whose parents came from the town, but it was never necessary to invoke this means of deciding who to admit. Owens' money was not spent on buildings, but on funding lectureships and professorial chairs. Owens College, as it became known, was established in 1851 in a building on Quay Street that had been owned by Richard Cobden. Over the next twenty years, the number of students and the reputation of the college grew, with the result that it became necessary to find alternative premises. In 1873, the college moved from central Manchester to a new site in Chorlton-on-Medlock where new buildings designed by Alfred Waterhouse were erected. Gradually the size of the college increased. New buildings were added, including the Manchester Museum and the Whitworth Hall, which is the main building in this picture. Up to 1880 Owens College had to award London University degrees, but in that year it became the first college in a federal university. Eventually, in 1904, the federal university was broken up and the constituent colleges, including Manchester, formed independent universities. Today, Manchester University extends over a large area; modern buildings were added during the middle quarter of the twentieth century.

This photograph was probably taken towards the end of the nineteenth century and seems to show one of the suburbs of the city where there was a demand for fresh fish, poultry and game. The photograph must have been taken before Christmas because there are geese hanging up in front of the window and bunches of holly on either side of the door. The shop also appears to have sold vegetables. The lad on the left may have been a delivery boy for the shop.

In 1857, Manchester Free Libraries began a programme of extending into the suburban areas of the city. Initially, three branches were opened – in Ardwick, at New Cross and in Hulme – and proved to be very popular with the local residents. For instance, in Hulme the demand for books was such that the library outgrew its original premises and had to move to larger ones until a purpose-built library could be erected next to Hulme Town Hall on Stretford Road. Other branches followed in areas including Chorlton-on-Medlock and Cheetham, the aim being to ensure that all Manchester's citizens were within easy reach of a library. In addition to lending facilities, many libraries also included a newsroom and even children's rooms. When Manchester expanded its boundaries and took over formerly independent districts, a policy of extending library provision into these areas was implemented. Initially, these libraries tended to be in temporary premises, but gradually purpose-built facilities were constructed to meet the needs of local communities. Crumpsall Library opened in temporary premises in 1897, but in 1911 moved to a new branch building on Cheetham Hill Road, close to the local shopping centre. This photograph was taken at the laying of the foundation stone on 20 October 1909 by Edward Holt, Lord Mayor of Manchester. The new library not only included lending facilities, but also a large room in the basement which was eventually used for adult education classes.

Didsbury, situated close to several crossing points on the River Mersey, was probably founded as a small farming community before the Norman Conquest. In the thirteenth century, the Barlow family of Barlow Hall built a chapel in Didsbury for their own use, but it was also used by local people because the parish church was several miles away in what is now central Manchester. During the Black Death in the fourteenth century, permission was granted to open a graveyard in an attempt to prevent the plague being transmitted between Manchester and Didsbury. It was around this chapel that the original village of Didsbury grew up. However, during the nineteenth century, when Didsbury began to develop as a residential area, the centre of the village moved to the junction to Wilmslow Road, Barlow Moor Road and Hardman Street (now School Lane), close to the railway station. This photograph, taken in 1924 by a photographer with his back to Barlow Moor Road, shows the junction of Hardman Street and Wilmslow Road. It clearly reveals how narrow this portion of Hardman Street was (and still is). In the background is the bridge over the Midland Railway's line from Manchester (Central) to the Peak District and London (St Pancras). To the right of the picture was a coal yard that was first mentioned in the trade directories in 1858 when the agent was Samuel Sharples. Hardman Street was renamed School Lane in 1930 when the cottages on the left-hand side of the street were demolished and plans made to widen the road to make it part of the main road to Stockport. With the outbreak of war in 1939, the proposals were not implemented. The site of the coal yard and cottages is now a car park. The shop on the right, with its fine painted advert on the gable wall, was built early in the twentieth century, replacing a two-storey block which appears to have been shops at street level and to have had living accommodation above. The building on the left was erected in 1881, shortly after the opening of the station a few yards away, and is a sign that the railway was expected to increase the number of people in the area, creating a demand for more goods.

Unlike suburban railway stations today, Didsbury had its own staff, some of whom stayed for many years. This undated picture shows them in the days when the Midland Railway operated services through the area. According to a Mr Alfred Marlow, who wrote during the interwar years, there was a stationmaster, booking clerk and head porter, but there must have been others as well. Does this photograph show any of these people? In addition, the station had a bookstall which was well patronised by passengers. It would be interesting to try to identify these smartly dressed employees of the Midland Railway who served the residents of Didsbury. (*J. Ryan*)

As the population of Didsbury grew in the nineteenth century, the original parish church of St James became too small. Coupled with this, the centre of the village moved closer to the junction of School Lane and Barlow Moor Road. To meet the needs of the growing number of people living in this area, Manchester Diocese decided to create a new parish in the new centre of Didsbury. Emmanuel Church was built close to the junction of Wilmslow Road, School Lane and Barlow Moor Road. The church was consecrated in 1858 and cost £3,000. However, there was no endowment for a permanent vicar or a home for one. In addition, there was still money owing from the actual building of the church. In order to clear the debt and build a vicarage, a bazaar was held in 1859, which was attended by local people and dignitaries to help raise money. This photograph shows a performance by a band, possibly one of those from a regiment based in Manchester. It is interesting to note how many of the people must have arrived by carriage – their transport is waiting for them to leave.

Opposite: In 1880, the Midland Railway rerouted its services between London (St Pancras) and Manchester from London Road station to the newly completed Central station. Several new stations were built in south Manchester to cater for the communities through which the new line passed. One of the most important was Didsbury, which opened in 1880, and provided a fast, efficient way to get into central Manchester. The new station was opened where the railway passed under Wilmslow Road, close to the junction of Barlow Moor Road and Wilmslow Road, and near to where the new centre of the village was developing. Initially, the trains tended to cater for the businessmen and merchants who lived in the area, getting into Manchester after 9 a.m., but gradually the number of services increased so that by the beginning of the twentieth century, there were both early morning and late night trains to and from Manchester. In addition, some of the long-distance trains also stopped at Didsbury, including services travelling between London and Manchester. This photograph of the front of the station shows the monument erected in memory of Dr J. Milson Rhodes who took an active part in local politics and was involved with attempts to improve the lot of those in the workhouses, especially those who had epilepsy. He died in 1909 and the memorial was put up the following year, incorporating a clock, drinking fountain and horse trough. (*J. Ryan*)

One of the curiosities of Manchester is the way certain areas have always been referred to as 'villages', even today when they are part of the city. This stems from the time when they were separate communities whose only links with Manchester were the fact that they were within its ecclesiastical parish and within areas owned by the lords of the manor of Manchester. The best known are Didsbury and Chorlton but others, including Rusholme, Withington and Fallowfield, were also called 'villages' by local people. This postcard shows the centre of Fallowfield in the early twentieth century with no traffic at all on Wilmslow Road. Today, the road is choked with vehicles, but the buildings on the left of the picture have survived and are still shops. The ones on the right, however, have disappeared. When this photograph was taken the shops were occupied by a wide range of firms catering for the local community, including a branch of the Manchester & Liverpool District Banking Co., a greengrocer, a confectioner, a milliner, an ironmonger, the offices of the *South District Advertiser*, a newsagent, butcher and fruiterer. On the opposite side of the road (the right-hand side of the illustration), were a wine merchant, a fishmonger, a tailor and many others.

In December 1901, Gorton was presented with its first public library as a result of the generosity of local mill owner John Buckley. The family had lived in Gorton for many years and John Buckley was well known in the district as a member of the local board of health and later the Gorton Urban District Council. According to a report of the speech he gave at the opening of the library, Buckley said that he wanted to 'make a gesture in his lifetime to the people of Gorton where he has always lived and worked'. The library, which cost £3,000, was also a commemoration of the golden jubilee of Queen Victoria's reign. It was on Cambert Lane and provided Gorton with a facility for which other districts would have to wait. The books were provided not by the council, but by donations, in both cash and kind, from prominent local residents including £100 from Colonel Peacock of Beyer Peacock & Co. Across the road from the library was St James's Church, where Buckley was buried in 1916. This photograph dates from 1906.

STRETFORD STREET, MANCHESTER

One of the main routes through Hulme was Stretford Road. (The person who put the caption on the postcard had got his details wrong because Stretford Road has never been known as Stretford Street.) It leaves Oxford Road at All Saints and eventually meets up with Chester Road in Old Trafford, providing a spine for this important residential suburb. There were not only many shops along its length, but also Hulme's Town Hall and library, focal points for the community, and the Chorlton Union Town Hall until it moved to Withington. This postcard shows Stretford Road between the wars when motor vehicles were becoming much more common. The photograph was taken at the junction of Stretford Road with Great Jackson Street and Upper Jackson Street. On the left the building occupied by Woolworth's can be seen, while on the right are the premises of C.R. Russell, piano dealers. This firm had taken over the building from another piano dealers, William Kenna Smith, in about 1927.

Levenshulme Tram Terminus

Although Levenshulme remained independent of Manchester until 1909, the district relied on its larger neighbour for certain services including gas, water and electricity. In 1901, when Manchester took over the running of the electrified tramways, Levenshulme granted permission for electric trams owned by the city to run into the area, subject to the drivers and guards being licensed by the Levenshulme Urban District Council and Manchester paying a fee for this licence as well. The first electric trams ran into Levenshulme in 1902 terminating near the junction of Albert Road and Stockport Road. Eventually, services were extended through to Stockport and Hazel Grove. This photograph shows the tram terminus in around 1902 or 1903 when the main road to Stockport was relatively quiet and peaceful. It was Manchester's responsibility to ensure that the roadway was maintained where the tram tracks were located. The introduction of electric trams provided the first real competition for the railways, especially when the tram service started early in the morning and ran at a frequency which the railways could not match. On the right, just behind the children, is the Railway Inn, which was probably built around the time the railway opened in 1842. On the left is Pack Horse Hotel which claimed to have been licensed in the sixteenth century and was rebuilt in 1907. This public house may have taken its name from the fact that pack horses probably stopped here on their way into or out of Manchester because the road was the main link between the city and Stockport.

When and why this photograph was taken is not known. All that can be ascertained is that it was taken by someone named 'A. Lister' and that it was posted in Levenshulme to a Miss S. Evans at 25 Kensington Road, Rusholme, on 18 June 1906. Examining the photograph, it appears that the children are all dressed in their best clothes and that there are adults present, also dressed in their best. This might have been a school or Sunday school outing in connection with Whit Week.

A well-known landmark on Stockport Road, Longsight, was the Wagon and Horses (on the corner of the street, with the lamp attached), which was demolished in about 1998. The site appears to have been occupied from around 1690 although the building in the picture was probably erected later in the eighteenth century. The public house probably derived its name from the fact that it was a stopping place for wagons on their way into and out of Manchester. An indication of the amount of horse-drawn traffic that passed through the area is the notice over one of the shops: 'C. Howarth – Hay and Straw and Corn Dealer'. This type of business was a vital part of the economy in the nineteenth century as everything had to be carried within towns by horse-drawn vehicles. Between Howarth's and the public house is a 'mechanical' dentist, who appears to have operated a sort of 'hire purchase' arrangement for treatment, an indication that those who lived in the area were not wealthy and could not afford to pay outright for their dental treatment.

Opposite: In 1919, Manchester Education Committee issued an important report stating that it was 'to take immediate steps for the development and provision of secondary education within the City, with the ultimate object of granting free secondary education to all children . . . who are desirous of, and who show capacity for, such education'. In order to meet the growing demand for secondary schooling and the expected increase in the number of pupils as a result of this new policy, the committee decided that three new schools would be required and that they should be built as soon as possible. The last of the three to be completed was Levenshulme High School for Girls, whose first pupils arrived on 3 September 1929. The new school was set in 12½ acres of grounds, which meant that it had its own playing fields, and had places for 540 girls. The buildings cost £77,000 and included seventeen classrooms, a lecture room, laboratories, library, hall and domestic science rooms. This photograph, taken in 1931, shows not only the buildings, but also the school uniform which included a hat. When the school was built, this part of Levenshulme was gradually being developed as both private and council houses were erected here.

One of the most important routes leaving central Manchester in a southerly direction is Stockport Road, better known today as the A6. It roughly follows the line of a Roman road between Manchester, Stockport and Buxton, and became a turnpike route as a result of an Act of Parliament passed in 1724. After the Act it was widened and improved, and the original legislation was renewed on many occasions until 1885 when it lapsed. At regular intervals along the turnpike were toll-houses where travellers paid a fee for the privilege of using the well-maintained road. One was situated at the junction of Slade Lane (on the right) and Stockport Road (on the left). It was reported in 1803 that this toll-bar took over £1,000 a year from passing traffic. This amount probably did not include the fees paid by stagecoaches, whose owners often compounded the tolls and made an annual payment. The toll-house seen in the centre of the photograph was demolished in 1934 when improvements were proposed at this major road junction. This photograph was taken in March 1924 and shows the building in the centre of the junction with its advertisements for Bovril and Lyons tea. The shops on the right are still there and many now sell foodstuffs associated with the Indian subcontinent and the West Indies. The post office has also survived.

This image shows the other part of the Slade Lane/Stockport Road junction – the photographer is looking along Stockport Road. Like the previous picture, it was taken on 13 March 1924 at a quiet time of day. Behind the toll-house, on the right-hand side of the photograph, is the bridge which carries the main Manchester to Stockport railway line, opened in 1842 and widened in the late nineteenth century as the amount of traffic increased. The bridge was rebuilt in the late 1950s as part of a programme of modernisation and electrification of the line to London. For a short time, there was a station known as Rushford near the bridge, but it was closed when Longsight station was opened. The row of shops and the short street on the left between the public house and the railway bridge have been demolished and the site landscaped. The shops which can be seen on the far side of the railway bridge still remain, although some are in poor condition. Taken together, this and the preceding photograph provide a fascinating glimpse of a major road junction in the days when cars and motor lorries were few and far between and when trams were the main means of public transport.

In the late nineteenth and early twentieth centuries, Longsight was a desirable residential suburb for the increasing number of people employed in the shops, offices and warehouses of Manchester. Efficient horse trams, and later electric tram services, coupled with workmen's fares, made it possible for working people to move away from the overcrowded areas near to the centre of Manchester and live where houses had small front and back gardens together with facilities like running water and gas. This photograph, taken in 1914, shows Stanley Grove, Longsight, at its junction with North Road. This was the residential part of the Longsight, away from the hustle and bustle of the main Stockport Road. The houses all have front gardens and several appear to have rooms in the attic as well. According to the 1914 directory, the residents of this part of Stanley Grove included a potato merchant, several householders, a portrait painter, a clerk, a physician and a surgeon, a clerk, a plumber, an insurance agent and a grocer. In the background is a bridge carrying the railway line between Manchester and Stockport. The tram route was the well-known no. 53, which carried vehicles that were specially constructed to allow them to pass under the railway bridge.

This photograph shows the opposite end of Stanley Grove to the previous picture, and it too was taken in 1914. This was the junction with Stockport Road. The character of this end of Stanley Grove was quite different. Although there were a few houses here, most of the property was of a commercial nature. On the left-hand corner is Briggs & Co., which made and repaired shoes. Beyond the shop are several houses occupied by a clerk, a decorator and people described in the directory for this year as 'householders'. Further along is a short row of shops which included a baker, a hairdresser, furniture broker and a shopkeeper with no specified type of business. On the right is a branch of Seymour Meads, a well-known and well-respected grocer in the Manchester area, the address of which was given as Stockport Road. The first building actually to have a Stanley Grove address was the local Conservative Club beyond which was a boot and shoemaker, a laundry, a confectioner and a watchmaker. All the properties in this photograph have now gone. The left-hand site is part of a shopping centre which includes a supermarket, while the site occupied by buildings on the right is still vacant and being marketed for development.

This postcard view of Stockport Road, Longsight, from about 1904 was taken looking northwards towards Manchester from the junction with Plymouth Grove. The church on the right was Longsight Independent Chapel, designed by Travis and Mangnall and built at a cost of £5,000, including fittings and fixtures. It opened in 1853 and was often known as 'Ivy Chapel' because the front wall gradually became covered with the plant. During the nineteenth century, the chapel was a fashionable place of worship, but as the character of the area altered, its congregation declined and it closed in 1933. For a short time it was occupied by a fun fair, but after the Second World War the building was demolished. Across the road, on the extreme left of the picture, is the Farmer's Arms pub and next to that is Longsight Public Hall and what a directory refers to as 'Fire Escape Station'. It was in the public hall that Longsight Mechanics Institute was founded in 1850s, a library developed from the institute. The building housed the Longsight branch of Manchester Public Libraries until 1978 when the present one was opened a few yards away on the opposite side of the road.

Opposite: Miles Platting is an area that people tend to pass through unless they either work or live there. This photograph was taken five days after the one at the top of page 373, by which time the weather had changed. It shows the junction of Oldham Road with Hulme Hall Road. The lack of people around and the fact that the shops appear to be closed and have their blinds down suggests that 23 March 1924 was a Sunday. The importance of such a photograph is that it shows the type of shops that were to be found in many of Manchester's suburbs, even the working-class ones. On one side of the road is the store run by John Bloom, draper, who also occupied 124 Oldham Road, two doors down from the shop on the right of the photograph, where he described himself as a 'costumier'. Next door to the Bloom's store on the left was a small shop belonging to Joseph Pearse, draper. The residents of houses on the left-hand side of the road included a bricklayer, a piano dealer, a milliner, a farrier and a spinner.

Miles Platting has been described as one of Manchester's inner city suburbs although it lies over a mile from the city centre at the junction of the railway lines from Manchester Victoria to Yorkshire via Stalybridge or Rochdale. The area was divided by several main roads, including Oldham Road and Hulme Hall Road. This photograph, taken in mid-March 1924 looking towards Oldham Road, shows some of the houses that lined Hulme Hall Road. The houses all have small front gardens and would have had small rear yards or gardens. The houses on the left appear to be older than those on the right. Their front gardens are surrounded by wooden fences while those on the right, with their bay windows, have small walls topped with railings. However, these front gardens were not very large: when the window cleaner called, he had to put his ladder on the pavement to be able to set it at a safe angle. In the background it is just possible to make out the railway bridge on the other side of Oldham Road where Miles Platting station was located. In 1924, the people who lived in the houses on the right of the photograph included a platelayer (no. 58), a plumber (no. 56), a warehouseman (no. 46), a mechanic (no. 42) and a tailor's presser at no. 40. On the left, the residents included a nurse (no. 61), a draughtsman (no. 59), a foreman blacksmith (no. 55), a solicitor (no. 47) and a cycle dealer at no. 43. Further along the road, behind where the photographer stood, was the Albion Iron foundry, occupied by West's Gas Improvement Co., manufacturers of gas meters.

The photographer who took this image of Queen's Road, Miles Platting, on 23 of March 1924 must have had a busy morning for he also took several other shots of this area at the same time. Some of the properties appear to be older than those on Hulme Hall Lane as they have no front gardens and many come quite close to the edge of the pavement. The fact that the adjacent properties are set back provides an ideal location for a Bovril poster, which appears to be offering a special deal on the railways. The shops on the right-hand side of the photograph are just a few of the many on this section of Queen's Road. Among them were a pork butcher's, the British & Argentine Meat Co. (1923) Ltd, Meadow Dairy Co., and a grocer's. The butcher's shop next to Collinge's fish and chip shop was owned by a Mrs Smith. The shop with its shutters up was a clogger's, next door to which was a cycle repair shop. The block was completed by a hairdresser and a fishmonger. Hidden from view is the town sub-post office and money order and telegraph office. Other traders in the block include a tripe shop, another clogger's shop, Mrs Walton's dining rooms, a wallpaper distributor, another café, a tobacconist and a confectioner's – certainly all the shops local people required. On the left is the local United Methodist Church and its associated buildings.

Until 1904, Moss Side was separate from Manchester and it tried to retain its independence longer. It asserted this in education. In 1870, the Forster Education Act introduced the concept of compulsory education, although at this time it was not free. School boards were to be elected and charged with the responsibility of ensuring the implementation of the act. Those elected to school boards stood for various reasons. Some became involved because they had an interest in education while others did so in an attempt to ensure that a particular viewpoint was represented. One of the major problems facing many boards was the lack of adequate school buildings. Although some church schools were handed over to the boards, many remained in the hands of the churches, who preferred to ensure that children were given a Christian-based education rather than a secular one. In Moss Side, the school board tended to include a number of representatives of the various religious denominations who were always jockeying for position. Despite the disagreements, new schools were built in the area to meet a growing demand. In 1895, plans were drawn up and work began on the construction of a new board school on Princess Road in Moss Side. This photograph shows the large crowd which assembled to witness the laying of the foundation stone on what was originally a green field site.

The main route from central Manchester through Moss Side is Princess Road, which until the late nineteenth century terminated at Clarendon Street at the entrance to Alexandra Park. In 1893, there were still a number of vacant sites awaiting development on Princess Road including the one opposite St James's Church, the tower of which can be seen in the centre of the picture. St James's was built between 1887 and 1888 to the designs of John Lowe. Within a short time, the empty land was built on. Some plots were used for housing while others were used for shops and Princess Road School, which is the tall building in the background on the left-hand side of the road. The houses shown in this picture can also be seen on the photograph of the laying of the foundation stone of Princess Road Board School on page 375.

This photograph of Oldham Road, Newton Heath, was taken in 1909 although the exact location is not recorded. It is possible that it shows an area close to St Wilfrid's Church. The photograph depicts the type of cottages originally built along this important arterial road. The delivery van belonging to Globe Express was the forerunner of the modern parcels delivery service. Other vehicles shown in the photograph include a water cart and a lorry piled high with what appears to be cotton on its way to a local mill from the docks or the railway in Failsworth or Newton Heath.

Opposite: Moston is one of Manchester's north-eastern suburbs and derives its name from the fact that it was originally a small farmstead on the edge of mossy land. The *Victoria County History* commented that it 'had a hilly surface' and that it 'had various works including a wire manufactory and a colliery'. It was not the type of area that appealed to the editors of the series because it had no large stately houses or old churches. However, the area does have its own history of which the local people are very proud. This photograph, like so many that were taken of groups, contains no information about the date, what the event was or where it was held. One can only surmise from the dress and the costumes which the children are wearing that it might be between the wars and that it marked Empire Day, which was held in the spring each year.

Newton Heath was included in the parliamentary borough of Manchester in 1832, but when it was proposed that it should also be completely incorporated within the borough in 1838, there were many objections and the decision was taken to exclude it. It was not until 1890 that Newton Heath became part of the city, by which time the population had reached over 36,000. In the nineteenth century a report by an inspector from the General Board of Health concluded that the sanitary condition of the township was very bad and that there was widespread opposition to the introduction of any aspect of the recently passed Public Health Act, which allowed local boards of health to be established. He went on to argue that effective drainage of the land was essential and that there should be proper house drainage together with well-laid sewers. Eventually, Newton Heath did have its own local board of health and conditions in the township started to improve, but it was a long process. This photograph shows the junction of Oldham Road with Dean Lane in 1924. The cottages on Dean Lane were built in the nineteenth century and in 1924 were occupied by several people who described themselves as householders. Some listed their occupations, which included a tram driver, a fireman, a boot repairer, a coal lifter and a greengrocer. Further along the road were Dean Lane station and Newton Heath Locomotive Depot, which provided engines for many of the services operating from Victoria and Exchange stations. The bank in the photograph claims to be Parr's Bank, but by the time the picture was taken, Parr's Bank was part of the Westminster Bank. Next door was Freize Ltd, who were costumiers. George Mason's was a well-known grocer's with several shops in the Manchester area. The other two shops which can be seen were those of Gent Brothers, who were watchmakers, and Joseph Hall, a herbalist, on the far left. Other shops in the area included a butcher's, a greengrocer's and a milliner's.

In 1861, communications between Northendon and Manchester were improved by the construction of what the *Stockport Advertiser* of 13 December 1861 called a 'footbridge' to link Northendon with Palatine Road. The new bridge was about 10ft wide and was described as being a 'light and elegant lattice girder bridge'. It replaced a 'cumbersome' and apparently 'dangerous' ferry across the river at this point. The new bridge could probably take a horse bus, but by 1874 there were demands for a wider structure, which could take traffic in both directions at the same time and provide a footpath for pedestrians. The replacement bridge was built by the Manchester and Wilmslow Turnpike and taken over by the East Bucklow Highway Board in 1881. The widening of the bridge and the abolition of the toll bar at Barlow Moor in Didsbury encouraged people not only to travel to Northendon and enjoy the countryside, but also to consider moving out to the area from Manchester. Gradually, large houses were built and businessmen began to make their homes in Northendon. This photograph shows the River Mersey with the Palatine Road bridge across it. If the visitor was to follow the river behind the photograph, he would reach the Tatton Arms, which was a popular place of refreshment. The number of visitors was such that as well as the pub, there was at least one café on the Northendon side of the river. Whether the building in the picture was the Northendon Café owned by a Monsieur Logios is not clear. If it was, then the photograph was taken prior to November 1904 when the café was burnt down for the second time in five years. In the 1920s, the site appears to have been occupied by the Riverside Café. It had a stadium attached which was used for wrestling, boxing, skating and local events such as fund-raising bazaars. The complex closed in 1962 after fire damage. From this photograph, it is possible to see why so many people travelled out from Manchester during weekends to enjoy the scenery and even boat on the river.

Boating on the River Mersey was confined to the stretch west of the Tatton Arms because there was a large weir there which had been constructed to allow a water mill to be built. The Tatton Arms, which can be seen in the background, was built in 1875 and replaced the Boat House Inn from which the ferry across the river to Didsbury operated. In the early twentieth century, boats were very popular at weekends with those who travelled out to Northendon from Manchester to enjoy the countryside. This photograph also shows what appears to be a small steamer which took people on trips towards Didsbury and Cheadle in the early twentieth century.

Opposite: When the first bridge across the River Mersey was opened in 1861, it enabled some horse-drawn traffic to travel between Northendon village and Didsbury and so into Manchester. In order to provide a link between the bridge and other roads in the district, a new thoroughfare was constructed, which adopted the name of the street on the Lancashire side of the river, Palatine Road. The result was that the old route along Church Lane to the ferry across the river became less busy. Gradually, shops began to appear on Palatine Road, especially around its junction with Church Lane. The top photograph was taken in about 1913 and shows that only one side of the road was built up. Although the shop in the foreground appears to proclaim its owner was Henry Handforth and that he was a provision dealer, by the time this photograph was taken, Henry appears either to have retired or died as the person recorded in the directory for this year as being at the building is Mark Handforth, provision dealer. In the early twentieth century, the stores on this stretch of Palatine Road included a hardware shop, a shoe shop, a confectioner's, a greengrocer, a milliner, an ironmonger, a draper and two other provision dealers. The choice of shops was to increase dramatically when Northendon was taken over by Manchester after the Wythenshawe estate was purchased and incorporated into the city in 1931. The area was to become a 'new town' with the result that more shops and facilities were built, including a cinema. The bottom photograph shows the shops that lined Palatine Road in the 1950s. Those on the right are where the hedge can be seen in the photograph above.

When the Manchester, Sheffield & Lincolnshire Railway built its line to Sheffield via the Woodhead tunnel, it passed through parts of east Manchester, including Gorton and Openshaw. It was here that the railway line and the natural ground level met and when Richard Peacock sought a site for his company works, he chose Gorton. In addition to the topography, another factor influenced him: the fact that the area was outside the boundaries of the borough of Manchester and therefore the rates were lower. At the same time, the area was close enough to Manchester to attract the skilled workers he required. Other companies were probably influenced by the same considerations when they came to establish their factories. Ashbury's Railway Carriage & Wagon Works was built on the edge of Gorton. Here, a substantial factory was constructed which was capable of turning out large numbers of both passenger carriages and goods wagons. It is said that the railway station at Ashbury's, shown in this photograph of about 1910, was built for the employees of the company to enable them to get to work because it was next to the factory. Ashbury's station was opened in 1855 and is still in operation today although the original buildings were demolished in the 1990s. (*J. Ryan*)

In order to get an impression of what an area looks like, it is often necessary to take several photographs that overlap each other slightly. This is exactly what the photographer who took this image and the one on the preceding page did. This shot shows the other side of Sandywell Street where there is a wall which appears to go uphill. The reason for this is unclear unless there is a slight rise in the land and as a result houses were built in such a way that there was a sharp drop from the pavement on to the road so the wall was erected to prevent accidents. The people who lived here would probably have been employed locally in the engineering works, mills or by the railway company. At the end of Sandywell Street, emerging out of the gloom is a tall building. This is Wheeler Street School, which was opened in 1902 and closed in 1967, becoming Wheeler Street Community Centre. How long the photographer waited to get the road clear of traffic will never be known as Ashton Old Road was always busy with trams passing and vehicles going to the various factories in the area.

Opposite: According to the *Victoria County History* for Lancashire, Openshaw stretches for 'over 2 miles along the Ashton Old Road, a long straight road leading east from Manchester to Ashton . . . the district is now urban, though a little open land remains on the northern border.' Between 1866 and 1890, Openshaw was a board of health like many other of Manchester's townships, but in 1889, the board decided that it would be in the best interests of the area if it merged with Manchester, a move which took place in 1890. For much of its length through Openshaw, Ashton Old Road was lined with shops and terraced houses. Behind the houses on the south side of the road were several large industrial concerns such as the Carriage & Wagon Works on the Great Central Railway (known locally as Gorton Tank and not to be confused with the Beyer Peacock works which was known as Gorton Foundry and lay south of the railway line), Armstrong Whitworth's works and the Otto Gas Engine works. The shops served the local community, providing it with everything it required. This photograph, taken in 1924, shows not only the pawnbroker's, which had been in existence since 1840, but also a greengrocer's, a newsagent's, a dress shop and a printers. From the posters on the building, it appears that Hardons were not only pawnbrokers, but also house furnishers and drapers. The houses on Sandywell Street are typical of those found in the area, built without front gardens and with the front door opening directly on to the street.

Manchester Grammar School was founded in 1515 by Hugh Oldham, Bishop of Exeter, to educate boys from Manchester and the surrounding area so that they might go to university and enter one of the acknowledged professions of the day – the church or the law. The school began in premises on Long Millgate on a site which was to become very confined because it was hemmed in by Chetham's School at its rear. As the school expanded during the mid-nineteenth century, it became apparent that the site was not ideal because there were no playing fields, no playground and the buildings had to be designed to fit the site. The number of pupils was seriously limited by space. Suggestions were made in the later nineteenth century that the school should move, but it was not until 1926 that the decision was finally taken. The school purchased the site of Birch Hall and its associated farmland in Rusholme and the new buildings were completed and opened in 1931. The new school, seen here in about 1933, was a vast improvement on the long draughty corridors, flights of stone stairs and lack of playground which the boys had previously endured. Proper science labs as well as a gymnasium and swimming pool were incorporated into the new site. Once the school had moved, the old buildings, which were said to cover 3,989 square yards, were sold and used first as a college to train mature people for teaching and more recently as part of Chetham's School of Music.

The prospect of Platt Hall and its associated estate being sold off to developers in 1905 and 1906 roused the residents of Rusholme who, under the leadership of William Royle, fought a campaign to save it for Manchester and convert it into a public open space. This photograph appears to have been taken when the estate was first put on the market in 1905, but as it did not reach the reserve price, the sale was withdrawn. The notice was very carefully sited on the corner of Platt Lane and Wilmslow Road. Platt Hall was the home for several centuries of the Worsley family. Lieutenant-General Charles Worsley was involved in the removal of the mace from Parliament in about 1651 and also represented Manchester in Parliament in 1653.

Victoria Park was created in 1837 as a residential area for the businessmen of Manchester who wanted to escape the increasingly unpleasant conditions in the centre of the town and yet be within easy reach of their firms. The development of the horse bus gave an impetus to this outward expansion. In 1837, a company was created to develop a residential estate on the edge of Rusholme and Chorlton-on-Medlock, sandwiched between Wilmslow Road and Plymouth Grove. The area was walled off and the erection of large houses began, the estate being laid out by Richard Lane. However, the development company collapsed in 1842 and it was another three years before the Victoria Park Trust was created to complete the plans. In order to keep the estate as select as possible, the entrances were protected by gates and porters were engaged to keep out unwanted visitors. This gate, photographed in about 1900, was located on Anson Road, where those who wished to use the road to leave Manchester were charged a toll. Even in the 1920s, trams were subject to restrictions when they passed along Anson Road. It is said that children used to play a game of trying to creep into the park under cover of a tram. The toll-gates were eventually abolished in 1937 and access to the park became open to all.

In 1874, a new church was built on the edge of Victoria Park, dedicated to St John Chrysostom. The new church, which cost £13,000, was dedicated in 1877 and served not only the residents of Victoria Park, but also neighbouring parts of Chorlton-on-Medlock. In 1904, the church was destroyed by fire, the damage being so great that only the tower and the four walls were left standing. In 1906, the church was re-opened, having been rebuilt with the help of John Ely, a local architect, who tried to reproduce faithfully G.T. Redmayne's original designs. This postcard shows the church standing in its dominant position on Anson Road, but there is no date on the card and so it is impossible to say whether the picture was taken before or after the fire.

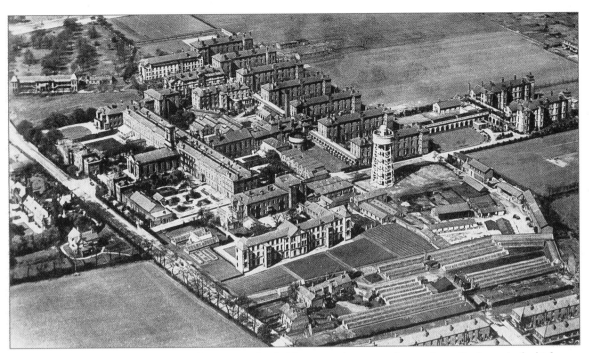

During the nineteenth century, Manchester was divided between three poor law unions, the largest of which was Chorlton, stretching from the River Medlock to the River Mersey. The union included densely populated suburbs such as Hulme and Chorlton-on-Medlock, as well as the residential villages of Didsbury and Withington. The original workhouse was on Stretford Road in Hulme, but by the mid-1850s it had become apparent that the existing buildings were inadequate to cater for the rising number of applicants for shelter. A decision was taken to move to a green field site in Withington where there was room for expansion and land for the workhouse to grow some of its own food. The original buildings, including the chapel, are on the left-hand side of the photograph. The seven parallel buildings behind were added later as hospital blocks designed by Thomas Worthington with advice from Florence Nightingale. When the workhouse opened on its new site, there were around 750 inmates, but by the end of the century the total had risen to over 1,100, many of whom were elderly and infirm, suffering from problems such as epilepsy, or were 'lunatics', orphans or abandoned children. When the poor law system was finally abolished in about 1928, the former Withington workhouse was handed over to Manchester City Council, which improved it and converted it into a general hospital. The hospital, seen here in about 1945, was taken over by the National Health Service in 1948/9. Recently its future has been in doubt.

Opposite, bottom: Whalley Range came into existence after Samuel Brooks, a Manchester banker, acquired land on the edge of Moss Side and Stretford in 1836. When he purchased the site, it was said that the only way across it was a footpath and that there was a need for the area to be properly drained before it could be developed, which cost him £12,000. Brooks named the area after the place of his birth, Whalley in Lancashire. Many of those who moved there were professional people who wanted to have easy access to Manchester, yet live in pleasant surroundings. This picture shows Withington Road which started at Brooks Bar and terminated at Wilbraham Road, although in the early twentieth century there was no development beyond Manley Road. Although many of the houses were numbered, they also had names such as West Bank, Thorncliffe, Hughendon Villa and Alton Towers. At the junction of College Road and Withington Road stood Withington High School for Girls, while further along College Road was the Lancashire Independent College where ministers for the Congregational Church were trained.

When Manchester embarked on a programme of slum clearance in the 1920s and 1930s, the main problem that faced the city council was the demand for land on which to build council houses to replace the homes that were to be demolished. In 1926, Manchester was given Wythenshawe Hall and Park by the Simon family and then purchased a considerable amount of extra land on which it planned to create a 'new town' with all its own facilities. Work started on putting in the infrastructure and building the houses before the outbreak of war in 1939, but during hostilities the project was suspended and some of the facilities were not completed until the 1970s. Among the earliest areas to be built up were those which bordered existing streets like Wythenshawe Road, shown here in the early 1950s. Although there were some maisonettes constructed, many of the new properties were houses with their own front and back gardens – facilities the new occupants would not have had in the inner city. Where possible trees were planted along side roads and grass verges were introduced. It must also be pointed out that not all the development which took place in Wythenshawe was carried out by the council. Some was undertaken by private companies to meet the growing demand for houses in the suburbs. The properties in this photograph were privately owned and at least one has a garage, something which the council houses did not have because only a few people owned cars.

CHAPTER SEVENTEEN

WHEN AT WORK . . .

From the end of the eighteenth century and throughout the nineteenth century, there was tremendous growth in industrial production in and around Manchester brought about by the use of steam power to drive machinery. Previously men and women had worked at home or in small, water-powered mills and factories, often in remote areas where there were fast flowing streams. Now men, women and children worked in larger numbers in mills and factories in the towns. Not only were the mills and factories getting bigger, machinery was also going faster, enabling production to be increased and new ideas pushed industrialisation forward. Manchester was regarded not only as the 'capital of the weavers and spinners', but also as a place to see steam power fully exploited.

Large towns have always attracted men and women in search of work and wealth. This had certainly been the trend throughout the eighteenth century, but with the end of the Napoleonic Wars, large numbers of men discharged from the services made their way to the growing industrial centres in the hope of making a fortune. Some were successful, but many were not. During the years after 1815, there was a good deal of unrest as factory owners struggled to adjust their production to the peacetime economy. Unemployment rose and there were demands for both economic and political reform. One of the largest meetings ever held outside London took place on 16 August 1819 at St Peter's Fields in Manchester. The dispersal of the meeting by the military on the orders of a frightened magistracy resulted in eleven people being killed or dying from their injuries; several hundred were seriously injured. The event became known as the Peterloo Massacre.

Although Peterloo ushered in a period of repression, it was not long before some of the legislation was amended. For instance, in 1824, the Combination Acts were repealed and trade unions were able to form. This prompted a rash of strikes, often led by spinners whose lack of activity could paralyse the textile industry. As a result of the strikes Richard Roberts, a Manchester engineer, was asked to develop a self-acting mule. This machine was designed to enable many of the operations carried out by mule spinners to be done automatically. This allowed the spinning of cotton yarn to be undertaken by semi-skilled hands rather than specialist workers who could bring the industry to a halt if they became involved in an industrial dispute. It took six or seven years before the self-acting mule was perfected. Roberts was one of a number of inventors who lived and worked in Manchester during the nineteenth century and helped to make it such an important industrial centre.

Although Manchester had a large number of different types of industry, producing goods for sale was not the only way people earned a living. During the nineteenth century, the centre of the city gradually became dominated by warehouses, offices and shops. The warehouses connected with the textile trade employed large numbers of people and generated much business. The first modern textile warehouse on Mosley Street by Edward Walters for Richard Cobden. Many of the new warehouses had impressive entrances with the ground floor reached via a flight of steps, while inside there were large open spaces. Here the products of the various mills could be viewed by potential customers without having to travel to the mill. This was a development of the

Manchester is regarded as an industrial city, but when it absorbed Wythenshawe in 1931, it acquired a large rural area in north Cheshire. The City Council intended to develop the area for housing so that residents from the slums could be relocated in what Lloyd George had described in 1919 as 'homes fit for heroes'. It was some time before the first houses were built and not until after the Second World War that development began in earnest. This photograph shows a farmer ploughing land in Wythenshawe between the wars. The scene looks very rural, but within thirty years, farms like this had almost disappeared under a sea of new housing. Wythenshawe's farmland was not the only property to be taken over for development. Many of the small farms which existed in Manchester, especially in the southern part of the city, gradually disappeared as more council houses were erected.

system whereby mill owners brought their goods to Manchester and lodged them at inns on certain days of the week. It also ensured that unwelcome visitors, especially from abroad, did not visit the mills and see machinery which they might try to copy when they returned home. The warehouses not only brought employment for warehousemen and mill operatives, but also business for the post office, railways and carriers. There was also the Royal Exchange, the focal point of the textile industry and all those industries whose commercial success relied to some extend on the cotton trade. It too was based in central Manchester.

Much of the production of the Lancashire textile industry and Manchester's engineering industry was for export. Those involved in the trade complained of the rising value of the pound, of American industry dumping goods on markets and the problems of high transport costs. The skill of the exporter was to gauge when the market was flooded in order to avoid having large stocks abroad or at sea which had to be sold at a loss as prices fell, and to judge when stocks were sufficiently low abroad to start exporting again. At the same time, falling export demand often led to rising unemployment at home and depressed prices, so good bargains could be had, and if the timing was right, the exporter would get his goods into the overseas market when stocks had run out and prices were rising. Some were very successful. For instance, John Owens, a merchant whose father started as an umbrella manufacturer, left over £168,000 when he died. Of this, over £98,000 was given to establish Owens' College, now Manchester University, in 1851. He was involved in the export of woollens to South America in the 1820s and 1830s.

During the mid-nineteenth century, Manchester was one of the leading centres of economic theory in England. The Manchester School of Economic of Thought promoted free trade of goods. By adopting this policy the academics believed other countries would be encouraged to remove their barriers and so help trade develop which would benefit the manufacturers back home. The movement developed out of the Anti-Corn Law League, whose aim was to achieve the repeal of the Corn Laws. This legislation had been introduced to protect farmers from foreign competition and only allowed grain to be imported when prices reached a certain level. It was finally repealed in 1846.

As well as large manufacturing industries, there were many small businesses in Manchester. Some grew into industrial giants while others continued to serve local or home markets. In Manchester there were one-man firms as well as companies employing over 1,000 people, small factory and workshop owners who managed just to survive as well as multi-millionaire industrialists, merchants and financiers.

The selection of photographs in this chapter shows aspects of both manufacturing and commercial life in Manchester during the last 150 years.

In 1931, Wythenshawe was absorbed by the city and became the location for a 'new town'. At that time, Wythenshawe was still largely rural with scattered farms and country lanes. This photograph, taken a few months before the outbreak of the Second World War, shows Greenbrow Lane at Baguley as the grass verges are cut by a workman using a scythe. The farmhouses and barns in the background and the trees spreading across the road give the impression of a corner of rural England, yet only a few miles away, council estates were being constructed and the quiet of a summer's day was occasionally punctured by the noise of aircraft using the newly opened Ringway Airport.

Until the internal-combustion engine became widely used, horses provided the power to haul wagons carrying goods to and from factories, mills, railway sidings and quayside and to haul buses and trams. The large number of horses meant that there was always plenty of work for blacksmiths and farriers. According to the 1836 Manchester trade directory, there were forty-six blacksmiths in central Manchester and this number had risen to over 162 by the 1870s. However, by 1900, the figures had begun to decline with only about 140 listed in the directory for that year. In addition, blacksmiths made an important contribution to the local economy in the surrounding districts like Rusholme, Withington and Didsbury where two or three would serve the local community. Whitehead's smithy in Rusholme, shown here in about 1900, was founded by Thomas Whitehead about 1845 and continued to operate until the 1930s when the number of horses in use declined sharply and the demand for the services of blacksmiths fell away. The firm was originally at 80 Wilmslow Road, but as the business expanded, new premises were taken at 3 and 5 Monmouth Street. Finally, Whitehead's moved to 546 Claremont Road, where it ended its days. Whitehead's were also farriers and wheelwrights.

Opposite: During the nineteenth and early twentieth centuries, horses and carts were as common as motor cars and lorries are now. Where and when this horse and cart were photographed and what it was carrying or where it was going, is not recorded. All that can be ascertained is that it was photographed making its way up a ginnel or entry between two rows of terraced houses. It is possible that at the end of the passage there was a small yard and stable where the horse and cart were kept overnight. The passage itself is an indication that the houses were probably built in the latter half of the nineteenth century when every property was supposed to have its own ashpit or privy in a small backyard. The night soil carts which emptied these privies used the passages at the rear of houses to do their job, hence they had to be wide enough to take a horse and cart. Sometimes, drains were laid down the centre of the passage to take surface water and water from the houses.

When the Manchester Ship Canal was opened in 1894, the slogan 'Manchester Goods for Manchester Docks' was introduced. Whether these carts piled with bales were used by the Manchester Ship Canal Co. as mobile advertisements or whether some manufacturers were prepared to allow the slogans to be attached to their carts as they made their way to the docks is not certain. The fact that the slogan was one which the Manchester Ship Canal Co. itself used is clear from the wall of the warehouse behind. Even today, the slogan can be seen from a train passing over the Manchester Ship Canal at Irlam – it is painted on the walls of the lock facing the railway line. The opening of the docks in Manchester and Salford enabled ocean-going vessels to reach within a couple of miles of the centre of Manchester and provided new employment opportunities for people of Manchester and Salford.

With the advent of the railways, several firms in Manchester began to manufacture locomotives, including Sharp Roberts, which made its first in 1833. However, after initial attempts, the firm gave up making locomotives to concentrate on manufacturing textile machinery, in particular the self-acting mule which had been developed by one of the firm's partners, Richard Roberts. In 1837, the firm resumed locomotive manufacturing with an order for ten for the Grand Junction Railway. These locomotives with their single pair of driving wheels were known as 'singles' and over the next twenty years the company produced over 600 of this type and its derivatives, not only for English railways, but also for European countries including France, Belgium and Holland. *Flora*, the locomotive shown in this photograph from about 1850, was typical of many built at the Atlas Works in Manchester. It was constructed for the Manchester, South Junction & Altrincham Railway, which commenced operation in 1849 as the area's first commuter line. When the line opened, there were thirteen trains a day in each direction taking between 20 and 30 minutes to complete the journey, much faster than the stage coach or horse buses. The firm continued to make railway engines in Manchester until the 1880s when it moved to Glasgow because there was no room for expansion at the Atlas Works, which were sandwiched between the Rochdale Canal, Oxford Street and Chepstow Street. In 1903, the company became part of the North British Locomotive Co. which continued to make railway engines until 1962.

Although nineteenth-century Manchester is associated with textiles, it was also an important engineering centre with several large firms including Whitworth's, Sharp Roberts and Beyer Peacock & Company. Beyer Peacock was established by Charles Beyer, Richard Peacock and Henry Robertson in 1854 to 'make locomotives and other such light machines as the . . . works are adapted to make'. The original works covered just 1 acre of the 10-acre site in Gorton which the partners purchased. Throughout the nineteenth century further land was acquired and the works was considerably expanded. By 1902, the workshops covered 9 acres of a 20-acre site with a narrow gauge railway linking the workshops. At the beginning of the twentieth century, the company employed 2,000 people and was capable of manufacturing 150 locomotives a year. By the time the firm closed in 1966, it had made over 7,000 locomotives, around two-thirds of which were exported to countries including Holland, Sweden, Argentina, Australia and South Africa. In the early 1900s, the company developed the Beyer-Garratt articulated locomotive for which there was a large overseas demand especially in southern and central Africa, where some are still working. A number of the firm's locomotives have been preserved including at the Dutch railway museum at Utrecht in Holland, Thirlmere in New South Wales and elsewhere in Australia. One of the South African Railway's Garratt locomotives can be seen in the Manchester Museum of Science and Industry. This photograph shows one of the workshops at the turn of the twentieth century with a large number of locomotives under construction.

Another well-known engineering firm which had its origins in Manchester was Whitworth's. It was founded by Joseph Whitworth in 1832 in a small workshop on Port Street. The following year, Whitworth moved to Chorlton Street, where the firm stayed until 1880 when it transferred to Openshaw. Whitworth is credited with having started precision engineering when he developed a micrometer accurate to a millionth of an inch. In the late 1830s, the firm made lathes, planing machines, other machine tools and engineering equipment in standard sizes. It claimed that all were checked for accuracy. Another development was the Whitworth thread, used on screws, nuts and bolts, which became the accepted standard and is still used today. Higher engineering and machining standards enabled other firms to improve their products. For instance, it enabled Beyer Peacock to build more economical, more reliable and more powerful locomotives. The armaments industry also benefited from Whitworth's work. Whitworth made higher muzzle velocities and accuracy possible when he introduced the rifled barrel to the field gun. This photograph shows Whitworth, third from the right, and those involved with the gun's development testing it on the beach at Southport. Whitworth was also involved in less glamorous developments such as a street cleaning machine which he developed in about 1843 and used in Manchester until 1848. Sir Joseph Whitworth, who died in 1887, was one of a group of engineers who made Manchester an important centre of innovation in engineering in the nineteenth century.

The 1830 Beer Act allowed anyone to establish a beer house, even in their own front room, provided they paid the £2 for a licence. Within a short time, a large number of beer houses had opened in Manchester and other towns and cities, often on street corners. As the nineteenth century progressed, many became tied to the larger brewers who supplied them. This photograph, taken in the 1890s, shows a brewer's dray delivering barrels to what is probably a tied beer house in a street which may be in the Ancoats area of Manchester. It is interesting to note that the way the kegs were lowered into the cellar has changed little even today: a rope is used to steady the progress of the full barrel and there is possibly a ramp down which it would roll. It appears that this house was doing a brisk trade judging by the number of barrels on the pavement. It is not recorded whose beer it was selling, but it would have been from one of the breweries which existed in Manchester at that time.

Sometimes those who worked did so to earn a night's accommodation rather than pay. This was the case for men who applied to the Manchester and Salford Methodist Mission for accommodation. Rather than charge the men, many of whom had come to Manchester seeking jobs, the Mission employed them to chop firewood, which was then sold to householders, offices and factories. The usual procedure was that men seeking accommodation would arrive around 1 p.m. and spend the rest of the day chopping wood or bill posting. In return for their labours, they received an evening meal and a bed for the night. Next morning, they left early to seek work, returning at about 7 a.m. for breakfast. Presumably those who found jobs reported the fact and were able to reserve accommodation for the following evening, for which they would pay a small sum. If they found a permanent job, the Mission made arrangements so that they had a cubicle as a bedroom rather than an open dormitory and they kept this until they had found somewhere suitable to live. This 1890s photograph shows some of the men in the wood yard with the results of their labour.

Knife grinders were a common sight in the nineteenth century and first half of the twentieth. Today, however, this useful travelling tradesman has completely vanished from our streets. The man would go from door to door with his grindstone on a trolley operated by a treadle via a belt which ran from a wheel to the spindle on which the stone was located – a simple sort of line-shafting that was found in factories all over the country at that time. When the belt was disconnected, the wheel could be used to move the equipment to the next customer. In this photograph of the 1930s, the knife-grinder appears to be wetting the grindstone, a process which resulted in a more effective sharpening surface.

Occasionally, strange illustrations make an appearance in collections. This card, with the photograph of the two men, possibly Messrs Schedule and Starbuck, appears to date from the early 1940s. Who they were and why the card was issued is not known, but it may have been an advertisement for their company or they could have been playing a joke on some of their customers.

WHEN AT WORK . . . 401

When both cotton and wool are turned into cloth, the resultant colour is rather inconsistent, tending to be greyish and not particularly attractive. From the earliest times, cloth has been bleached and dyed using naturally occurring materials such as logwood and madder. However, natural dyes produce a limited range of colours. In the late eighteenth century, the first steps were taken towards synthetic dyes by Thomas Hoyle. This resulted in a colour known as 'Hoyle's Purple'. By the middle of the nineteenth century, experiments were undertaken to produce a wider range of synthetic dyes using coal-tar. One of the earliest of these was 'mauveine', produced by W.H. Perkin senior in 1856. Gradually the number of factories producing synthetic dyes increased to meet the demand from the textile industry for a wider range of colours. In 1876, Charles Dreyfus founded the firm known as Clayton Aniline to produce dyes from coke oven benzole. The firm was very successful, gradually increasing not only its range of colours, but also its size. In 1911, it was taken over by CIBA Ltd and eight years later, CIBA joined with Geigy and Sandoz to form CIBA-Geigy. Throughout the interwar period, production and the range of colours continued to expand as dyes had to be found for the increasing number of synthetic materials which were being developed. This photograph, taken in 1933, shows part of the Clayton Aniline Plant. Note that belt-driven machinery is still the order of the day, that much of the equipment is made of wood and that the men are not wearing shoes or boots, but wooden clogs, which were not corroded by the acid used in the manufacture of the dyes and other chemicals at the factory. There is no form of protective clothing, not even goggles.

There was an explosion at Roberts, Dale & Co. in Cornbrook, on the boundary of Manchester and Stretford, just after noon on 22 June 1887 when a stove used for drying prussic acid blew up, killing one person. The explosion, which devastated the works and the surrounding area, was said to have been heard in Oldham. The local press reported the event extensively, the *Manchester Guardian* taking 3½ columns to describe the event and a further 1½ to cover the inquest into the death of the person who tried to extinguish the fire. Asked to comment on the explosion, one of the partners, Mr Roberts, told the reporter he did not know the cause, but the reporter added that 'Mr Roberts did not seem in a communicative humour'. The firm never fully recovered from the explosion.

Although Manchester was an important manufacturing centre, it was not a large producer of cotton yarn or cloth. Manchester's importance to the textile industry was its commercial and finance business. It was in Manchester that many of the mills had warehouses where they could display their products to would-be customers from both Britain and overseas. In 1838, the first purpose-built textile warehouse was constructed for Richard Cobden on Mosley Street. Within a short period of time several more warehouses had been erected, each bigger and grander than the last until the completion of Watt's Warehouse on Portland Street in 1858. Whole areas became devoted to warehousing with their grand entrances up a flight of steps, open rooms where cloth could be examined and basements where packing took place. This photograph shows the basement of one of Manchester's warehouses where cloth is being packed in waterproof fabric and hessian. Work was very hot and dirty for those in the packing rooms, yet all the men are wearing waistcoats, which was an accepted part of the period's dress code.

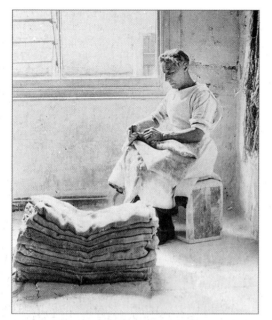

Although some firms employed large numbers of people, there were also a great many small ones involved with producing a wide range of products. A glance through a trade directory for the end of the nineteenth century reveals a vast range of small manufacturers; many were either one-man concerns or employed only a few people. The three illustrations here show three examples of small firms or businesses found in Manchester in the late nineteenth and early twentieth centuries. The photograph on the left shows a man quietly stitching bags. They appear to be made of hessian or a similar material and could have been used in the textile industry for carrying cotton between mills or for foodstuffs such as flour. The illustration below shows a carpenters' workshop where three men appear to be discussing a problem with a job, some aspect of the news or just generally chatting before resuming work. The picture on the right is again of a small workshop, which appears to be a joiner's shop, with a man, possibly the owner, posing for the photographer with what looks like a chisel.

In the middle of the nineteenth century, there were three prominent architects working in Manchester whose surnames began with the letter W. These were Edward Walters, who designed the Free Trade Hall and numerous warehouses, Thomas Worthington, who was responsible for the Memorial Hall, the Albert Memorial and the Minshull Street Police Courts, and Alfred Waterhouse, who designed the Town Hall, Strangeways Prison, Owens College and the Assize Courts. The work of these three stands out as making a major contribution to the townscape of Manchester. Fortunately, many of the buildings which they designed have survived the passage of time and can still be admired today. However, the Assize Courts, which stood between Bury New Road and Strangeways Prison, have vanished. The building was designed by Waterhouse and completed in about 1868, at the same time as the prison. This photograph is one of several taken during construction and shows some of the men responsible for the work. The balustrades give the impression of grandeur. Around some of the columns inside were carvings of old punishments, a sort of warning to those who were on trial of what might have happened to them under earlier regimes. The Assize Courts were seriously damaged in the Christmas and Whitsun air raids of 1940 and 1941 and had to be demolished.

Opposite: In 1840, Rowland Hill introduced the Penny Post which enabled letters to be sent any distance for the sum of 1*d*. Previously letters had been charged both by distance and weight. The new arrangements resulted in a gradual rise in the volume of mail. Sorting offices became hives of activity as outgoing mail was organised for despatch to other parts of the town or country and incoming mail was made ready for delivery. These two photographs show the letter sorting room at the main post office (top) and the parcel sorting department (bottom) in about 1900. The busiest time in the sorting office was around Christmas when there were complaints that the public tended to leave posting to the last minute. For the parcels department, it was busy all year round, handling over 100,000 items every week in 1900.

Between the two world wars, local authorities were allowed to begin building council houses in an attempt to eliminate the slums which had grown up in the nineteenth century. In order to embark on a programme of slum clearance, new housing had to be built on the outskirts of the city. One such area was Newton Heath around Ten Acres Lane and Briscoe Lane. Here, the houses had to have very deep foundations to provide stability on account for the nature of the land. The house on the left had to have foundations 8ft 10in deep while on another part of the site, the foundations are shown as being over 13ft deep. Whether these houses were popular with their tenants is not certain because they were close to a gut works, the smells from which would have been very unpleasant. The factory took the parts of animals that could not be used for food, rendered them down and converted them into products for the textile industry.

This corner shop clearly sold groceries and provisions and employed a delivery boy to take customers' orders to their homes. The full name of the firm that owned this store was Meadow's Dairy Company and it was a provision dealer with about sixteen shops in 1938. These shops were to be found in Salford, north and east Manchester and the Moss Side area. The location of this shop cannot be identified from the photograph as there are no street names and no house numbers visible. In the window there are numerous bills which give details of prices. Over the entrance is the statutory notice which indicates that the premises were licensed to sell either tobacco goods or alcohol, or even both. At the side of the delivery boy's bike is a pram, which from its size seems to be one which a little girl would have used for her dolls.

Opposite: An important part of any community was the corner shop. Some were tobacconists and sweet shops while others sold food. This particular store, pictured in the late 1920s, stood at the corner of Princess Road and Royle Green Road in Northendon. The local directory gives the address as 42 Royle Green Road. In 1938, the occupier was a Henry Hudson Moult, shopkeeper. The advertisements on the shop itself are typical of the 1930s. Some of the products will be familiar to the older generation of readers – Lyons tea, Fry's cocoa and chocolate, Black & Green's tea, Player's Weights cigarettes, which were still being produced in the 1950s, and Player's Digger tobacco, which was still available until about 1998.

The summer of 1911 was a period of much industrial unrest which affected both industry and transport. In Manchester, trams failed to run, carters went on strike and railway services were decimated. The military had to be brought in to protect carters who were prepared to work and deliver food to the markets. This photograph shows a detachment of the 16 Lancers at Hulme Barracks whose task it was to protect food supplies. The effects of the strike were felt across the whole community, even by holidaymakers who found that although they could get back to Manchester, there was no one to help them with their luggage when they reached the city.

These two have just arrived at Victoria station in August 1911 and cannot find a porter to help them with their luggage. According to the original caption, when the photograph was published, a kind member of the public helped them with their bags. Although the 1911 strikes affected the mining industry and transport system in the main, there were also strikes for higher wages in Manchester's engineering industries.

These demonstrators are outside the works of Armstrong, Whitworth & Co. in Openshaw reading the notice which the management had pinned to the door announcing that the firm would pay the workers the going rate as agreed in what were described as the 'recent settlements'. Other engineering employers took the same line and gradually the men returned to work and the strikes ended.

Between 4 and 12 May 1926, Britain was affected by a general strike. Manchester was relatively peaceful compared with some other towns. There were spasmodic outbreaks of violence, such as the destruction of two vans belonging to the LMS at Smithfield Market and a lorry being set on fire by Oldham Road Goods Depot. There were also reports of a van driven by a volunteer being attacked by a crowd at London Road station, but intervention by the police prevented it being destroyed. This photograph shows tram drivers and other involved in the General Strike attending a rally in Albert Square.

Transport was heavily disrupted. Although electricity supplies were maintained, the unions threatened that if any attempt was made to run the trams, they would shut down all the power stations – no attempt was made to run the trams throughout the period of the strike. Trains were also badly hit with few services at the beginning of the strike, but gradually the number increased, making it slightly easier to get to work. In this photograph, striking Manchester Corporation Transport Department employees are seen marching along Hyde Road to a rally in central Manchester. They are watched by other workers.

For those not involved in the strike, there was the problem of getting to work. Some were able to get lifts with friends while others cycled, walked or made use of transport run by private bus and coach companies. Even lorries were pressed into service, as this photograph shows.

CHAPTER EIGHTEEN

. . . AND WHEN NOT
AT WORK

Many people believe the nineteenth century was a period when there was little time spare for activities other than working, sleeping and eating, that lives were ruled by the factory bell or hooter and that for the average working man or woman, wages were only just sufficient to provide for food, heating and the rent. However, this picture is far from accurate: working hours were gradually reduced and the Saturday half-holiday movement, led by William Marsden and George Wilson, became established, allowing firms to close at 1 p.m. on Saturdays, and this became noon in the early twentieth century.

During the nineteenth century the average working person saw a gradual increase in the amount of money they had to spend. This was brought about by a combination of steadily rising wages and relatively stable prices. It has been said that in the middle of the century the habit of saving, either with a friendly society or a bank, began to filter down to the working classes. In addition, having 'a little to spare' was no longer the preserve of the upper classes. The existence of this extra cash, according to James Walvin in his book *Leisure and Society, 1830–1950*, was 'a fact of major significance in the evolution of new recreations'. It must, however, be remembered that there were still many who could not afford to save and who continued to have a hand-to-mouth existence.

The nineteenth century also saw the beginnings of annual holidays, or wakes weeks as they were referred to in the north-west. Employers began to appreciate that maintenance on machinery could be carried out more efficiently if their employees were absent and so they started to grant a week off work – without pay of course. There were also 'unofficial holidays' when workers took an extra day off without permission. The best known of these was 'Saint Monday', when you either did not turn in for work or if you did, achieved very little.

There was a realisation that those who were employed in warehouses, offices, banks and shops did not get the same time off as those in mills and factories because there was no need for these organisations to close down for maintenance purposes. Then, in 1870, the Bank Holiday Act was passed. In the eighteenth century, the Bank of England was closed for 47 days a year, which was reduced to 44 in 1808, to 40 in 1825, 18 in 1830 and just 4 in 1834 (Christmas Day, Good Friday, 1 May and 1 November). The 1870 Act forced banks, warehouses and shops to close down for certain days and created long weekends.

The greatest changes took place in the latter half of the nineteenth century as the benefits of giving people an opportunity to take a break began to be appreciated. Before about 1850 any kind of break was frowned upon. Alexis de Tocqueville, visiting England in 1835, commented that one 'Never heard the gay shouts of people amusing themselves or music heralding a holiday. You will never see smart folk strolling at leisure in the streets or going on innocent pleasure parties in the surrounding country.' In the same year, another visitor to Manchester, Van Raumer, wrote that 'the working people have generally no means of excitement or amusement at their command during the week . . . and even Sunday, stern and rigid as it is here, brings no recreation or enjoyment'.

Sundays tended to be dominated by those who believed that people should do nothing on the Sabbath except go to church or sit at home. These people represented all denominations and were generally referred to as Sabbatarians. In fact, many working people did not go to church on Sunday, but instead went to the local pub. The only people who benefited from the Sabbatarians' approach were the publicans. In 1856, Manchester introduced band concerts in parks in the city, but there was strong opposition from the Sabbatarians and the experiment was not repeated in following years. However, it is worth noting that during the period when the concerts were held, there was a marked decrease in drunkenness according to the police and that when the concerts stopped, the rate of drunkenness rose again.

De Tocqueville and Van Raumer echoed comments made by a local man, James Philip Kay, who had written in 1833 that 'the entire labouring population in Manchester is without any season of recreation, and is ignorant of all amusements, excepting that very small proportion which frequents the theatre. Healthful recreation in the open country is seldom or never taken by the artisans of this town.' Even Parliament recognised that lack

During the late nineteenth century there were several references to parks having 'gymnasiums' for boys and girls. This description gives the impression that these were purpose-built specially equipped, supervised facilities. However, nothing could be further from the truth as this photograph of a 'gymnasium for children' at an unnamed park in Manchester shows. The word meant that more pieces of equipment than usual were installed. It appears that by the time this photograph was taken, in about 1914, the policy of having one such area reserved for girls and another for boys had been abandoned and that all children played together.

When Whitworth Park was established in the 1890s, the main intention was to provide a place where children could play away from the roads and streets. Consequently, many of the restrictions found in other parks were not enforced here. For instance, there was no attempt to stop the children playing on the grass, while the lake was shallow and toy boats could be sailed on it. The one concession made to adults was the erection of a bandstand. This Edwardian photograph shows children, who appear to be in their best clothes, sitting on the grass while the adults listen to a concert.

of open spaces and other recreational facilities were an evil. In 1844 the Short Time Committee reported that 'Schools and libraries are of small use without the time to study. Parks are well for those who can have time to perambulate them and baths of little use to dirty people who do not leave work until 8pm.'

Many of the problems which arose in the first half of the nineteenth century had been caused by rapid industrialisation and the growth in the industrial towns of the north of England. Open space was at a premium and it was not until the early 1840s that reformers began to appreciate the importance of creating areas where working people could walk and get away from their overcrowded living conditions. It was claimed that the lack of open space had caused the decline in certain sporting activities such as football. However, by the end of the century, organised sport, including football, rugby league and cricket, was beginning to make a come back.

This selection of photographs aims to give an impression of the wide range of activities which people enjoyed in Manchester in the latter half of the nineteenth and early twentieth centuries.

Heaton Hall and its associated park were owned for a long period by the Egerton family, later to become the Earls of Wilton. The present Heaton Hall was designed by James Wyatt in 1772 to replace an earlier building. The new house was sited in an elevated position with extensive views over to the Pennines and the Irwell and Irk valleys. In 1902, the Wilton family were faced with heavy death duties after two earls died within a few years of each other.

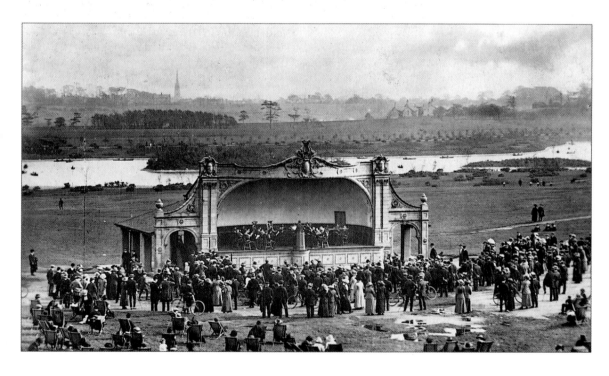

Although Manchester decided not to landscape the park at Heaton Hall, certain alterations were made to the area in the years before the First World War. In order to attract visitors, a lake was constructed and when, in 1912, the former Town Hall on the corner of Cross Street and King Street, was demolished, it was decided to re-erect the columns from the front portico by the lake in Heaton Park. This atmospheric photograph was taken in the 1930s and shows the columns standing high above the trees.

Opposite: There were suggestions that Heaton Hall and its parkland might go for housing or even to be turned into an industrial estate, but in 1902, Manchester City Council purchased the hall and the 600-acre estate to preserve it as an open space for the residents of north Manchester. The following year, the estate was incorporated within the boundaries of the city of Manchester. The council decided to maintain the openness of the estate although flower beds were planted close to the hall, giving it a somewhat formal setting and contrasting this area with the rest of the park.

Some developments did take place at Heaton Hall including the construction of a 12-acre lake, capable of accommodating 2 motor launches and 100 rowing boats, which can be seen behind the bandstand in the picture at the top of page 417. The park soon became popular with visitors and was a venue for Whit week trips by Sunday schools.

Opposite: Official openings provide the opportunity to photograph civic dignitaries and other leading citizens taking part in activities that they would not otherwise consider. For instance, this photograph was taken in 1910 after the Lord Mayor and the Lady Mayoress officially opened Platt Fields Park. As part of the opening ceremony, the official party was taken for a boat trip around the lake watched by large numbers of people who had turned out to attend the event. One gets the impression that some of those in the boat were not really enjoying the trip and considered it beneath their dignity.

When Manchester acquired the Platt Hall estate in 1907 and converted it into a public park, William Royle, who led the campaign to save the estate for the public, ensured that the opening of the new park was a grand civic occasion. Although the weather was wet, a large crowd turned out to witness the event. The speaker is believed to be William Royle himself and there is a note at the bottom of the photograph, added when it was printed, which says 'This is a grand day for Rusholme.'

One of the events that took place for many years in Didsbury was the annual show, which was held on the Simon playing fields. The first was organised in 1901 although there is evidence that there were agricultural shows in the area in the nineteenth century. The Didsbury Show was organised by a body known as the South Manchester Show and was held on August Monday (the first Monday of that month) each year. Entry was free and it always attracted a large crowd. This photograph was taken at the 1910 show and records the judging of the horse and carriage class. The event was last held in 1966 when the fields were taken over by Manchester City Council which refused to allow the land to be used for the show.

In 1911, Didsbury marked the coronation of George V and Queen Mary with a procession through the streets of the village to Ford Bank. The local papers described the event as 'a pretty little spectacle' which 'did great credit to the organisers'. The procession included floats entered by various Didsbury organisations together with representatives of the council and organisers. According to Fletcher Moss, Didsbury's local historian at the beginning of the twentieth century, everyone in the village was expected to take part and make some contribution towards the event. The floats had themes including 'The Union Jack', 'Maypole,' 'Army and Navy' and decorated prams. This photograph shows just one small portion of the procession as it passed Didsbury police station in the centre of the village.

During the 1920s, outings in charabancs and large cars became very popular with groups from pubs and large families. This photograph was taken in the mid-1920s and shows a family from Moston about to set out for a day trip either into the country or to the coast. As many people could not drive or even afford to buy a car of this size, it is probable that the one in the picture was hired for the day together with the driver. (*Mrs L. Connor*)

The arrival of the railway train ushered in the era of mass transportation not only to and from work, but also for recreational purposes. During the 1840s, there were a number of well-reported railway excursions from Manchester and other parts of industrial Lancashire to the coast, usually to Fleetwood and then Blackpool. Trips to the countryside and seaside were also organised by Sunday schools, churches, trade unions and many other bodies. The Factory Inspectorate even gave information to firms on how to book a train or arrange an excursion for employees. This photograph, probably taken in about 1910, shows a group of young people waiting at a Manchester suburban station for a train. It is not clear whether this was a Sunday school trip or one organised by a local firm. However, there is a clue in that the card was sent to someone in Droitwich and the sender gives the address from which it was despatched as Alma Park School, which is in Levenshulme. It is possible that the station might be Levenshulme Hyde Road, which was on the Chorlton-cum-Hardy to Fairfield line and that the people in the photograph are in some way connected with the school. (*J. Ryan*)

During the last two decades of the nineteenth century, interest in football revived. Many teams were established by Sunday schools, clubs and factories, attracting large crowds of spectators. Some of these amateur clubs gradually became professional and entered the football league. The two Manchester clubs were not admitted to the league until some years after it was established. Manchester City and Manchester United have very different origins. Manchester City began as a church team which merged with another run by a youth club, whereas Manchester United began as a works team. Manchester City was known as Ardwick FC until 1894 and had its ground at Hyde Road until 1923. Manchester United started life as Newton Heath Loco and had several grounds in the Clayton area before moving to Old Trafford in 1910. This photograph shows the crowds at a football match in Manchester sometime before the First World War, but unfortunately the location and teams are not recorded. Note that the spectators are all standing and are exposed to the weather. Seating and covered stands are the order of the day now.

On 10 October 1851, Queen Victoria paid her first visit to Manchester and was warmly received by large crowds lining the streets. The Queen entered Manchester over Victoria Bridge from Salford, where she had inspected a huge gathering of Sunday school children in Peel Park. Triumphal arches were erected across Victoria Bridge and in St Ann's Square while the streets were decorated for the visit. Her route to the Exchange, where she received an address of loyalty from the Mayor and Corporation, took her along Market Street, High Street, Swan Street, Oldham Street, around Piccadilly to Mosley Street, Peter Street, Deansgate and St Ann's Square. As a result of the reception she received, Victoria authorised the Exchange to be known as the 'Royal Exchange' and two years later, Manchester was granted city status. This photograph, taken on the day of the visit, shows the royal procession entering Manchester. The arch and the carriage are clear, but as the length of exposure was long, anything moving appears to be blurred.

In 1887, a large exhibition was held just outside Manchester in Old Trafford at which the products of the various firms in the region were displayed. It was organised to mark the fiftieth anniversary of Queen Victoria's accession to the throne. The exhibition, which was on the same site as the Art Treasures Exhibition of 1857, attracted a large number of visitors and included a large re-creation of the Market Place in Manchester. In order to attract members of the public to the event, the station which had been built for the 1857 exhibition was re-opened. Special trains were run from Manchester as well as from other parts of the country. Firms took their employees to the exhibition not only for a day out, but also to enable them to see their own products on display alongside those rival firms were producing. According to reports, the event attracted huge crowds during Whit week and they appear to have consumed vast amounts of food and drink. This photograph shows the station and the staff required to operate it for the duration of the exhibition – May to October. When the event closed, the station remained open, becoming known as Warwick Road, and was used extensively by those who attended Lancashire County Cricket Club's matches at Old Trafford, just a short walk away.

The exact location of this street party is not known, but the photograph was taken on 22 June 1897 during the celebrations of Queen Victoria's diamond jubilee. According to the newspapers, Manchester treated the day as a public holiday with church services and a civic lunch in the Town Hall. School children were provided with a breakfast while 'waifs and strays' who did not bother people by trying to sell them firewood and matches were provided with a meal by the city council. The parks were full of people with children playing and bands performing to appreciative audiences. The *Manchester Guardian* applauded the wisdom of the City Council in spending a 'few thousand pounds' on events in Manchester which attracted visitors from the surrounding area.

The Manchester and Salford Methodist Mission was not only involved in helping those who lived in the poorer parts of central Manchester and Salford, but also held religious services both in the Methodist Central Hall on Oldham Street and in the open air. This outdoor service in about 1897, which appears to have been well attended, was being held in Stevenson Square, only a short distance from the Central Hall. The arrangements appear to have been very thorough for not only is there a choir on the platform, but one of the sisters is playing what looks like a harmonium. The platform was a very simple structure – a cart with planks laid across it, the shafts of which can be seen to the right of the choir and person leading the service.

In the mid-nineteenth century, some lamented the gradual disappearance of old customs but in some parts traditions continued to be observed and became focal points for local events. One such area was Gorton where the annual rush cart procession continued until about 1875. This photograph appears to be of the Gorton rush-bearing, probably towards the end of its existence. Rush carts were certainly in use in Gorton before 1775 when there is a reference to two. The idea was that fresh rushes were provided for the floor of the church. According to Higson in his *Gorton Historical Recorder*, there was rivalry between Gorton and Openshaw for many years as to which district produced the best rush cart, but after 1775, only the people of Gorton continued with the tradition. Not only did the event enable the local people to show their skills in decorating a rush cart, but it was also a chance to have a good time.

Opposite: As this group of people approaches, the man on the right of the picture respectfully touches his cap, but is it out of politeness for the lady or is it out of recognition for the gentleman on the left of the group? The gentleman is Keir Hardie, leader of the Labour Representation Council. When Hardie returned from his foreign visits in May 1908, he attended two meetings in Manchester on 3 May. The second was for members of the Manchester and Salford Independent Labour Party (ILP). It was held at the Co-operative Hall, Downing Street. Both events were chaired by Councillor J.M. M'Lachlin from Levenshulme and he may be the person on the lady's right.

During the latter part of 1907 and early 1908, the leader of the Labour Representation Council, Keir Hardie, made visits to several countries including South Africa and India. Travel was slow compared with today as long overseas journeys had to be made by boat. When Hardie returned home, the first event he attended was in Manchester, which was reported as being a 'welcome home' meeting. In fact, there were two meetings held in the city. The main one was at the Free Trade Hall, which was filled to overflowing. Hardie gave a wide-ranging speech about his overseas visits, what he had seen and learned about the conditions and problems in India and South Africa. Not only did he attack government policies, blaming the presence of plague in India on 'western commercialism', he also criticised politicians like Churchill for their attitudes towards the problems he found in the countries he visited. It is not certain where this photograph was taken or what the men in the picture are reading, but in the background, covering some posters for a temperance 'Ham, Tea and Social' evening, is an advertisement for Hardie's visit.

The first Whit walks were organised by the Church of England in 1801 to ensure that children from the various Sunday schools visited Manchester's parish church at least once a year. Gradually, other denominations adopted the idea of a religious walk during Whit week, which was a sort of 'wakes week' in Manchester and the time when Manchester races were traditionally held. One of the most colourful of the Whit walks, especially in the twentieth century, was the Roman Catholic event, which was held on the Friday in Whit week until the religious connection with the late May holiday was broken in the 1960s. Many of those who attended Roman Catholic churches came from other parts of Europe and the Whit processions enabled them to dress in national costume. In 1936, 18,000 people took part, representing twenty-six churches and accompanied by thirty-six bands. They walked 4 miles from Albert Square, Peter Street, Deansgate and Market Street to Piccadilly. This photograph of the late 1930s shows the Italian community in Piccadilly with the Madonna from St Michael's Church, George Leigh Street in Ancoats. When the procession finished, the walkers returned to the church where the statue was set down. The people sang the English and Italian national anthems followed by the 'Ave Maria' and 'Faith of Our Fathers'.

Opposite: Sitting and watching the world go by was a popular pastime for some sections of the population. This photograph was taken in the late 1890s and shows the walls of the Infirmary in Piccadilly. The original photograph was published by the Manchester and Salford Methodist Mission in one of its annual reports and then turned into a postcard; it may be that these people, who were either casual labourers or out of work, were photographed to illustrate the type of person the Mission was trying to help. Sitting in either Piccadilly or other places in central Manchester was and still is popular at lunchtime on warm summer days.

Although meetings were known as 'Manchester Races', the racecourse was never in the city – races were always held in Salford. The earliest reference to horse racing in Manchester goes back to 1687, but races did not become regular until 1772. The original racecourse was at Kersall Moor, but in 1847 the events were moved to Castle Irwell, where they stayed for twenty years until new owners of the land refused to renew the lease. They were opposed to horse racing, arguing that it encouraged betting which led to poverty and misery. A new racecourse was built at New Barns, where it remained until 1902 when the land was used to build no. 9 dock. Manchester races returned to Castle Irwell, where a modern course was laid out on a 116-acre site. The races always attracted large crowds, even in wartime as this 1941 photograph shows. The most famous event was the Manchester November Handicap. The racecourse closed in 1963 and the site is now part of Salford University. It should be noted that horse racing was held at Heaton Park between 1827 and 1838 on a track laid out by the Earl of Wilton and intended for the entertainment of his guests, although members of the public did manage to gain admittance.

ACKNOWLEDGEMENTS

In the first two volumes of this series on Manchester, I expressed my gratitude not only to all those who have collected and preserved photographs of Manchester in the past, but also to those who are still doing it today. As towns and cities change, it is very important that a pictorial record of the town is maintained for future generations of historians and Mancunians so that they can see what the city looked like at the end of the twentieth and beginning of the twenty-first centuries. The thanks of the current generation of local historians should go to all those in the past who have kept photographs and postcards of places so that we can see what the city of out forefathers looked like. New material keeps coming to light.

At the same time, thanks should be expressed to all those who have written about their experiences in Manchester as these accounts can often help to identify a picture or the picture can enliven what they have written. Nor should newspaper reporters be forgotten; they assiduously collected news stories in the past, and wrote detailed reports, far more detailed than anything which appears in the press today. Their work can provide the background to an event or street scene.

My grateful appreciation is due again to Manchester Central Library, to John Ryan for the loan of some of the more interesting postcards, the Manchester and Salford Methodist Mission, Mrs L. Connor and Manchester City Planning Department for allowing the use of photographs from their collections. If I have forgotten anyone, I am very sorry and hope that you accept my apologies.

I would also like to thank David Brearley who has copied many of the lantern slides which have been used in this book. Without his help, the reproduction of some of these images would not have been possible. I would also like to thank Simon Fletcher of Sutton Publishing for his interest and helpful comments and Sutton Publishing in general for their policy of trying to make illustrations of times gone by more generally available.

Finally, I would like to express my grateful thanks to my wife, Hilary, for reading through the drafts of the captions and making helpful comments, spotting things I had overlooked or not explained clearly enough. Also, thanks are due to Peter and Anna who tolerate their father's enthusiasm for Manchester and collecting materials on the city.